NOTES

OF

TRAVEL AND STUDY IN ITALY.

BY

CHARLES ELIOT NORTON.

BOSTON:
HOUGHTON, MIFFLIN AND COMPANY.
The Riverside Press, Cambridge.

PREFACE.

A PORTION of the following Notes appeared in "The Crayon" during the year 1856. The larger part of this volume, however, is now published for the first time.

I am well aware that a traveller is likely often to draw false inferences from what he sees and hears, especially in a country whose people are of a different race and whose institutions are of a different character from those of his own. This has led me to be sparing in my deductions from my personal observation and experience.

But there are certain principles in religion and in government of universal application; and how far these principles are adopted or rejected in any special state is a subject upon which an intelligent man is bound to form and at liberty to express a distinct opinion.

I have not hesitated in the following pages to express myself strongly in regard to some of the corrupt doctrines, of the Roman Church and methods of the Papal Government. But while condemning much in the practice of the authorities of the Church, I retain the highest respect for many of its members, — and I am bound to some of them by ties of warm affection. I regret that what I have said may, if it come before them, give pain to persons whom I should wish only to please.

The present condition of Italy is full of hope for the future. A new life seems to have begun for her, and every lover of freedom will join in the wish that Carlo Alberto's vigorous declaration may now prove true, *Italia farà da se.*

Shady Hill, Cambridge, Mass., 5th December, 1859

CONTENTS.

THE RIVIERA. GENOA. FLORENCE.

DECEMBER, 1855.

THE Var forms the geographical boundary between France and Italy; but it is not till Nice is left behind, and the first height of the Riviera is surmounted, that the real Italy begins. Here the hills close round at the north, and suddenly, as the road turns at the top of a long ascent, the Mediterranean appears far below, washing the feet of the mountains that form the coast, and stretching away to the southern horizon. The line of the shore is of extraordinary beauty. Here an abrupt cliff rises from the sea; here bold and broken masses of rock jut out into it; here the hills, their gray sides terraced for vineyards, slope gently down to the water's edge; here they stretch into little promontories covered with orange and olive trees.

One of the first of these promontories is that of Capo Sant' Ospizio. A close grove of olives half conceals the old castle on its extreme point. With the afternoon sun full upon it, the trees palely glimmering as their leaves move in the light air, the sea so blue and smooth as to be like a darker sky, and not even a ripple upon the beach,

1

it seems as if this were the very home of summer and of repose. It is remote and secluded from the stir and noise of the world. No road is seen leading to it, and one looks down upon the solitary castle and wonders what stories of enchantment and romance belong to a ruin that appears as if made for their dwelling-place. It is a scene out of that Italy which is the home of the imagination, and which becomes the Italy of memory.

As the road winds down to the sea, it passes under a high isolated peak, on which stands Esa, built as a city of refuge against pirates and Moors. A little farther on,

> " Its Roman strength Turbia showed
> In ruins by this mountain road," —

not only recalling the ancient times, when it was the boundary city of Italy and Gaul, and when Augustus erected his triumphal arch within it, but associated also with Dante and the steep of Purgatory. Beneath lies Monaco, glowing " like a gem " on its oval rock, the sea sparkling around it, and the long western rays of the sinking sun lingering on its little palace, clinging to its church belfry and its gray wall, as if loath to leave them.

COGOLETTO.

As I passed through the lower room of the poor. inn in ʼhis dirty little town, which is one of the many that claim the honor of having been the birth-place of Columbus, I was attracted by seeing a Franciscan holding a tin money-box, on which was painted a figure of the Virgin, and engaged in close conversation with the master of the house. The room was used as a *caffè*, and idlers of various sorts were standing at the door, or sitting at the table in the middle of the room taking their coffee or their glass of *vermuth di Torino*. Some of them were listening to the talk between the friar and the landlord ; and it appeared that the Franciscan was trying to persuade the innkeeper to purchase from him the secret of the lucky numbers in the lottery which is to be drawn next Saturday in Genoa, — a secret which he declared had been revealed to him in a dream. The friar was successful, and, after some haggling about the price, took a bit of money which jingled into his box, giving in return a slip of paper on which were inscribed the desired numbers.

The Middle Ages still possess Italy. In these country-towns, even in enlightened Sardinia, one feels himself a contemporary of Boccaccio, and might read many of the tales of the " Decameron " as stories of the present day. The life of the common people has much the same aspect now as it had centuries ago. Italy has undergone many vicissitudes, but few changes. *Il vecchio pianta la vigna e il giovine la vendemmia :* " The old plant the vine and the young gather the fruit from it," says a common proverb. The Italians of to-day are gathering the fruit off the ancient stock.

GENOA.

The success of the experiment of constitutional government in Sardinia is at this moment the chief hope of Italy. A liberal and wise spirit of reform is uniting the interests of all classes, and a steady, gradual progress proving the ability of Italians to govern themselves without the excesses of enthusiasm or the evils of extravagant and undisciplined hopes. While Milan and Venice are hemmed round by Austrian bayonets, and Florence is discontented under the stupid despotism of an insane bigot, — while Rome stagnates under the superstition of priests, and Naples under the brutality of a Bourbon, Turin and Genoa are flourishing and independent. The old traditions of the commercial enterprise and warlike expeditions of the Genoese are being renewed, and the prosperity of this great port is one of the most important elements in the present political prospect of Italy.

Every gain of material power is at the same time a gain of moral power for Sardinia. The regeneration of Italy depends on the renewal of her ancient material prosperity. Commerce is the support of liberty. Free trade opens the way for free speech and free thought, and leads to freedom in politics and in religion. Railroads are more subversive of ecclesiastical supremacy than the ablest tracts against Popery. To develop her internal resources is the true policy of Sardinia. Her increasing strength at home gives her new strength abroad; and her example is a daily growing danger to the despotisms that lie around her borders. Lombardy belongs by nature to Piedmont; and no cordon of Austrian troops, no legion of spies can keep Lombard eyes from casting longing looks toward the west, or Lombard hearts from being touched into flame by the breath of liberty that invisibly blows over the frontier. Every ship that Genoa sends from her harbor carries away, as its unregistered cargo, something of the superstition and ignorance of Northern Italy. Her trading-vessels are the peaceful, but irresistible fleet of Freedom. Piedmont was the last retreat of Liberty in Italy, and it is now becoming her stronghold.

It is not to be overlooked, however, that the present condition of the mass of the people of Piedmont is so low in point of education and of desire, that it is difficult to make them take any hearty interest in the cause of constitutional freedom, or to bear their part in the working of the government. They are led just now more rapidly than they can well follow. The difference between the views of the common people and those of such men as Cavour and d'Azeglio is a difference, not of degree, but of kind. The peril of Sardinia arises not so much from the neighboring hostility of Austria and the dull opposition of Rome, as from the inevitable internal weakness which must for a time be the result of such forcing processes as she is compelled to undergo.

PIETRA SANTA, 9th December, 1855.

A year ago the dogma of the Immaculate Conception of the Virgin was pronounced at Rome, and the first anniversary of this event, " which spread joy through the heavens and the earth," as an inscription that I read declared, has been celebrated to-day as a *festa*. The streets of the towns through which we have passed have been filled with bright crowds of people keeping the holiday, and all the bells of the churches have been ringing. We

stopped at Pietra Santa just at sunset, and I went down
through the narrow street to the square of the little city,
where the old church of San Martino, and its tall, rough
brick campanile, form, with the smaller church of Sant'
Agostino, a group of buildings of striking peculiarity and
interest. The square was almost empty, except immediately around the doors of St. Martin's, through which
people were passing in and out. Going into the church,
I found it full of worshippers. The high altar was
lighted with a hundred candles, that burned in the midst
of brilliant decorations and hangings of crimson drapery.
The light about the altar was the only light in the church ;
the nave and aisles were dim in the twilight. On the
step of the altar, in front of the railing, were kneeling
a band of the Fratres Penitentiæ, in black dresses with
white capes, girt with a cord about their waists. Immediately behind them sat the Gonfalonieri of the city, in
purple cloaks lined with yellow, and black velvet caps
with white plumes. Soldiers kept the space around
them clear, but all the rest of the church was filled by
men and women of every class, in characteristic and
picturesque varieties of costume, standing or kneeling;
while the priests chanted, and the choir, supported by
the organ and trumpets, took up in turn its parts of the
service. It was a scene from the Middle Ages. It
seemed as if the old church were filled with such a
crowd as might have collected within it five centuries
ago. All was in keeping: — the strange dogma which
was being celebrated as a doctrine of pure religion, —
the growing darkness in the church, save where the can-

dles shone on the gold and silver ornaments of the altar,
— the voices of the priests, interrupted now and then by
the clink of the metallic money-box in the hands of the
beadles, as they passed round to collect the offerings of
the pious, — the chanted litany, with the loud murmur of
the responses through nave and aisles, — the dead language of the service, — all seemed to partake more of
the spirit of the past than of the present, to be an inheritance from Heathenism rather than the natural growth
of Christianity.

When the service had ended, it was growing dark out
of doors. The Gonfalonieri were accompanied by their
guard and a band of music to the city-hall, and the
illumination which had been prepared for the evening
celebration was begun. As the night became darker,
the scene became more beautiful. From the gate in
the old wall down through the main street leading to
the square, the houses were prettily lighted up; but
in the square itself, the churches, and all the buildings round them, were brilliant with lamps, while lights
shone down from the ancient castle crowning the hill
that rises above the city. In a little chapel, whose outside was covered with colored lamps, a choir of boys
was singing. The townspeople and the peasants, in holiday costume, were assembled in great numbers to see
and take part in the show. The night was calm, so that
the lamps burned steadily ; and the pleasure of the time
was increased by the mildness of the air, which had no
touch of winter in it. The great church, such a church as
is found only in Northern Italy, with the irregular mould

ings of its doors, its quaint carvings, and its beautiful rose-window, stood upon its platform, raised above the level of the place, looking only the more venerable in the imperfect brilliancy of the illumination, which, while it sharply defined some of the main lines of the *façade*, left broad spaces of wall in dim and shadowy obscurity. An illumination is, perhaps, always quite as fine in its effects of darkness as of light; and while the eye is charmed with the shining and brilliant lines cut sharp against the dark sky, or with the fiery ornaments of crosses and stars that lie against the black walls, or with the pencillings of light that show the exquisite delicacy and gracefulness of some ancient stone-cut ornament, — the imagination leaves all these, and wanders off to lose itself among the hidden secrets of the dense masses of blackness that catch not even a reflection of the brightness around them, but lie deeper and darker than night, vague and mysterious, in the very heart of light.

PISA.

There are few buildings in the world so complete in their effect, so impressive at first sight, and of such increasing interest upon longer acquaintance, as the Duomo group at Pisa. Forsyth has expressed a portion of their peculiar charm, in one of those vivid and poetic half-lines with which he redeems his cynical criticisms, when he speaks of them as "fortunate alike in their society and their solitude." Pisa has an air of repose, but not the air of decay which is usually associated with it in Italian cities. It is at once quiet and cheerful, and in its most

retired part, close to the battlemented wall, remote from
bustle, but not secluded from approach, stand the Cathedral, the Baptistery, the Campo Santo, and the Leaning
Tower. To their original beauties time has added those
which come only with age, softening and harmonizing all
that was rough and incongruous, and giving to their white
marble a hue which can be described only as that of
marble interfused with the yellow rays of sunshine, and,
while adding these beauties, has accumulated with them
all the charms of Art and of association. The contrast
between the color of the buildings and the blue sky is
beautiful; and the slanting shadows, thrown by a clear
afternoon sun from the seven circles of the pillars of the
Tower, from the pillared stories of the front of the Duomo,
and from the exquisite tracery of the arches of the Campo Santo, produce effects which show how Nature delights
to adorn and embellish the well-executed works of man.

For the student of the works of the early artists, there
is no place in Italy of greater interest than the Campo
Santo. Its treasures have often been described; but
description can convey only an imperfect impression of
the solemn beauty and sacred interest of the place. All
its frescoes have suffered from the injuries of weather,
and the worse injuries of re-painting; many of them are
almost obliterated, many have been shattered by careless
work upon the building, many broken away to give place
to worthless modern sepulchral monuments; some are
patched with bits of coarse raw plaster, or clamped with
bands of iron that interrupt their finest passages; yet they
still retain enough of outline and of color to indicate what

they must once have been, and to give a strong impression of the character and motives of their authors. Nor
is their interest only that of works of genius. In this
consecrated burial-place, these pictures were to prepare
the soul for life and for death. They were not the vain
imaginings of the fancy, not for mere delight of the eyes,
but they were representations of the deepest and most
essential realities. It is in them that one may find the
religious ideas of the Middle Ages exhibited in their
most impressive forms ; and, spite of all grotesqueness of
arrangement, deficiency of drawing, ignorance of composition, and absence of the graces of a later age, it is from
them that one may learn the power of an art, which,
though it embodies crude and false religious notions, does
so with a simple and sincere faith. In seeing these frescoes, one feels that the *picturæ ecclesiarum* were indeed
in those times the *libri laicorum*. The lessons they
taught were easily learned, and the stories they told were
too plain to be misunderstood.

There are few places which are so harmonious in their
character with the works of Art they contain as this
Campo Santo. The cloistered aisles paved with sepulchral slabs, — the sun falling through the Gothic tracery
of the arches, and casting down dark shadows upon the
effigies of crusaders and religious men, worn with the
steps of centuries, — the relics of ancient sculpture, and of
Middle-Age carvings, placed around the lower walls, —
the sarcophagi in which the ashes of kings have lain, —
the chains that marked the ancient servitude of Pisa, now
restored by Florence, and hung up here, where jealousies

and rivalries are to be forgotten, — the consecrated earth from Palestine, covered with the greenest grass, — the dark cypress, the closed-in quiet and solitude, — all give to this Campo Santo that solemnity and beauty of aspect, that air of peacefulness and repose, which befit the burial-place where a city has laid its chosen dead for more than five hundred years.

There is one other scene in Pisa of such great beauty that it deserves to be remembered even with the cathedral buildings. It is the Lung' Arno at sunset. The sun goes down behind the Ponte a Mare and the Torre Guelfa. The heavy, irregular arches of the bridge, and the tall, square mass of the tower, stand out against the red sky, and are reflected in the rapid water. On the southern bank stands the little gem-like chapel of the Spina, — its white marble pinnacles, crockets, and finials catching something of the sunset glow. On the other bank is the line of houses and palaces, conspicuous among which is that which bears the chain over its door, and the words, " Alla Giornata," cut on the block from which it hangs. To the north and east, miles away, the mountains rise blue above the city, their snow-tipped summits tinged with a golden rose-color. And

" On the surface of the fleeting river
The wrinkled image of the city lay,
Immovably unquiet, and forever
It trembles, and it does not pass away."

FLORENCE, 16th Dec., 1855, Sunday.

For some days past, notice has been given, by a placard posted at the church-doors, and in other places, that to-day the Compagnia della Misericordia (the Brotherhood of Mercy) would visit the church of the Santissima Vergine Annunziata, the protectress of Florence, to render solemn thanks to her for having delivered the city from the scourge of cholera. This Compagnia is one of the most remarkable institutions, and this church one of the most interesting churches of Florence. The church derives its name from a wonderful picture, in which the head of the Virgin is said to have been painted by angels while the artist slept, and which was formerly venerated for its miracle-working power throughout Northern Italy. The picture is not shown except on occasion of the most solemn ceremonies. It is usually kept covered by a veil, upon which is painted a head of the Saviour by Andrea del Sarto. The *cortile* in front of the church contains several frescoes by the same artist, and over the door of the cloisters at its side is his famous Madonna del Sacco, which, although faded, and otherwise injured by time, still retains enough beauty to justify its ancient reputation, and to place it among the finest works of this unhappy painter. The chapel of the Virgin, overloaded with the rich gifts and votive offerings of her worshippers, is decorated with lilies, which are at once the device of the city and the emblem of its protectress. Round about it burn forty-two lamps of silver; and no chapel in Florence is more brilliant, or more frequented. The worship of the Virgin seems now to be at its height in

Italy, * and her churches and chapels are everywhere receiving new honors.

* That the Virgin has long been the chief object of worship among the common people in Italy is notorious, and the present Pope has done much to increase the devotion to her. Since the dogma of the Immaculate Conception was pronounced, this devotion has prevailed to a greater extent than ever before, and becomes, apparently, more and more exclusive. The present condition of Christianity in Italy is one of the most striking and sad of the many sad aspects that she presents. In a little book of services for the use of the devout at this church of the Most Holy Maria Annunziata, it is said that the Pope, by his Brief of the 10th of July, 1854, has conceded an indulgence of three hundred days to whoever shall recite devoutly the following prayer: —

> A Voi, O Vergine Madre,
> Che mai foste tocca,
> Da reo alcun di colpa
> Nè attuale nè originale
> Raccomando ed affido,
> La purità del mio cuore.

The pamphlet closes with a hymn of praise to the Virgin, of an extraordinary character. It reminds one of a political song. It will hardly bear translation: its first stanza is as follows: —

> Or l' Inno s' innalzi,
> Del fervido Evviva,
> Che dolce alla riva
> Dell' Arno echeggiò.
>   Sul labbro devoto,
>   Continovo sia,
> Evviva Maria, e chi la creò,
> Evviva l' Angelo, chi l' annunzio.

Eleven stanzas of a similar nature succeed to this, all ending with the same burden; and to the recitation of this hymn, also, Pius IX. has annexed an indulgence of three hundred days.

Some time before three o'clock, which was the hour fixed for the departure of the procession of the Misericordia from its chapel at the corner of the Via della Morte, in the square of the Duomo, the streets in the neighbor- hood of the Annunziata, and the piazza in front of it, were filled by crowds of people desirous to see the show, and to gain even a distant share in the blessing that might attend the performance of the ceremony. The church was already filled to overflowing, except the por- tion of it which was reserved for the Brotherhood. A lit- tle after three the procession began to appear, walking up a pathway opened for it by soldiers. At its head were several priests in their robes, one bearing a cross ; then followed the brethren in their long black dresses and black masks, which are so familiar to every one who has been in Florence, their faces wholly concealed, except where their eyes appear through narrow slits. Their black hats hung upon their backs, and each man carried in his hand an unlighted candle. They walked two and two ; and it was only by differences in their gait, and now and then by some stray lock of hair, or by some wrinkle seen through the opening in the black mask, that the difference of age amongst them could be discovered, — while by the contrast in the character of their hands something of the diversity of their callings in life might be guessed at ; for this Brotherhood of Mercy includes in its ranks young and old, noblemen and mechanics, — and distinctions disappear beneath its black hoods.

The popular tradition in regard to the origin of the Misericordia, taken from a book written in the sixteenth century, by Messer Francisco Ghislieri, a citizen of Florence, is as follows : —

"It was in the year of our Lord Jesus Christ, 1240. At this time the city of Florence and her citizens were engaged in the traffic of merchandise, or rather in dealings in woollen cloths, which, by their excellence of fabric, supplied all the cities of the world, so that two fairs were held every year, on St. Simon's and St. Martin's days, at each one of which were present the richest merchants of Italy, who came from abroad to provide themselves with all sorts of stuffs. And so great a sale was there, that the least that was spent at each one of those fairs was fifteen or sixteen millions of the florins of this city. Wherefore many porters and carriers of burdens were needed to carry the aforesaid cloths and wools to and from the shops, the dye-houses, and wash-houses, and other places needful to the making of these goods, all for the greater convenience of the workmen who were engaged in the forementioned manufacture. Now the greater number of these porters used to assemble on the piazza of San Giovanni, or of Santa Maria del Fiore, as a place assigned to them by the Republic of Florence, to await there the opportunities of employment, which continually occurred. On this place was a range of vaults, supposed to belong to the Adimari, which stood always open, on account of being subject to inundation. These cellars the porters made use of for shelter, especially in the winter, against the rain and the rigor of the cold, collecting around the fire, and amusing themselves with play, when they had no work to do, which, indeed, occurred but rarely. It happened that among the seventy or eighty porters who assembled there, was one Piero di Luca Borsi, a man advanced in years, who held in devout regard the most holy name of God, and who was greatly scandalized at hearing every little while the Maker of Every Good abused by the blasphemies of his wicked companions. He therefore resolved, as their elder, to propose to them that every time any one of them should dare to utter blasphemies against God, or against his Most Holy Mother, he should immediately without fail put a bit of copper coin into a box destined to this object, in penitence for his fault, and in order utterly to root out so pernicious an abuse and so grave a sin. The proposition pleased his companions, who promised to adopt it, and so maintain it that it might result to the greater glory of the Divine Majesty.*

"Much time having passed with this devout custom, and a good sum of money having accumulated in the box, it seemed well to Piero di Luca to make another proposition to them, which might be of no less profit than the first, since it was to serve for the benefit both of soul and body. He proposed to them to make six dresses

---

* Old institutions appear under new conditions. The following paragraph was published in the New York *Evening Post*, in June, 1859, in the summary of news from California. —

" An ' Anti-Cursing Club ' has been formed at Grass Valley, Cal., the members of which are fined twenty-five cents for every oath, the money to be appropriated to some worthy purpose from time to time. At the last accounts, the club had cursed enough to buy a pew, and there was a balance on hand."

with masks, large enough to fit a person of common height and size, and to allot one to each section of the city, choosing one or more porters who should wear it from week to week, and should receive from the box a giulio * for each journey that they might make through the city, in order to carry to such place as they might wish, or to the hospitals, the sick poor, as well as those who might fall from buildings, or might fall dead or fainting, and those murdered, and those who might be found in the streets in any condition that needed human aid. The wise proposition and good counsel of Piero pleased all his companions, who swore carefully to observe, and with all diligence and charity to maintain this project. And it was also agreed by them to do so without receiving the pay proposed ; for the reward of charity is to be required in the other life, from the hands of God, who recompenses each man justly.   Thus for the space of many years they continued to engage in this exercise of mercy, with such applause from the citizens, that, had they wished to accept great sums of money, which were offered to them, they might have gained as much as three *giuli* each time they went out, if their excellent leader, Piero, had not refused them, in the hope of winning an eternal blessing.

"At this time the above-named Piero passed to the other life, and another of them was moved by a divine inspiration to provide a picture of Christ Dead, at whose feet he placed a little box, with an inscription upon it,

---

* A small silver coin.

2

which said, 'Give alms for the poor, sick, and needy
of the city,' and to put this, with the picture of Christ
Dead, near to the church of San Giovanni,* on the day
of Pardon, which falls on the 13th of January. His
thought was to make use of the money in buying some
chambers for a chapel for the use of the Company, that
they might there make prayers, and discourse of the
affairs pertaining to this pious exercise of mercy. His
good thought was finally approved by all, and so put
in practice, that on that day so many devout people
united in giving alms, that the little box was not large
enough to hold all the money that was offered by the
faithful at the feet of the Saviour for the poor and
distressed; so that they found about five hundred florins, which were enough to buy some chambers above
the vaults that have been spoken of, and to arrange them
for the use of the Company."

This quaint tradition, which even in its form bears
the mark of age, may or may not contain the true account of the beginning of the Misericordia. It is well
to believe a story which reflects so truly the national
pride of the Florentines, representing the goods of their
city as the best, her fairs as the most frequented, and her
very porters as the worthiest of the time, — and which
gives such a vivid illustration of the power of pictures,
when men painted them from their hearts, and the
figure of the Saviour stood for the real image of Him

---

* Dante's "Il mio bel San Giovanni," now the Baptistery of Flor
ence, with the bronze gates by Andrea Pisano and Ghiberti.

who died on the Cross. Those were the days when
Florence was capable of the noblest things, — the days
just before Dante's time, just before Giotto began to
build his Campanile. What is certain in regard to the
Company is, that its earliest records are lost, but that in
1361 a new body of statutes was adopted for its government, and that still earlier, in 1348, during the terrible
plague, made famous by Boccaccio, which in the course
of six months carried off more than half the population
of the city, that is, more than fifty thousand out of its
ninety thousand inhabitants, this brotherhood had so distinguished themselves by their self-devotion and their
fidelity to duty in the season of hardest trial, and had
so gained the attachment of their fellow-citizens, that
their treasury was enriched by legacies amounting to
thirty-five thousand golden florins, a sum equal to at
least three hundred thousand dollars at the present day.

From this time the sphere of their charities went on
continually enlarging. They no longer took charge of
the sick and the dead alone, but large sums were annually set apart for clothing the naked, liberating prisoners, and giving dowries to poor maidens. They also
took charge of children who were abandoned by their
parents, and it would appear from some of the early
records that they paid for the bringing up of the children in different trades. The Florentine statutes, towards
the end of the fourteenth century, order that all wandering and lost children should be carried to the House of
the Misericordia; and as a proof of the estimation in
which the Company was held, it is mentioned that in 1365

the monks of Camaldoli petitioned that the great chapel of the new church they were building in Florence might receive its title from the Misericordia, and that the church might be one of those where once a year, on the day of Santa Lucia, the Company caused the Mass of the Abandoned to be celebrated. *

In 1368, a new pestilence gave occasion for fresh displays of the good works of the Brotherhood and the gratitude of the people. A curious story remains to show the uprightness of the spirit by which the Company was ruled. It appears that in those days, when the wicked believed that by a pious legacy they might gain absolution for their crimes, one Neri Boscoli, a banker, who had passed many years in Naples, made the Misericordia the heir to his great property, which report said had been gained by evil usury. The Company, fearing lest it might become, as it were, the accomplice and the heir of wickedness, if it should receive ill-gained money, called to their council the most famous theologians of the city, and did not accept the legacy until it was determined, in a solemn and extraordinary assembly, that it might

---

* The Mass of the Abandoned is a mass said for the souls of those who, from poverty or other cause, have been unable to provide for the masses to be said for their repose after death, or have left no friends by whom this pious charge may be undertaken, and, thus "abandoned," need the aid of charity. Dante affords many illustrations of this doctrine of the Church: for example: —

"Io fui di Montefeltro, i' son Buonconte:
Giovanna o altri *non ha di me cura*,
Peroh' io vo tra costor con bassa fronte."

Purg. V. 88.

be received for use in works of charity, because thus
that could be returned to the poor which had been un-
justly taken from them, — with the additional provision,
that restitution should be made to all who could prove
that they had suffered from the usury of which this legacy was the result.

During the unhappy period when Cosmo de' Medici
was ruling and corrupting Florence, the Misericordia, of
which he was jealous, as a body possessing too much
power over the affections of the citizens, and as likely to
act by itself too independently, was gradually deprived
of its ancient statutes, and forced to accept essential
changes of organization.   By degrees it lost its old character, its funds were misused in lavish profusion and
worthless bounties, the patrimony of the poor became
the plunder of the rich, and only the memory of the good
name of the Company remained.   But, sixteen years
after the death of Cosmo, in 1480, an incident occurred
which revived the half-extinguished flame of charity, and
gave new existence to the Brotherhood.   It appears that
a very poor man died, and no one came to bury him.
Then one who lived in the same house took the body
upon his shoulders, and carried it to the Palace of the
Signoria.*   The Gonfalonier, at the sight of this specta-
cle, said, struck with wonder, "What is this?" "Behold," replied the man, "the result of the neglect of the
laws, and of good customs!"   And leaving the corpse at
the feet of the magistrate, he went away.   This circum-

* Now called the Palazzo Vecchio.

stance caused a great commotion among the people.
They recalled the good old times, when, if the poor man
had no friends to bury him decently, the Misericordia
took charge of his funeral, and bore him to the grave
with prayers and all the offices of religion. They remembered and repeated the good deeds of the Brotherhood in tending the sick and providing for the needy,
and they lamented that it no longer existed. Not long
after this, it was determined to reconstitute the Society,
and in 1489 new statutes were established, and the
Misericordia once more began its unending work. The
number of the brothers was fixed at seventy-two, thirty
priests and forty-two laymen; and this number was
chosen, "inasmuch as our Lord Jesus Christ, besides
his apostles, instituted and ordained seventy-two disciples,
who were to go through the world with charity, preaching and scattering the seed of his doctrine; so we wish
that the aforesaid number of our fraternity and company,
seventy-two, should go through our land of Florence, ex-
ercising the works of mercy and charity, and especially
in regard to the burying of the poor and wretched dead,*
without any pay or reward, but only for the love of
Jesus Christ, who, through love of us, underwent his
death and passion."

The Company was not reorganized too soon. In 1495
the plague once more appeared in Florence, again in

---

* In respect to this particular injunction in regard to the burying
of the poor, the importance attached by the Roman Church to the
funeral rites is to be remembered.

1498, and still again in 1509. In all these years, the Misericordia discharged its part with its ancient fidelity and courage, and added to its other cares that of a hospital, in which the brothers took charge of the sick.   During the last dark years in which Florence retained even the name of a republic, from 1520 to 1530, pestilential diseases seem to have broken out from year to year, and to have kept pace with civil discord and political calamities. But the bitterness of party rage found no place under the dark gowns of the Misericordia, and political enmities never interfered with the discharge of the offices of charity. The Company survived the fall of the city, and from that time, for the last three hundred years, has pursued its unintermitting course of benevolence, — sometimes called on for special exertion, never without duties, ready for all seasons of trial, never failing, never disappointing the confidence reposed in it.

The present organization of the Misericordia is as follows : — There are seventy-two chiefs of the watch, of whom ten are dignitaries of the Church, fourteen noble laymen, called freemen, twenty priests, not dignitaries, and twenty-eight laymen, not noble, called wearers of aprons, or artisans ; and these preside, four every day, over the arrangement and good order of the expeditions to be made through the city. In addition to these, who form the body of the Company, there are numerous novices and volunteers enrolled under different titles ; so that the whole number of the members now amounts to 1440, a number sufficient to meet all the usual demands upon the Society. The members take their turns of ser vice in a regular succession of days ; and whenever they are needed, they are called to assemble at the house of the Society by a bell, whose tolling may be heard over all the city. A day scarcely ever passes without its solemn summons being sounded. The members on duty collect at their place of meeting, and, putting on their black gowns and masks, depart together, generally bearing upon their shoulders a bier hung also with black. As they pass along the streets, every one who meets them lifts his hat, and the soldiers on guard present arms in token of honor. Having accomplished their duty, they return to their chapel, and, in entering it, each says to the one at his side, "May God give you your reward !" Then, after saying the Lord's Prayer, they take off their disguise, and return to their usual occupations.

In the year that is just going out, Florence has been exposed to great trial, and the Misericordia has given fresh proofs of its devotion, and of the value of its pious services. The cholera broke out early in the summer. At the commencement of the epidemic, the Company called together its members with the accustomed sound of its bell. But the tolling became so frequent that it increased the alarm which the disease created. Then the members assembled in numbers at their chapel, and stood waiting in readiness for the calls, which were not long delayed. On one day seventy-seven biers were counted, borne by them through the city. The number of members at last became too small for the increasing need, and a hundred temporary assistants were added There was no pause in their indefatigable labors

With the danger their courage increased," says the account from which a great part of the preceding narrative has been taken; * "and during this period, the Company of the Misericordia showed itself not only admirable, but sublime."

It was to render thanks for the ceasing of the epidemic that the Brotherhood went in procession to-day to the Church of the Annunziata. Remembering the long series of years, stretching back from century to century, through which this society has carried on its unbroken course of benevolence, recalling the principles upon which it was founded, seeing in it the visible token of the desire of men to conform themselves to the example of Christ, beholding in its mask the sign of that humility which desires not to have its good deeds known of men, it was impossible to stand by unmoved, as the procession passed; and one could not but feel a thrill of sympathetic pleasure in the pride with which poor Florence regards these sons of hers, who do so much to keep up one of the best traditions of her Past.

* *La Compagnia della Misericordia di Firenze.* Cenni Storici di Celestino Bianchi. Firenze, 1855.

See also Passerini, *Storia degli Stabilimenti di Beneficenza e d' Istruzione elementare gratuita della Città di Firenze.* 1858.

ROME.

STENDHAL begins the Roman entries in his brilliant
" Promenades dans Rome" with the following words :
" C'est pour la sixième fois que j'entre dans la *ville
éternelle*, et pourtant mon cœur est profondément agité.
C'est un usage immémorial parmi les gens affectés d'être
ému en arrivant à Rome, et j'ai presque honte de ce que
je viens d'écrire."

Three days ago, the old Prince Corsini died, and to-
day his body has been lying in state in the great palace
of his family.   It was in this palace that Christina, Queen
of Sweden and daughter of Gustavus Adolphus, died.

To-day the doors have been open, and every one who
desired has been admitted to see the state apartments
and the dead Prince.   All sorts of persons have been
going up the magnificent double flight of stairs, — ladies
and gentlemen, poor women with their babies in their
arms, priests, soldiers, ragged workmen, boys and girls,
and strangers of all kinds.   There were no signs of

mourning about the house, but in the first great saloon
sat two men in black gowns, busily employed in writing,
as if making inventories; and in each of the next two
rooms were two priests in their showy robes, performing
separate masses, while many people knelt on the floors,
and others streamed through to the apartment in which
the corpse was laid out.   Here, on a black and yellow
carpet, in the middle of the floor, surrounded by benches
which were covered with a black cloth on which was a
faded yellow pattern of a skeleton with a scythe, lay the
body of the old man.   He was eighty-nine years old; but
here was nothing of the dignity of age, or the repose of
death.   The corpse was dressed in full court-costume, — in
a bright-blue coat, with gold laces and orders upon the
breast, white silk stockings, and varnished pumps. It had
on a wig, and its lips and cheeks were rouged.   At its feet
and at its head was a candle burning; two hired mourners
sat at each side, and two soldiers kept the crowd from
pressing too near or lingering too long.   The room, which
was not darkened, was hung with damask of purple and
gold, and the high ceiling was painted with gay frescoes of
some story of the gods.   It was a scene fit for the gravedigger's grim jokes and Hamlet's sad philosophy.

Many years ago, Prince Corsini held the office of Senator of Rome, and at the time of his election the lions
of the Capitol and the Barberini Triton spouted wine
instead of water, as when Rienzi was made Tribune; but
he Prince's name will hardly be remembered by another
generation, unless it be by the readers of Landor's "Im-
aginary Conversations."

The palace has that air of incomplete magnificence
and partial neglect which belongs to so many of the palaces of Rome, and of the South. There are statues in
the halls, but the tiled floors are coarse and damp, the
large windows are filled with rattling and dim glass.
Painted wooden columns are set up opposite marble ones.
The beautiful garden, stretching behind the palace toward
the Janiculum, has been left to decay. Its iron gate is
rusted, its regular walks overgrown with mould and green
moss. Its alleys, arched over with myrtles, are weedy
and dark and damp. Everything wears a look of dilap-
idation, and the sentiment of the place is that belonging
to declining splendor and neglected beauty.

In the evening, a showy funeral procession, with carriages, and long trains of priests with candles and chanting, accompanied the body of the Prince to the church of
St. John Lateran, where, in the gorgeous family chapel,
it was once more laid in state, as a show for indifferent
spectators. His servants for the last time rouged the
wrinkled cheeks, and arranged the dyed moustaches, and
then left the body to the care of the priests, who sat
drowsily reading their services over it. The chapel
itself was not brilliantly lighted, though it appeared so
by contrast with the rest of the church. A few candles
were burning at the high altar, but their rays were soon
scattered in the immense spaces of the nave and aisles.
Now and then, some attendant, with a candle in his hand,
passed across, — his light making the surrounding darkness darker, and the distance more obscure. In this
dimness, the vastness of the church became far more

impressive than in the daylight. The fluttering statues in the piers lost their air of dressiness and disquiet, and looked down from their niches like the peaceful shades of Saints and Apostles.

18th January, 1856, Sunday.

The annual festival called the Festa delle Lingue has taken place at the Propaganda to-day. This college was founded by Pope Gregory XV., in 1622, under the impulse, as it seems, of a sincere Christian spirit. In his bull relating to the institution he said: "Christ's charge to the successors of Peter is, 'Feed my lambs.' But how many strayed sheep still remain, — sheep who have never known the fold of Christ, or who have wandered away from it!" And it was to accomplish this charge, so far as lay within his power, that the Pope established a college into which students from distant infidel or heretic countries were to be received, and whence, having been instructed in the doctrines of the Church, they were to go out as missionaries to their native lands. Gregory died before his institution had received its full development; but it was warmly supported by his successor, Urban VIII., from whom it took its name of the Collegio Urbano de Propagandâ Fide; and from that time until the present it has flourished under the protection of successive popes. During the past year, one hundred and hirty-three pupils, from every quarter of the world, have received instruction within its walls. Italian is made the common language of communication and instruction, but each of the pupils is required to keep up his acquaintance with his native tongue, that he may preserve the power to address his own countrymen.

Once a year, on the octave of the Epiphany, an exhibition is held, at which the pupils recite compositions upon the same subject, but each in a different language. It is always an occasion of interest, and to-day the little chapel of the Propaganda, which is in the large and ugly brown building forming one end of the Piazza di Spagna, where the College has its seat, was crowded by an audience which seemed composed of persons of almost as many nations as were represented by the pupils. The chapel is badly arranged and badly lighted. It is hung with red and yellow curtains, and pervaded, if one may use the expression, by an absence of simplicity and good taste. The pupils were placed upon a platform at its end. Immediately in front sat two or three cardinals and the instructors, while all the rest of the room was filled by the spectators, amongst whom a few of the Swiss guard were stationed to keep the passage-ways from being choked up. The services were commenced without any special form and with no ceremony. One of the pupils delivered a short prologue in Italian, from which it appeared that the subject which had been chosen for the compositions of to-day was the miraculous escape from injury of the Pope and many other distinguished ecclesiastics, together with a portion of the students of the Propaganda, in the giving way of the floor of a room in the convent of Sant' Agnese fuori le Mura, in which they were assembled. The accident took place last April. The Pope had gone out in the morning to visit the re-

cently discovered church of Sant' Alessandro, and on his
return had stopped at the unoccupied convent of Sant'
Agnese. Here there was a considerable assemblage of
persons, including those who had accompanied him, and
others who here joined his suite. The floor of the room
in the second story in which they were collected suddenly
gave way. Most of the company fell with the floor; the
Pope was overthrown, but not precipitated to the lower
story. Several persons were more or less injured; there
was a scene of great confusion, but no one was killed or
irrecoverably hurt. In the performance of this afternoon, the escape of the Pope, and the comparatively
slight harm caused by the accident, were ascribed to the
miraculous interposition of the Virgin, and, in addition to
her favor, to the good offices of the three holy Magi, who
are regarded as the special patrons of the Propaganda.
Their relation to this institution arises from the belief
that the visit of the three kings to the manger, and their
adoration of the Infant Saviour, were typical of the final
subjection of all heathen nations to the throne of Christ.
The legend of the Church represents them as returning
from Bethlehem to their own distant lands as the
first missionaries of the gospel of Christ, and their
story has from very early times been considered as
significant of the calling of the Gentiles. They are,
therefore, regarded as the patron saints of missionary
enterprise.

The prologue in Italian was followed by a series of
performances in the Eastern languages, and, for the benefit of those who understood only the common tongues, a

programme in Italian was distributed which contained an abstract of the different parts. The first was in Hebrew, upon the delight of Satan at the danger of the Pope and of the pupils. The next was in Chaldee, a dialogue between two young men from Mesopotamia; and this was followed by parts in Syriac, Armenian, Arabic, Chinese, Georgian, Bengalee, and so on, each spoken, with very few exceptions, by young men to whom these languages were their native tongues. The Persian, for instance, was delivered by Signor Luigi Sciauriz, of Mardin in Mesopotamia, and the Koptic by Angelo Kabis, of Achmin in Egypt; Mardin and Achmin being places which it is hard to believe have as actual a reality as those which we hear of every day, and in the midst of which we live. In the second portion of the exhibition, the portion that was made up of parts in the Western tongues, occurred some more familiar names. For instance, a boy named Thomas Pinckney, from Walterborough, U. S., took a share in an Italian dialogue, and Thomas Beeker, of Pittsburg, delivered an animated poem in Irish. Most of the parts were in verse; but it would have been dull work to listen to them, had they all been in one language. In the sounds of thirty-seven different languages it was easy to find entertainment; and in the sight of young men from so many countries, united in one common object and mode of life, there was interest enough to overbalance their individual dulness. It would have been hard to find a subject less suited for the average of poetic and oratoric power than the one chosen for this display; and it was a curious specimen of bad taste and bad judgment that such a topic should have been selected for a commemoration that might be made so striking by a proper choice. On one occasion, not many years since, the subject given out was "The Tower of Babel," or the confusion of tongues. A more appropriate topic could hardly have been found.

January 20th, 1856.

The Festa of Sant' Antonio commenced three days ago, at his little church just beyond Santa Maria Maggiore, and will continue for two or three days longer. It is the occasion of one of the most curious customs of the Church, — the blessing of the animals. Sunday is generally the day upon which the ceremony may be seen to most advantage, for then the country people have leisure to come into the city with their horses and other creatures to get the blessing of the priest; but to-day has been gray and wet from the beginning, so as to prevent as large an attendance as usual. This afternoon, a good many people were in the church, looking at the coarse frescoes which represent the temptations of the Saint, and there was something of a crowd, chiefly made up of boys and beggars, about the doors. At the side door, just out of the rain, stood a good-natured, dirty-looking priest, with a brush in his hand and an earthen jug full of water at his side, who, when a carriage or a wagon drove up or passed by, shook his brush, dipped in the holy water, at the horses, and muttered some words of benediction. A good many of the country carts came along and stopped at the door; their drivers gave the priest a little fee for shaking his brush, and then went on. Many of the car-

riages came, apparently, to bring persons who wanted to
see the show, if by chance there were any; but others
were brought up with the express purpose of getting a
blessing for the horses, which was paid for according to
the wealth of the owner, or perhaps according to his
superstition or his love of display. It is a rule here, that
those blessings which we are accustomed to consider the
free gifts of God must be paid for in some way, either in
hard money or in harder penance. Heaven is not given
away in Rome. The Pope himself, the cardinals, and
the nobles, all send their horses, during the course of the
feast, to be blessed. Torlonia sends his best carriage
drawn by eighteen horses. The coachmen are in their
best liveries, and the footmen splendid in powder and
lace. . It is said he pays a thousand dollars for the
benediction.

Beside the wagons and carriages that came this afternoon, (the air was so gray and thick that one could not
see the Alban Hills,) there were a good many horses and
donkeys ridden up one by one, or sometimes two or three
together. Some of them had ribbons braided in their
tails and manes, and hanging about them in streamers,
and their riders looked as fine as the horses; while others
were such rough, uncared-for, bare-boned, worn-looking
creatures, that one could not but wish that the blessing
would turn into a good supper and shelter for them.
This odd custom is a very old one, and strikingly illus-
trative of the character of many of the observances cherished by the Church in Italy, as means by which the
superstition of the poor may be turned to the benefit of

the priests. I say the superstition of the poor, though
Torlonia's thousand dollars may outweigh all the pence
of the peasants; for such a custom can last only while it
is founded on the popular belief. If the poor should
learn to distrust St. Anthony, and neglect to send their
scrubby donkeys for his blessing, the princes would not
be long in following their example. But in these States
of the Church the progress of intelligence is stopped, and
a spiritual police, more watchful than any municipal one,
takes good care that it shall not, by force or by stealth,
break through the barriers imposed upon it.

At a little distance from the church was a thick crowd
of children, who were making such a noise that I went to
see what it was about. I found they were surrounding a
man who was making and selling what looked like molasses candy. He could not sell it fast enough for his
customers, who squeezed him and shouted at him without
mercy. He had a pot boiling over a fire of small sticks,
and when his supply of the ready-made article was
fairly exhausted, he poured out the contents of his pot
(a mixture of honey and sugar) upon a white marble
slab which he had upon a chair at his side, and after it
had sufficiently cooled, he began to pull it in the same
way in which molasses candy was pulled when we were
young. It quickly began to change from black to white,
and at the same time the uproar, which had somewhat
abated while the little children were watching the progress of the manufacture, began with redoubled energy.
The smallest boys crept between his legs and stuck up
their eager heads, with a half-*baiocco* in their hands, in

the hope of getting a chance at one of the pieces of a fin-
ger's lengtl that he broke off from the long stringy mass.
Little girls carrying babies, big boys who with a whole
baiocco could buy two pieces, others who had no money
and could only look at what they wanted to eat, all
crowded up, shouting and laughing.   Children are alike
the world over, but these were more charming than a
common crowd of children, for every one was full of excitement, which yet was not so intense as to threaten any
sad revulsion of feeling.   Their eyes were glittering,
their voices raised to the highest point, their hands fuller
of eagerness than of money; but as one by one got his
piece, there was such absolute sweetness in their mouths,
such a cessation in their shouting, and such a perfect content over their dirty, happy, pretty faces, that, in seeing
them, the bystanders had almost as much satisfaction as
the children themselves.   It was by far the best part of
the show of the blessing of the horses.

A celebration has been going on for two or three days
past at the church of Sant' Andrea delle Fratte, — one
of the oddest and most irrational of Borromini's fantastic
erections, — in commemoration of the miraculous conversion of a Jew that took place here in 1842.   The occurrence is remarkable as being one of the latest and best
authenticated miracles of the Roman Church, and it
affords an illustration of the origin and adoption of
many of those miracles with which the annals of the
Church have been full, since the apostolic days.   I
bought the authorized narrative at the church-door

this afternoon, and this is the account which it contains : —

"In January, 1842, a young and wealthy Jew of Strasbourg, named Alfonso Maria Ratisbonne, came to Rome on a journey of pleasure. Here he met an old friend of his, the Baron de Bussierre, who was residing in Rome, and who accompanied him in many of his visits to the places which every stranger desires to see. The Baron, being a good Christian, was grieved to find his friend fixed in his belief as a Jew, and frequently urged upon him the arguments in favor of Christianity. One day he begged him to accept a medal with the effigy of Our Lady the Queen of the Angels upon it. Ratisbonne, more to satisfy his friend than to profess the least veneration for the Madonna, with a smile hung this miraculous medal about his neck. The Baron, rejoiced at his success, did not delay to address daily the most fervent prayers to the Most High for the conversion of his friend, and directed his two young daughters to recite every evening some Ave Marias for the conversion of Alfonso. Moreover, he went to the Count Laferronays, his confidant, who was most devoted and attached to the Catholic religion, and begged him also, with the same object, to address fervent prayers to the Most High, and to the Great Mother, the Most Holy Mary. A few days afterwards, Count Laferronays suddenly died. On the 20th of January, Bussierre met Ratisbonne, who told him that he was about to leave the city, his affairs not permitting him to make a longer stay. The Baron, regretting to hear this, begged him to accompany him to the church

of Sant' Andrea delle Fratte, whither he was about to go
to make some arrangements with one of the friars for the
Count's funeral. Having arrived there, he left Ratisbonne
in the church, while he went for a few minutes into one
of the adjoining apartments. Ratisbonne was looking at
the objects of interest, and observing the ceremonies of
the funeral of a noble lady, when all of a sudden the
church disappeared and a dazzling light shone round
about him. He was transported, without knowing how,
before the altar of Saint Michael, where the light ceased,
and, raising his eyes, he saw upon this very altar the Most
Holy Mary, beautiful and shining, who with her hand
made a sign to him to kneel down, and he, obeying, knelt.
Bussierre, at this moment returning, saw his friend upon
his knees and weeping. He asked him what was the
matter, but Ratisbonne did not reply. Then Bussierre
went to the College of the Propaganda, which stands just
opposite the church, to beg some of the Jesuit Fathers to
come with him and speak with Ratisbonne. They hast-
ened back, and Ratisbonne, then drawing the medal from
his breast, said, 'I have seen her! I have seen her!' and
then proceeded to give an account of the appearance of
the Virgin, ending with the declaration of his desire to
be baptized. And so, on the 31st of the month, he was
baptized by the Cardinal Patrizi, and received the sacraments of Regeneration, of Confirmation, and of the Most
Holy Communion, in the presence of a great crowd of
people. Shortly after, he entered the order of the Jesuits
in France, and is still living."

This is the story, whose facts may, it seems to me, be

fully accepted and believed, without regarding them as
miraculous.   The excitement, which no one is exempt
from, in first visiting Rome, — the knowledge that his
conversion was an object of desire to his friend, and the
consequent dwelling of his own mind upon the subject, —
the impression made upon him by the ardent and imaginative fervor of Bussierre, — the superstitious feeling
very naturally produced in a weak mind by the wearing
of an image of the Virgin, — were enough, even if we
exclude the operation of other very probable influences,
such as fatigue, and the confusion of ideas to which one
not versed in the groundwork of his own faith is exposed
when surrounded by the exhibitions of the prevalence and
power of another, — were enough to produce in Ratisbonne a condition of the nervous system in which visions
are no longer improbable, and credulity accepts them as
miraculous realities.   Explanations of this sort seem to
be applicable to many of the stories of the Saints.   I see
no reason to distrust their visions, and can easily believe
that it was only the coarser conceptions of his followers
that changed St. Francis's vision of the Saviour, and his
imaginative reception of the *stigmata*, into the five actual
and visible wounds.   Multitudes of reported miracles
are nothing more than misunderstood natural events, and
many a good man has believed in miracles which were
only the result of the morbid action of his own mind.
Over the altar on which the Virgin appeared to Ratisbonne, there now hangs a picture of the Madonna as she
looked to him.   The chapel has been incrusted with the
most precious marbles, and many votive offerings are

hanging upon its walls. A miraculous image or picture is an immense advantage to a church; and Sant' Andrea delle Fratte, which was formerly rather poor and deserted, is now one of the most frequented and popular churches in this part of the city.

There is a *triduo* every year in honor of the appearance of the Virgin; and to-day, the anniversary of the miracle, services of great pomp have been going on from morning till evening. This afternoon a Dominican friar delivered an energetic sermon to a crowded and devout audience. It was an entertaining and picturesque composition. He described the rich and scornful Jew, visiting one after another of the holy places in Rome to scoff at them, laughing at the superstitions of his friends, and taking pride in the power of his own intellect and the antiquity of his faith; when suddenly, by the blessed interposition of the Most Holy Mother of God, all was changed. Then followed a long comparison of the conversion of Ratisbonne with that of St. Paul; and the sermon wound up with an address to the picture of the Virgin, appealing to her to protect her faithful and increase their number. During this invocation, the audience all turned toward the chapel of the miracle, and knelt. While the sermon was going on, the candles about the church had been lighted up, and the high altar shone with the hundreds that were arranged upon it. Then came some operatic sacred music; and finally a benediction, pronounced by a cardinal.

January 27th, 1856, Sunday.

A girl took the veil this morning at the church of Santa Cecilia, and entered the convent of Benedictine nuns.

Any one who desires to retain his imaginations of what this solemn and affecting scene might be should not go to witness the ceremony. I did not know this, and therefore went to the church to see it. In front of the *baldacchino* a temporary altar had been erected, and rows of chairs extended from this down the nave, leaving an open space in the centre. The church was gradually filled by spectators, who presented the strange variety usually found in the Roman churches on occasion of any peculiar solemnity. A large portion of them were foreigners attracted by mere curiosity, looking at the scene as at a show, and giving to the place the air of a theatre. There were many beggars and poor children, and a few Romans of the better classes. The seats in front were reserved for the friends of the girl who was about to leave them, and to enter those doors which open only to admit the living and to dismiss the dead. After waiting for some time, the cardinal who was to officiate — Cardinal Brunelli —entered with a small train of attendants, and took his seat in front of the altar. Very soon afterwards the novice came in, dressed in a ball costume, of white satin and laces, and with diamonds in her hair, followed by a lady also in full dress, and by two little girls in white, with wreaths of artificial flowers on their heads, and with wings of painted feathers fastened by silver buckles upon their shoulders. The novice knelt at the cardinal's

feet, repeated some few words, and then took a seat opposite a temporary pulpit, into which a priest ascended to
deliver a sermon.   It was a discourse upon the dove that
could find no rest for her foot upon the face of the earth
and sought for shelter within the ark.   One would have
thought that such a text, at such a time, could not but
give occasion to words that would touch the heart; but
the priest was a dry old man, with a husky and broken
voice, and he proceeded as if all feeling had left his soul
long ago.   He sat in the pulpit, and made up his sermon
of the emptiest commonplaces regarding the dangers and
miseries of the world, and the poorest compliments to
those who chose to quit it, and, by withdrawing themselves from its duties, to avoid its perils.   There was not
one word of earnest exhortation, of sincere joy, or of religious counsel.   The friends óf the girl were utterly
unmoved through the whole; she herself sat with little
expression of feeling; and the foreign spectators seemed
to care only that the sermon should be finished quickly.
When the priest had done, the girl rose and again knelt
before the cardinal.   After a few words, he raised her up,
and they proceeded down the church to the side door,
through which she entered into the convent.   While they
were going down the nave, a general rush took place
among the ladies to get standing-places upon a platform
erected in front of the grating, at which the remainder
of the ceremony was to take place.   It was an unseemly
and indecorous scene.   A few Swiss guards, in their har-
lequin dresses, endeavored vainly to preserve some order.
Men and women crowded and pushed each other, with no

regard to the sanctity of the place, the solemnity of the
occasion, or the rights of those most interested. Mean
while the cardinal came back, a way being with difficulty
made for him through the crowd, and took his seat at the
grating. In a moment the novice appeared behind it,
accompanied by nuns in their dresses of black and white.
The crowd was so restless that at first it was difficult to
catch the words of the service. Behind the grate, in the
dimness of the chapel in which the nuns stood, one could
see that the diamonds and laces were being taken from
her who no longer was to have use for them. Her long
hair was cut off. The veil, a piece of white cloth, was
put upon her head, falling down behind and at each side.
Prayers were chanted in the nasal, singsong way in
which prayers are said here, vows were made, the choir
sung, the cardinal gave his blessing, the nuns flitted to
and fro behind the grate, and the show and the service
were over. The cardinal, on his way out of the church,
stopped at the high altar to be disrobed, his lackeys in
their red-lined blue coats took snuff together, and he then
went out to the hall at the side of the convent, where the
new-made nun was to receive the congratulations of her
friends, and at whose door the crowd were already once
more jamming each other. An old man distributed two
printed sets of verses, copies of which had been posted at
the door of the church before the service. Each con-
ained three sonnets, "Upon occasion of the honorable
and pious Roman maiden, Annunziata Maria Anne
Sforza, on Sexagesima Sunday, the 27th of January,
1856, assuming the religious dress of the Holy Bene-

dictine Virgins, in the venerable convent of Saint Cecilia, and taking the name of Donna Maria Colomba Teresa of the Precious Blood of Jesus." The sonnets were as unpoetical as the ceremony had been.

In spite of all the want of feeling in the forms that had been gone through with, it was impossible not to have a profound sense of the melancholy of this ceremony. Whether the nun who has now to begin her convent life had before been happy or unhappy, it was equally sad to see her, a girl, thus renounce the world, and confine herself within limits so narrow that neither the affections nor the intellect could escape being stunted and crushed by them. If the heart beat against the bare convent-wall as against prison-bars, it would but deaden itself the sooner. If it found at first a pleasant sense of repose and shelter in the convent life's dull round of useless daily exercises, and in the seclusion of the small. white, silent chambers, it could not but gradually smoulder and die away in very inanition. It implies a curious deficiency of understanding, or an equally strange perversion of the doctrine of Christ, that one meaning to be a Christian should fail to reconcile the love of this world with the love of God, and should seek by desertion to win a victory. Here is faithlessness assuming the garb of faith, and love seeking to grow more pure and strong by crushing the very affections in which it lives. The gospel of Christ is read backwards, when that world which he came to save is regarded as a world which it is a merit to abandon.

And yet how explicable is this, explicable above all in

a society where domestic life is so ill-understood as it is for the most part here, where education is so imperfect, and religion so overlaid with superstition! Some souls may perhaps be made better, or, if not better, more comfortable, by thus sheltering themselves from the cares of common life; but, for one made better, how many suffer from want of the discipline of worldly duty! and how many, shunning known temptations, fall into others, greater, but unsuspected!

After the ceremony was over, I stayed in the church. It is as ugly as most of the modern churches in Rome, — disfigured with white paint, gilding, tawdry ornaments, dirty, showy hangings, and tasteless offerings; but, notwithstanding these, it is one of the most interesting churches in the city. It is built on the site of an earlier church, which in its turn was erected on the spot upon which, according to tradition, originally stood the house of Saint Cecilia. The touching story of her life and martyrdom is one of the most interesting of the saintly legends of Rome. She lived and died in the third century, and her memory seems to have been honored by those who knew her and had witnessed the excellence of her life and the constancy of her death. She was rich and beautiful and good. She so loved music, and sang so sweetly, that angels are said to have joined their voices with hers in the praise of God; and she died for her faith in Christ. The chamber of her house in which she was martyred is said to be preserved in one of the chapels of her church. It was a bathing-room, and the ancient pipes and furnaces still exist. The floor has a pavement of later date, made of bits of broken marble and colored stone. Upon one worn block of white marble, that had been brought from the place where it had originally served for the sepulchral slab of some Christian in early times, there was the rude and half-effaced figure of a dove bearing an olive-branch, with the words, *In Pace*. They were the only words which remained.

Under the high altar is a statue, which is one of the most affecting works of modern sculpture. It represents the body of Saint Cecilia as it was found in her tomb, when it was opened in 1599, at the time of the modernization of the church. She is lying upon one side. Her face is turned away, and a cloth is bound around her forehead. Her dress is perfectly simple, covering, but not concealing her form. Her arms are extended, and her beautiful hands rest one upon the other; her feet are bare. A little circlet round her neck seems to signify the mode of her death. There is an air of entire purity and grace about her form and position. It is not the statue of a living body, but it has none of the horror of death, — only its rest and its dignity. It is the statue of a noble, martyred woman, not in the anguish, but in the peace of martyrdom.

Rome, 21st January, 1856.

Cornelius, the distinguished German painter, who has just received one of the great medals for his cartoons at the Paris Exposition, has been living for two years past in Rome. He is now an old man, but he still occupies himself with his art, and has lately finished a design

4

which his admirers regard as one of his finest works, and in which he himself takes a pleasant, unaffected satisfaction. It is now in his studio in the Palazzo Poli.

The work is a highly finished sketch in tempera for a fresco, for the apse of the royal church in the burial-ground at Berlin. It represents the waiting for the Last Judgment, — the moment of expectation. The composition is a full, but not complete one. The immense space to be occupied by the fresco, a space of some ninety feet in height, (Michel Angelo's Last Judgment is but sixty feet high,) affords ample room for many figures, and for the noblest design. Cornelius has introduced certainly many figures, not fewer than one hundred and twenty. He has drawn part of his inspiration from the book of Revelation, but the types of the Apocalypse are strangely mingled with the realities of the Gospel and the traditions of the Church.

I dislike to describe pictures; no words can convey an adequate idea of a painting. Still, enough can be told to give an impression of the feeling manifest or the intellect displayed in a work of Art; and this picture seems to me so remarkable, as an exhibition of the character of much of the most applauded work of the present time, that I venture on a brief description.

In the upper centre of the picture is the Saviour, seated in a glory surrounded and supported by seraphs. At his feet are the four beasts of the Apocalypse. At his right stands the Virgin, and opposite to her St. John the Baptist. Immediately above the figure of Christ, and forming the upper group in the picture, are a band of angels, bearing the instruments of the passion, and on either side are the twenty-four elders, in white raiment, casting down their crowns. Beneath these, outside of the Virgin and of St. John, are two rows of figures, the upper representing martyrs with palms in their hands, the lower, apostles and saints.

Beneath the Saviour is a group of angels, of which the principal figure holds the not yet opened book of life, while the others have the trumpets of judgment in their hands, awaiting the signal for sounding them. Below, in a band stretching nearly across the picture, are the chief fathers of the Greek and Latin Churches. They rest upon a cloud, which serves, as it were, for the base of heaven, but is connected at each end with earth by aërial steps, as if to signify the union of the Church in glory above with the Church in conflict below. On these steps, at the right, ascends an angel with a censer, from which the smoke of the incense of prayer is rising; below is another angel, helping up a penitent; and at the foot is still another, defending a child from a serpent that has wound about his leg. On the other side, at the head of the steps, stands the Archangel Michael, with his sword drawn, waiting for the order of execution; at the foot, advancing toward earth, are three angels, one with the crown of thorns, another with the olive of peace, the third with the palm of victory. In the centre of the lower portion of the picture, between the two stairways of cloud, stands a bare, unadorned altar, surmounted by a cross. At the ends of the altar kneel the present King and Queen of Prussia, surrounded, at a little distance, by the other members of the royal family.

Such is the composition, which, by some of the German critics here, is declared to be the most wonderful of the age. But if my description has been at all intelligible, it is obvious that the first essential of a great composition is absent from this; — that essential is unity. No common sympathetic action, or mutual relation to be recognized by the imagination, combines these discordant groups into one common interest. The Last Judgment, however unsuitable it may be for painting, and although adapted only to the coarse materialism of the Middle Ages, is at least a subject controlled by one great motive. The emotions and the incidents belonging to it are all distinctly referable to a common end and a single overwhelming interest. But to attempt to represent the moment before the Judgment, the moment before the action has commenced, is an attempt at once profane and presumptuous. The more labored and elaborate in detail it may be, the more inadequate it is made. This picture is called a work of spiritual Art; but is it not rather a work of pure materialism?

No one ever looked at Michel Angelo's Last Judgment to have his conceptions of the awful day exalted or enlarged. To feel the power even of this most muscular of pictures, one must forget the subject, and look only at the separate figures as studies of anatomy and of drawing. One leaves the Sistine Chapel with no religious awe, with no sense of exaltation; but simply with a clearer acquaintance with Michel Angelo's unparalleled force as a draughtsman, and the conviction that the power exerted by the artist produces no corresponding effect upon the spectator, when that power is employed upon a subject before which all human strength is weakness and the clearest human conceptions only folly and confusion. But when one looks at this work of Cornelius, one finds not even that excellence in detail which might awaken an interest in the separate portions of the unconnected whole. It possesses no beauty of color, and no such pre-eminence in drawing as to give it any peculiar claim to admiration.

But, moreover, it is one of those pictures which have so far lost the characteristics of pictorial Art as to require an explanation in words of its meaning, — not merely of its meaning in details, for explanation of these is of course required in many of the greatest pictures, but explanation of its main object and purpose. However attentively it may be studied, it does not explain itself. What is the event for which all these figures are gathered together? No person, no action, no gesture indicates it. If you have seen other pictures, you may guess that it has something to do with the Judgment, or you may be told what it is by some person who has learned. But who are awaiting judgment? Are the doctors of the Church who sit on the cloud to escape the terrible day? Is the penitent whom the angel leads up the steps already judged and pardoned? Is Michael the Archangel waiting with drawn sword to descend upon the royal family of Prussia, who are the only people visible on earth? What bold and empty absurdity to put King

Frederick William in military uniform here! Cornelius may excuse himself by referring to the early masters, who insert the portraits of their patrons in their most sacred pictures. But there is no parallel. In the one case it was honest superstition combining with vanity on the patrons' part, that led to such a course; but in this latter instance there is nothing better than a courtier's flattery and the degradation of an artist.

In pictures by the old masters, where a story is treated in episodes, the idea of unity in the general design is lost sight of in the desire to convey the meaning more strongly by the introduction of various incidents, sometimes disconnected in time and place with each other, sometimes the successive scenes of a continuous story. These are narratives in painting instead of in words, and belonged to that age when pictures supplied the want of books, and when the object and limits of Art were most imperfectly understood. But the separate groups in this fresco of Cornelius, although remote from each other in all natural relations, have no episodic character. None of them are complete in themselves, and yet many have so little bearing upon the general design that one after another might be struck out, and no want would be felt.

This picture is a type of many works of recent Art, and especially of some of the most celebrated of the present German schools. It may or may not be soon forgotten; but the school of which Cornelius has long been the acknowledged head will, for some time at least, continue to exercise an effect more or less powerful upon

the progress and prospects of Art. The sooner the false
ness of the principles upon which it has proceeded, and
the consequent worthlessness of its results, are exposed
and understood, the better will it be, not merely for Art,
but for Religion.

Two great mistakes seem to be at the foundation of its
efforts, — one, the rejection of truth to Nature, as the sole
source of worth in Art, — the other, the frequent substi-
tution of mere intellectual force or fancy for spiritual sentiment; so that, in place of the harmonious combination
of thought and feeling, feeling has been sacrificed, and
the intellect itself dwarfed by its absence. Take, for instance, Kaulbach's famous picture of the Dispersion of
the Races, as an example in which both these errors are
peculiarly exhibited. Few pictures have been more
praised, or more circulated by engravings in the last few
years, than this; and yet it would be difficult to find a
picture, showing equal capacity on the part of the artist,
in which essential truth to Nature was more sacrificed.
It is a composition of powerful incongruities, and the
power is that of exaggeration. Nor is the absence of
truth to Nature greater than the absence of sincere feeling. It bears no marks of being an inevitable work
of genius. It is rather a block-house of the intellect, in
which piece after piece of study is filled up, to produce
what is meant for a great work. The signs of inspiration
are imitated, but its reality is not experienced.*

* Kaulbach was the pupil of Cornelius, though now the head of
a sect somewhat adverse to his old master. For other instances
of his manner, see his Illustrations to Shakspeare. They are pure
travesties.

A striking instance is afforded by another famous German artist, Overbeck, of the manner in which Nature has been disregarded out of deference to a preconceived ideal. In his works one may see how a man even of sincere religious conviction may fail, when by misfortune or by fault he prefers following other men, to following the simple truth. Overbeck's style is founded upon that of the masters of the fifteenth century. Charmed, as every one of sensibility cannot fail to be, with the simplicity, sincerity, and fervor exhibited in the works of the early painters, Overbeck has tried to adopt their manner, with the idea of producing the same effect. But the manner of the painters of the fifteenth century was often shackled and cramped by difficulties which have long since been broken away, and by ignorance which has long since yielded to knowledge. They painted the best they knew; their charm was not a mere charm of manner, but of character. A Fra Angelico would paint more angelic angels to-day than he could four hundred years ago, if he kept the same purity of soul that he then possessed. The beauty and the holiness of which their pictures are fuller than any others that the world has seen were often rendered in spite of and not by means of their technical manner. Had Overbeck lived in a cloister four centuries ago, and painted as he does now, his pictures would be precious as representations of the feeling and the power of an artist of that early time; but being painted to-day, they are only exhibitions of a talent that finds itself in the world out of season, and seeks its inspiration in the works of long past men, instead of in

Nature, fresh and full of beauty to-day as on the day when God first looked upon his work and saw that it was good. Truth and goodness are the same in one age as in another, and yet the manifestations of truth and goodness vary with every day and with every human soul. It displays a pitiful mingling of wilfulness and weakness to shut one's eyes to actual life and beauty, and in pietistic fervor to endeavor to revivify the meagre saints and mild Madonnas of five hundred years ago.

It is a greatly neglected canon of Art, that no work founded on the principle of imitation possesses any real vitality or genuine worth. If a man be truly an artist, he will find that he has a special message to deliver, which cannot be expressed in old forms. It is new wine, and needs new bottles.

Rome, February 10th, 1856, Sunday.

The Accademia Tiberina holds its sessions on Sunday evenings, in a hall in the Palazzo dei Sabini. It is one of those literary academies, of which there were formerly so many and some so famous in Italy, and of which the greater number have died out or been crushed out in later years. There is little to be feared or to be hoped from them now. They would not exist, were there any danger of their becoming too liberal.

This evening the large hall of the Academy was poorly lighted with a few oil-lamps, and a few priests and sleepy old gentlemen sat scattered about the room. By degrees the seats were slowly filled; a few ladies came in; a young man lighted up candles, so that one could see the dim frescoes on the walls; two cardinals shuffled in with some bustle and parade; and then the members of the Academy who were to take part in the evening's performances appeared from a back room, and took their seats upon the platform, fronting the audience. The cardinals, by the way, sat before the rest of the company on old-fashioned gilt chairs.

The performances commenced with the reading, by an architect, of a paper on the restoration of the curious Church of San Niccolò in Carcere. It was a good specimen of the old style of academic dissertation. It was the sort of thing in which one might sleep through a century or two without harm. Beginning with Tullus Hostilius, a thousand years before the church was built, continuing through the history of republican Rome, the essay arrived in due time at the commencement of the Christian era, and finally at that of the erection of the church. The narrative was broken by disquisitions on the value of the science of archæology, on the sufferings of the martyrs, on the virtues of his Holiness the reigning Pope, and other more or less remote topics. Then came a shower of facts about the church, rattling down dry and hard on the heads of the audience; and when at length the end arrived, it was received with undeniable satisfaction and applause. The subject was an interesting one, treated by an academician.

When this discourse was finished, the President announced the name of a young priest, who rose and recited a long series of Latin hexameters on the Sacrifice of Isaac. They might have been written two hundred years ago.

The priest took his seat, and the President said, " La Contessa Teresa Gnoli " ; and a young lady, who had been the only lady on the stage during the evening, rose and commenced the recitation of some verses upon the meeting of Beatrice and Laura. A delicate expression of sensitiveness and timidity was united with a dignified self-possession in her bearing and manner. Nor was the charm of her manner greater than the sweetness of her voice, the grace and dramatic energy of her gestures and expression, the simplicity and taste of her dress. Her poem was musical, and full of that tender feeling which the thought of Beatrice and of Laura might well awaken in the heart of a sensitive Italian woman. The audience were brought into sympathy with her, and, in a rapture of delight, broke in upon her recitation with cries of " Cara ! " " Cara ! " " Bella ! " " Bellissima ! " She sat down, almost overwhelmed by the applause of her enthusiastic listeners. For a moment, this one graceful woman, with the fire of youth and poetry, animated the old room, the languid audience, the pompous cardinals, and the decaying Academy, with a life and spirit to which they were little used. The Contessa Gnoli is a descendant of Ariosto.

It would have been well, had the performances of the evening ended here; but other poems followed. They were of that class which belong to a period of lifelessness, when originality is proscribed as a defect, imagination regarded as a heresy, and the copyist of ancient forms more praised than the creator of new spirits. One alone was good as a humorous piece of social satire ; most of the

others had the dull·and musty odor of the cloister ; all
were written by men living where liberty of speech is
dangerous, and liberty of thought only suspiciously and
irregularly indulged.   It is, perhaps, in such a place and
at such a period that the most verses and the least poetry
are written.

Everything is the subject of an ode or a sonnet, here
in Rome.   Six sonnets were written on occasion of the
nun's taking the veil at the convent of Santa Cecilia the
other day, — and this ceremony is not a rare one.   There
is a poetic chronicle of the commonest affairs ; and the
history of the Pope might be traced or lost in innumerable verses. Of pure improvisation there is little. Gianni,
who died some years since, was one of the last of the
famous *improvvisatori*.   An improvised sonnet of his, on
the Death of Judas, is a most striking specimen of rapid
composition, not merely on account of the difficulties of
the form and the complexity of the rhyme, but still more
from the vigor of expression, which runs, indeed, here
and there, into excess.   This sonnet has fewer faults than
are commonly found in such hasty performances.

> Al ora che Giuda di furor satollo
>   Piombò dal ramo, rapido si mosse
> Il tutelar suo demone, e scontrollo,
>   Battendo le ale fumiganti e rosse.
> E per la fune che pendea dal collo
>   Giù nel bollor delle Tartaree fosse
> Appena con le forti unghie avventollo,
>   Che arser le carni e sibilaron le osse.
> E giunto nell' ignivoma bufera,
>   Lo stesso orribil Satana fu visto

L' accigliata spianar fronte severa.
Poi con le braccia incatenò quel tristo,
E con la bocca insanguinata e nera
Gli rese il bacio che avea dato a Cristo.*

This is one of that class of sonnets which the Italians call *sonetti col botto*, " sonnets with a blow," the last line being concentrated and energetic beyond all the rest, and closing the sonnet with an explosion of force. It is a style less in favor now than of old ; and a better taste shows itself in less ambitious and less striking, but more simple and pleasing performances.

Monti wrote four sonnets upon the same theme with this of Gianni, but none of them seems to me to possess so much merit, and the horror of the subject is to be forgotten only in the display of the peculiar power of the *improvvisatore*.

It is a misfortune that the Italian language should lend itself so readily to the making of verses. Papal Rome has never had a poet.

* TRANSLATION. — That hour when Judas, filled with madness, hung from the tree, his guardian demon came with rapid flight to confront him, flapping his smoking and red wings. And by the rope that hung about his neck, down into the boiling of the hellish ditch hardly had the demon hurled him with his strong claws, before his flesh burned and his bones hissed. And when he reached the fiery whirlwind, horrible Satan himself was seen to smooth his wrinkled brow severe. Then with his arms he enchained that wretch, and, with his bloody and black mouth, gave back to him the kiss that he had given to Christ.

ROME, 6th February, 1856.

Rome possesses comparatively few works of those centuries when modern Art exhibited its purest power, and
reached a spiritual elevation from which it soon fell,
and which it has never since reattained. The decline
that became obvious in the sixteenth century stamped
its marks upon the face of the city. Raphael and Michel
Angelo were the forerunners of decay, and their works
and those of the host of their unworthy followers are the
works which give one of its most prevailing characteristics to Rome of the present day, and predominate over
all others. The spirit of the earlier artists was incongruous with the worldly pomp and selfish display of the
capital of the Popes; but Michel Angelo's genius gave
just expression to the character of the Papacy in its
period of greatest splendor, and Bernini is the fit repre-
sentative of its weakness and decline. The eye is
wearied and discouraged by the constant repetition of
monuments of Art which, the more skilful and elaborate
they may be, only the more exhibit the absence of noble
design and elevated thought. It is vain to seek among
them for that excellence which is at once the result and
the source of integrity of purpose and purity of affection.
The spirit of Christianity is not visible in them. Change
the attributes with which they are accompanied, (nor
would even this change be always required,) and the host
of sculptured and painted angels, prophets, and martyrs
of these later centuries might stand for heathen images
or for figures of the lowest earthly characters. Simplicity is banished and modesty proscribed. Instead of

being the minister of truth, the purifier of affections, the reveal r of the beauty of God, Art was degraded to the service of ambition and caprice, of luxury and pomp, until it became utterly corrupt and false.

The power of appreciating what was good was necessarily lost with the desire for it and the love of it; and the results of the last two centuries and a half in Rome are hardly more melancholy in what they have produced than in what they have destroyed. Works of such men as Giotto, Fra Angelico, Perugino, and Razzi have been effaced to make room for others worse than worthless; and even now the current of improved taste and feeling is not so strong as to save from the profanation of so-called restorers many most precious relics of the past. The example of destruction was set in Raphael's time; and whatever may be the estimate in which his Stanze are held, it is not to be forgotten that pictures by Perugino and Signorelli were obliterated to make room for them.

Amid this general wreck, a few of the earlier works have escaped; and after the ambitious effort and emptiness of the degenerate schools, it is a relief and delight to find here and there a specimen of the labors of those masters who regarded their art as a sacred calling, and worked not for the sake of applause or gain, but for the love and in the fear of God. The most precious of all these is, perhaps, the little chapel of Nicholas V., in the Vatican, whose walls are covered with a series of frescoes by Fra Angelico, illustrating the stories of St. Stephen and St. Lawrence. This chapel is said to be the oldest part of the present Vatican, and its preservation seems to have been owing more to accident than to any recognition of the beauty which it contained. For more than a hundred years the key to it was lost, and its door was unopened. Few, except the readers of Vasari, knew that such a chapel had existed, and as late as the middle of the last century the still smaller number of those who desired to see the frescoes were obliged to scramble into it through the single window over the high altar. Another chapel at the Vatican was painted by Fra Angelico, with scenes from the life of Christ; "an excellent work in his manner," says Vasari, and one of whose merit we may judge, not only by that of the pictures in the chapel of Nicholas V., but also by our knowledge of the manner in which this most Christian painter was accustomed to treat the subjects that he drew from the life of his Master. But this second chapel was destroyed less than a hundred years after it had been painted, by one of the Popes, (Paul III.,) who desired to straighten a staircase that ran by its side. It is fortunate that no crooked stairs passed by that of Nicholas V.

It was in the year 1446 that Fra Angelico was called by the Pope from his convent at Fiesole to paint at Rome. He was already an old man, for he was born in 1387. He had painted in Foligno and in Cortona, but his principal works were in Florence, and from there his fame had spread over Italy. His life had not been marked by great events, and among the biographies of artists there are few of less interest from their incidents, or of more interest from the character displayed in them than his. Vasari, usually little appreciative of the na-

ture and value of the moral relations and the religious
bearing of Art, is kindled into enthusiasm in writing of
this pure and holy man. Contemporary prejudices and
prepossessions are forgotten, and the biographer partakes
for the time of the spirit of the artist.* " Such superior
and extraordinary talent," he says, " as was that of Fra
Giovanni, cannot and ought not to belong to any but a
man of most holy life ; for those who employ themselves
on religious and holy subjects ought to be religious and
holy men." He was simple in his modes of life, and a
great friend of the poor. He might have been rich, had
he cared to be so ; but he used to say that true riches was
in being content with little. He said that he who employed himself in Art had need of quiet and of living free
from cares, and that he who would represent Christ
should always live with Christ. " He was never seen
angry with any of the brothers of the convent; which
seems to me," says the honest Vasari, " a very great
thing, and one almost impossible to believe. In fine,
this never sufficiently to be praised father was most humble and modest in all his works and discourse, and in his
pictures easy and devout ; and the saints that he painted
have more the air and likeness of saints than those of
any one else. It was his custom never to retouch or go
over his painting, but to leave it always as it first came,

---

* To such a degree is this the case, that many have supposed that
this Life could not have been written by Vasari; but there seems no
sufficient ground for depriving him of the credit of having composed
this delightful narrative   See Le Monnier's edition of Vasari's *Lives*.
Florence, 1848, Vol. IV   *Commentario alla Vita di Frate Giovanni.*

believing, as he said, that such was the will of God. Some say that Fra Giovanni would never put his hand to his brush before he had made a prayer. He never painted a crucifix but tears bathed his cheeks, and thus in the looks and attitudes of his figures is seen the goodness of his sincere and great soul in the Christian religion."

No artist ever more completely painted his own character in his works than Fra Angelico. The simplicity, the purity, and the spirituality of his life are visible in them all. The angels of other artists rarely seem angelic when compared with his, and the happy name by which he is known is at once expressive of his own virtues and of the preeminence of his conceptions of the heavenly host. Many faults of drawing, many limitations of technical skill, many of what in strict language are to be called *artistic* defects, are visible in his pictures; but these defects were common to all artists of the age; and it is to be remembered that even in artistic qualities he is the equal of the best of his time, while the spirit which pervades his works is such as to give a charm to their very deficiencies, and the stiffness of Fra Angelico is not only pardoned, but loved, for the beauty that lies behind it.

The chapel of Nicholas V. is very small, and its ceiling and walls are wholly covered with his paintings. Most of them, though faded, are well preserved; but a few have been ruined by dampness, and others have suffered at the hands of restorers. The ceiling is of a deep sky-blue color, pointed over with golden stars. In the four compartments into which it is divided are the

Four Evangelists. In the corners of the chapel are the Eight Doctors of the Church, — two in each corner, one above the other.*

On the walls are represented, in six compartments, the principal events of the lives of St. Stephen and St. Lawrence, so arranged that the correspondences in their histories may distinctly appear. These two saints have long been associated together in the legends of the Church. Their bodies lie in the same tomb, under the high altar of the venerable basilica of St. Lawrence without the Walls, one of the most interesting churches in Rome, from its antiquity, the beauty and solitude of its position, standing lonely on the edge of the Campagna, and from its air of undisturbed quiet and tranquil decay. It is said, that, when the relics of St. Stephen were lowered into the tomb, the bones of St. Lawrence moved to make room for them.

The most beautiful of these works of Fra Angelico — of which all are beautiful — are, perhaps, the Preaching of St. Stephen, and the Distribution of Alms by St. Lawrence. In the first the Saint stands upon a step, robed in a deacon's dress. Before him sit many women upon the ground, listening to his words. Behind these women stand "certain of the synagogue," laying plots against him. The background is occupied with the buildings of Jerusalem. The simplicity of the arrangement of the group of women is entire ; their attitudes are full of na-

* They are St. John Chrysostom and St Bonaventura (or St. Jerome), St. Gregory and St. Augustine, St. Athanasius and St. Thomas Aquinas, St. Ambrose and St. Leo.

ture, of dignity, and of grace; their expressions are of earnest attention; and their sweet, thoughtful, and serious faces, "looking steadfastly on him, see his face as though it were the face of an angel." The painter was too deeply impressed with the reality of what he desired to represent, to strive after those varieties of composition which, while showing his skill, would have interfered with the needed expression. The only collateral incident that he introduces is the represention of a little child seated by his mother, who holds his hand. There is nothing to remind one of the painter; St. Stephen and his audience are all that the picture brings before the mind.

In the Distribution of Alms by St. Lawrence, the subject is not less simply and nobly treated. The Saint stands in the centre of the picture, surrounded by the poor, blind, and lame. His face has a deep serenity of expression, as if his heart were filled with the foreknowledge of that horrible but triumphant death which awaited him on the next day. His dress is of the richest color, and ornamented with symbolic flames of gold. Two little children, with their arms about each other, are at his side, just turning away with the gift they have received from him. A blind man is feeling forward with his staff. A poor cripple is stretching up his hand for the alms which the Saint holds out. A woman approaches with her baby in her arms. Two old people draw near on the other side. All the figures are instinct with truth and life. It is like a real scene, and the benign spirit of charity gives it a celestial glory.*

* Small outlines from these two pictures are to be found in the last

In the pictures of the martyrdoms of the two Saints, it is curious to observe how the mild pencil of Fra Angelico has refused to represent the vileness of the executioners. He could not paint wickedness, and the bad themselves are saved from the hatred that is due to them by that sublime weakness which was unable to imagine evil. This chapel is one of the holy places of Rome.

Fra Angelico never returned to his well-beloved convents in Florence and in Fiesole. He painted other works in Rome, and for some months labored in ' that great storehouse of the best Art, the duomo of Orvieto. He died at Rome on the 18th of March, 1455. He was buried in the church of Santa Maria sopra Minerva, and the Pope, Nicholas V., who had held him in just esteem, caused a monumental slab, upon which his effigy was sculptured, to be erected to his memory.

This monument still remains in the chapel at the left of the choir of this splendid church. The artist is represented in the dress of his order, his head resting upon a pillow and his hands folded. The face seems to have been taken from a mask made after death. The closed eyes are deep-set, and the cheeks hollow, as if sunk with age and disease. The features are small and delicate, and marked with an air of grave repose. The lower part of the monument is worn by the passing by of the

edition of the English translation of Kugler's *Handbook of Painting;* and the Arundel Society has done a good work in publishing a complete series of outlines, on a large scale, of the frescoes in this chapel

generations that have stood and knelt at its side.   The
inscription under the figure is as follows : —

HIC JACET VEN. PICTOR FR. IO. DE FLO. ORDINIS PREDICAT.
14LV.

NON MIHI SIT LAUDI QUOD ERAM VELUT ALTER APELLES
SED QUOD LUCRA TUIS OMNIA CHRISTE DABAM :
ALTERA NAM TERRIS OPERA EXTANT ALTERA COELO.
URBS ME JOANNEM FLOS TULIT ETRURIÆ.

Here lies the venerable painter, Brother John of Florence, of the
Order of the Preachers. 1455.

Not mine be the praise that I was as a second Apelles,
But that I gave all my gains to thine, O Christ!
One work is for the earth, another for heaven.
The city the Flower of Tuscany bore me — John.

ROME, February, 1855.

It is a custom in Rome, when a house is completed,
that all those who have been engaged in building it
should have a little celebration together.   I met last
night an architect well known here, a man of education
and intelligence.   Not long ago, he was at a meeting of
this sort, to celebrate the completion of a building, the
erection of which he had overseen.   In the midst of the
proceedings, the police suddenly broke in, and arrested
the architect with several others of the company.   He
was thrown into prison, — and this is in itself a severe
punishment in Rome, owing to the ill condition and bad
management of the prisons ; he was not informed of the
nature of the charge against him ; for three months he
was in confinement ; he was then brought before one of

the courts, and learned that he was charged with having taken part in a seditious meeting. He was able to prove that the meeting was simply of the kind described, and that he and the workmen with whom he had been associated were infringing on no political reserves; and he was ordered to be discharged, but to remain for some months under the surveillance of the police. He received no apology or compensation, and he had no means of redress. The authorities took no account of the interruption of his social relations, or of the injury to his business. It would be dangerous for him, were he to complain, and no good could come of it; even the story must be told under one's breath. I heard it last night in a drawing-room, where ———— was delighting the company with the music of his wonderful violin. Under a despotism, the musician has a happy lot. No spy can detect the sedition that may lie within the compass of his instrument; and he may breathe out the longings of his soul for freedom in notes the secret meaning of which no police agent can detect. The Italian loves that music which expresses those passions the expression of which he may indulge in no other way. It is for this reason that Verdi is now the favorite master over all Italy; and it is not only because the librettos of some of his operas were too liberal, but because the music itself was instinct with the wild and vague liberalism of the time, that their performance has now and then been forbidden by suspicious authorities. But when the singers could no longer sing them, the organists began to play them in the churches.

Rome, February 22d, 1856.

The condition of public affairs here is thoroughly dis-
heartening. No state could be more rotten and retain
its vitality. " Our government," — a Roman, who is
neither revolutionist nor radical, said to me, — " our government is in the hands of three classes : bigots, knaves,
and fools." The principle of action of the larger number of these men is expressed in the concise words of
Louis XV.: " *Ceci durera plus que moi* " ; they are men
without religion, without probity, without patriotism, but
with power.

This year some of the annual taxes were laid for fourteen instead of twelve months. A piece of absurd chi-
canery. The government did not wish nominally to
increase the tax, and therefore ordered that the year
should be considered as containing fourteen months, and
the tax be reckoned by months, and paid accordingly.

No *employé* of government pays taxes.

Corruption rules supreme. It is acknowledged and
permitted by the highest authorities. Many officials receive a salary so small as to be utterly insufficient for
their support; they are told to depend for their livelihood
on the *incerti* of their office, — that is, on fees, whose very
name shows that they are regulated by no fixed scale,
but depend on the ingenuity and the impudence of him
who demands them.

Both justice and injustice are for sale ; and the first
price asked for either is often much larger than will be
finally accepted ; as is the case with that asked for most
articles in Rome.

One of the most amusing instances of petty and corrupt tyranny is that exercised by the servants of men in authority. These servants, coming from the very dregs of the people, with all the pretensions of full-blooded flunkies, and with all the dirt of a friar, keep a list of the persons who visit or have business with their masters; and twice a year, at midsummer and at the beginning of the year, call at the houses of these their masters' acquaintance, and demand a *mancia*, a " gift," or a " fee," for their services. If it is refused, they have a thousand ways of exacting their vengeance. Their master is not in when he who does not give the *mancia* calls; notes to him are mislaid; and all the petty vexations that the malice of servants can suggest are well worked out. To one whose social relations are extensive, the *mancia* is a serious tax. From three to five pauls (thirty to fifty cents) is a common sum to be given. It is plain how soon this would score up to a considerable amount.

The saddest aspect of things here arises, however, not from the weak tyranny of the government, nor from the corruption of officials, but from the character and condition of the people themselves. Society is divided into two great classes, — that of those whose interest it is to keep things as they are, and that of those who would change or overthrow the existing conditions, in the belief that change must be improvement. The first of these classes is a small minority, but united by discipline, by education, and by faith, and holding power, money, and troops in their hands. The other is made up of nine-tenths of the Romans, but without organization, without

confidence in each other, without intimate knowledge
of each other, and with principles so adverse on many
points as to desire completely different courses of action.
Distrust is the one prevailing element in society. No
one confides in the one who stands next to him. Hypoc-
risy is the rule, not only of Jesuits, but of those who
have been governed by Jesuits.

Meanwhile, moderate and thoughtful men live and suffer. Their daily lives are a daily struggle. To die
would be a happiness, if by their deaths any good could
be accomplished for Rome; but to offer themselves as
sacrifices, in a cause where the devotion of a single life
would seem like attempting to force a flood back with the
hands, would be the exhibition not of heroism, but of
impatience and of faithlessness. " But it is better not to
talk of these things," said an Italian to me; " for these
are the things that leave a bitterness in the heart." All
is darkness, and the wisest men are groping for light, not
knowing in what direction it lies. But perhaps the first
glimmer of a new dawn may even at this black moment
be springing fast forward, soon to break the blankness of
the sky. God deserts not the world. Trial, sorrow, and
suffering are the forerunners of justice, liberty, and truth.

> " I watch the circle of the eternal years,
>   And read for ever in the storied page
>   One lengthened roll of blood and wrong and tears,
>   One onward step of Truth from age to age.

> " The poor are crushed; the tyrants link their chain;
>   The poet sings through narrow dungeon-grates;
>   Man's hope lies quenched; and lo! with steadfast gain
>   Freedom doth forge her mail of adverse fates."

Rome, 28th January, 1856.

The Sala Regia at the Vatican serves as a vestibule for the Sistine and Pauline chapels. Few persons stop long to examine the frescoes with which its walls are covered; for Michel Angelo's great picture is too near, and Raphael's loggie are to be reached through the adjoining hall. The frescoes, indeed, are the work of second-rate artists, and do not, for the most part, deserve attention, except as affording some curious illustrations of the facts of history, as understood at the Papal court at the time when they were executed. In this respect, three of them are remarkable enough, and the story of their painting is entertaining; — they are the three by Vasari, representing scenes from the Massacre of St. Bartholomew.

In the beginning of 1572, Vasari, who was now sixty years old, was at work painting in this hall under the direction of Pope Pius V., with whom he was a great favorite. Other artists had been previously employed; but now Vasari was to do all that remained, and to go on until the work was completed. Suddenly, on the first of May, the old Pope died. Poor Vasari was bitterly vexed. " This is an infinite loss to me," he writes, the day after the Pope's death; " for I was just settling affairs for Marcantonio," (his nephew, for whom he had been endeavoring to secure some favor,) " and getting something for myself. . . . . I was just finishing painting in fresco the Battle of the Turks, and it is the best thing that I ever did, and the greatest and the most studied; but his Holiness has carried away with him all the hope of my labors, yet the fame of Giorgio will remain for ages of years; thus it is that the wind carries away vanity and our labors." * The honesty of Giorgio's letter is delightful, and his attempt at resignation has an amusing *naïveté*. His plans were for the time broken up, and it was doubtful whether the next Pope would stand his friend and continue him in the work that he had begun. He had to cover up his nearly finished Battle of Lepanto, and, leaving Rome, returned to Florence, where he was sure of employment under his patron, the Grand Duke Cosmo I. Here he remained through the summer, but, early in October, a letter came from Rome, summoning him thither, at the command of the new Pope, Gregory XIII., to finish the work he had begun in the Sala de' Re. He did not delay going, and on the 17th of November he writes from Rome to Prince Francis, afterwards Grand Duke of Tuscany, telling him of his arrival, and of his satisfactory interview with the Pope. "His Holiness intends to finish the hall entirely, and has a mind," says Vasari, "to have on the side not yet painted the affair of the Huguenots which has taken place this year under his pontificate." On the 20th, the Prince writes his answer to this letter. It was a short one, but there was room in it for the following sentence: "His Holiness does wisely in wishing that *so holy and noble a success as was the execution against the Huguenots in France* should appear in the Sala de' Re." The massacre of St.

---

* This extract and the succeeding one are taken from letters published by Dr. Gaye in his *Carteggio d'Artisti*, a book full of curious and often important information

Bartholomew had taken place but three months before this time. The Pope's design of having this "eternal infamy of France" painted upon the walls of the great hall of his palace, and the Prince's approval of the plan as one worthy of the head of the Church of Christ, would be like an extravagant travesty of reality, were they not so incontrovertibly true.

On the 12th of December is another letter of Vasari's to Prince Francis, in which he describes at some length his designs for the three pictures that were to be painted concerning the Huguenots. The first was to represent the death of Admiral Coligny, or rather his being borne wounded to his palace; the next was to be the breaking of his door by the Guises and their band, and the throwing of the Admiral from the window, with the slaughter of the Huguenots in the streets; and the third was to represent the King going to the church to return thanks to God, and sitting in parliament with his council. "These works, I am afraid, will keep me occupied a long while." On the 18th of February, 1573, Vasari writes to his friend Vincenzio Borghini, and in the course of his letter says: "I keep my hands going like a fifer, and, God be praised, every one of the six great cartoons for the six pictures in the hall is entirely finished; nor have I ever done better, God helping me. And in the hall are finished within eight days two pictures wholly colored in fresco by my hand, which means something; and if things go on so that next Tuesday Messer Lorenzo of Bologna, with two others, come to help me, I believe that by the end of April everything may be finished, and

everybody dismissed. But I do not believe that I shall
be able to get away from here before the end of May,
because I shall have to manage to get something for
Marcantonio, my nephew; and this court is very slow,
and, although I am a favorite and well looked upon, etc.,
this thing of making haste has the Devil on his back.
But I am skilful, and God will aid me, and I shall have
finished one of the greatest works that I ever did; for if
Malagigi had had this hall to do, it would have frightened him, both him and his devils; but because here,
Monsignor Mio, is God, and He does these things, and not
I, you may be sure it is so." *

Other letters, giving an account of the progress of
the work, follow from time to time, equally amusing from
their unreserve, the pleasant mixture of piety and self-
complacency, and the clear picture which they afford, not
only of Vasari's character, but also of the condition of
things at this period in Rome. At last, on the 1st of
May, the pictures were finished, and he writes to tell Borghini of a visit which the Pope had paid to him in the hall
the day before: "The Pope and the few gentlemen who
were with him were full of wonder, and his Holiness
stayed there more than a whole hour, and said many
kind words to me, and told me that I had never done
better, and promised that he would give something to my
nephew, Marcantonio, and that he would remember me;

---

* Vasari's sentences in these letters are frequently unfinished, and
with a syntax that is somewhat confused; obviously written offhand
and carelessly. The spelling, too, is often very bad; but his meaning
is generally clear

and this evening the court is full of admiration, the report having got about that I have finished." All through the month his content continues. "This is the best work of all that I have done in Rome." "God has granted to me the favor that the hall is finished, and yesterday morning [the 20th] it was opened with great praise and honor to me." In June, Vasari left the city, which, according to his own expression, had been so good to him, and returned to Florence. The pictures of the Massacre of St. Bartholomew were the last works that he accomplished in Rome. In June of the next year, he died.

These frescoes, spite of Vasari's own judgment of them, are hardly to be reckoned as his best works. They are cold in color and weak in design. "We paint," says he, "six pictures in a year, while the earlier masters took six years to paint one picture." And it would not be difficult to paint six pictures of this sort in so short a space of time. There is nothing, however, in their execution, any more than in his letters about them, to show that he regarded the subject of the massacre with dislike. It was a triumph of the Church, and it mattered little whether the Church triumphed over infidels or over heretics. The time of faith had passed, and had been succeeded by that of indifference to everything but the interests of the *visible* Church. These pictures stand not so much a monument to Vasari's fame, as a record of the approval bestowed upon one of the blackest deeds of intolerant and cruel passion by him who professed to be the Vicar of Christ upon earth.

Inscriptions were placed under these three pictures. The first read, —

GASPARD COLIGNIUS AMIRALLIUS ACCEPTO VULNERE DOMUM REFERTUR GREG. XIII. PONTIF. MAX. 1572.

The second was, —

CÆDES COLIGNII ET SOCIORUM EJUS.

And the third, —

REX COLIGNII NECEM PROBAT.

In 1828 these inscriptions still existed,[*] but now they are obliterated, and the space which they once filled is unoccupied. One might suggest that these blanks should be filled once more : that under the first picture one should read, Love your enemies ; under the second, Bless them that persecute you ; and under the third, Forgive us our trespasses.

The news of the massacre of St. Bartholomew arrived at Rome on the 5th of September, 1572. The letters announcing the event, which the legate of the Pope, Salviati, had sent from Paris, were read the next morning in the presence of the Pope, at an assembly of the Car-

---

[*] See Stendhal, *Promenades dans Rome*, I. 224. " Thus," says this clever writer, " there is one place in Europe where assassination is publicly honored." The upright President de Thou was accustomed to quote the following lines from Statius, applying them to the massacre. Their lesson seems to have been but half learned at Rome.

" Excidat illa dies ævo, ne postera credant
Sæcula : nos certe taceamus, et obruta multa
Nocte tegi propriæ patiamur crimina gentis "

dinals. Their contents were to the effect, that the Admiral and the Huguenots having entered into a conspiracy against the King, they had been slain by the royal will and permission. After the news had been heard, it was determined that there should be a solemn service in commemoration of the event, on the next Monday, in the church of Santa Maria sopra Minerva. From the meeting, the Pope and Cardinals proceeded at once to the church of St. Mark to render thanks to God the infinitely great and good, (*Deo optimo maximo*,) for the great favor He had vouchsafed to bestow on the Roman Church and the whole Christian world. The exultant joy at Rome was wonderful. A salvo was fired from the castle of Sant' Angelo, and in the evening fireworks were displayed and bonfires lighted in the streets. None of those rejoicings were omitted which the Roman Church observes on occasion of the most glorious victories.

The news of the massacre was received with especial satisfaction by the Cardinal de Lorraine, brother to that Duke de Guise who had been slain by a young Huguenot at the siege of Orléans in 1562. He hated the Huguenots with a personal and vindictive hatred. He gave publicly a thousand crowns to the courier who brought intelligence so welcome to him, and, on his demand, the Pope and the Cardinals went in procession, two days afterward, with the most splendid and stately pomp, to the church of San Luigi de' Francesi, to assist at a solemn festival in celebration of this triumph over the enemies of the Faith. The Cardinal placed an inscription above the door of the church, in which, in the name of his master, Charles IX., he congratulated the Pontiff, the Cardinals, the Senate, and the people of Rome, on the stupendous results of the prayers and the counsels of many years.* The church was crowded by the chief people of the city, and the Protestants were publicly cursed. A jubilee was proclaimed by the Pope, that thanks might be rendered to God for the destruction of the enemies of the truth, and of the Church in France, and by his direction a medal was struck, on one side of which were his own head and the date of his pontificate, and on the other a representation of an angel with a sword in his hand pursuing armed men, who are in flight, and some of whom have already fallen, with the inscription, *Strages Ugonottorum*, " The Slaughter of the Huguenots." †

Such was the spirit of the times, and such the condition of religion at Rome. All the facts above stated are taken from Roman Catholic authorities. It would be well to let them rest ; but in a series of tracts recently written by some of the English converts to Romanism,

---

* See Thuanus, *Hist.* LIV. § 4. De Thou was an eyewitness of the massacre at Paris, and the next year was at Rome.

† M. Artaud de Montor, well known as a zealous Romanist, gives a full account of this medal, the existence of which has been sometimes disputed, in his life of Gregory XIII., — *Histoire des Souverains Pontifes Romains*, IV. 410–415. It was contained in a collection of the Papal medals given to him by Pius VII. But it appears that some years afterwards he himself persuaded Leo XII. to order this medal, " *cette terrible médaille*," to be withdrawn from a similar collection which this Pope was about to send away as a gift.

and much in favor here at present, there is an able and curious defence of the proceedings of the Court of Rome in this affair. The writer assumes that at the time of these rejoicings nothing was known of the indiscriminate nature of the massacre. "The Court of Rome rejoiced and returned God thanks, not for a massacre, but for the detection and suppression of a bloody conspiracy; a legitimate and righteous cause of pious congratulation in the eyes of every reasonable man." *   And again: "In short, the undoubted facts of history — and, I may add, every new fact which is established — entirely acquit the Pope and the Church of France of all sort of connection with the massacre, whoever may have been its guilty contrivers. The accusation has not only no grounds, but no shadow of a ground to rest upon; and is the pure invention of a stupid and malignant bigotry, regardless alike of rational probability and of historical truth." †   This statement may be literally correct; one may admit that neither the Pope nor the Church of France had any connection with this massacre as its contrivers or instigators, but this is all.   To rejoice in and honor the performance of a deed after its commission is generally the token of a spirit that would not have prevented its possessor from taking share in the deed, had his circumstances allowed. The Cardinal de Lorraine, whose vindictive exultation over the massacre was exhibited in the most notorious manner, was one of the highest dignitaries of that Church which is said to have had no connection of any sort with

* *Clifton Tracts*, Vol. I.   Tract V., p. 29.   † Id., p. 32.

the deed. The Pope marked his satisfaction in the most
durable of methods, and reckoned the event the chief
glory of the first year of his reign. It will not do to say
that he was ignorant of the horrid nature and the worse
than barbarous cruelties of the massacre, when he regarded it in this manner; for it was three months after
it had taken place, a space too long for ignorance, that
he gave Vasari the order to paint those monumental pictures which still bear witness to the truth on the walls
of the Sala de' Re.

It will be a happy day for truth, when Catholics and
Protestants alike become ready to acknowledge that men
of both names have, in all ages, done deeds for which
there can be no defence. To labor to obscure the truth
concerning guilt, and to seek for false or fallacious ex-
cuses of a crime, is to become a sharer in the crime
itself.

ROME, February 28th, 1856.

Gas-works have recently been established in Rome,
under the charge of an English contractor. The tall
modern chimney of the works rises near to the Tiber,
under the Palatine Hill, and is somewhat incongruous,
both in appearance and association, with the character
of the surrounding objects.

The contractor is a monopolist, and carries things with
rather a high hand. One of his late proceedings exhibits
the manner in which justice reaches its end in Rome.
He was desirous of introducing gas into the house in
which he himself occupied hired apartments. The pro-

prietor, however, was averse to the proposal ; whereupon the pipes were carried in by the Englishman, spite of all opposition. The proprietor brought the case before one of the courts, and a surveyor was appointed to examine the premises and adjudicate upon the matter. He reported, that the rights of the owner of the house had been clearly violated, and that the English contractor ought to be compelled to restore things to their former condition. From this decision the contractor appealed to another court. The decision was, however, confirmed, and an architect appointed to oversee what was necessary to restore the house. The architect was beginning to carry out the order of the court, when a notice was served upon him by the police to proceed no farther in the business. The explanation of this is simple. The Englishman is rich ; the police can be bribed. *Omnia Romæ cum pretio.*

Rome, 12th March, 1856.

The prevalence of beggary has been for centuries one of the discredits of Rome. It has existed in spite of the efforts and the bulls of successive Popes, and in spite also of the abundant almsgiving of Catholic charity, — or rather, not in spite of, so much as in consequence of, this indiscriminate almsgiving. Perhaps no city in Europe is furnished with more numerous or more wealthy institutions for the care of the poor, and yet few cities have a larger or more unblushing host of beggars. The beggary of Rome is a reproach not so much to the charity as to the good sense of the Romans. Poverty has been increased

by the means taken to relieve it, and mistakes of judgment and of doctrine have produced evil consequences,
for which no excellence of intention can serve as excuse.   But in the midst of much false benevolence there
has been much of that true charity which does not confine itself to the relief, but considers also how best to
secure the prevention of pressing want.   Some of the
public charities in Rome are institutions of the most efficient character; and many private individuals now devote
themselves, and have in generations past devoted themselves, with self-forgetful energy, and an intelligence un-
blinded by the fallacies of the Church, to the improvement of the condition of the poor.

I had the good-fortune, the other day, to find a little
book, printed in 1625, which contains the life of a man
who, in his time, did much good; whose name, hardly
known at all out of Rome, and but little known even
there, deserves remembrance, as that of one who very
early saw and attempted to deal with the evil which is
pressing so heavily upon us, and to remedy which so
many attempts are being made in our cities, — that of
the destitution and misery of young children.   His name
was Giovanni Leonardo Ceruso.   He was born near
Salerno, not far from Naples, in the year 1551.   His
parents were neither rich nor poor; they lived happily,
and brought up their children in the fear of God, and as
good Christians.   The elder brother of Giovanni became
the priest of the village where they lived, and put Giovanni at the head of the parish school.   Here he taught
the children with fidelity, and, as he almost always spoke

n Latin to them, and used often to write upon the ground with a stick which he held in his hand while he was in school, the older scholars gave him the nickname of *Letterato*, by which name he was afterwards generally known. During all his early life he appears to have shown a devout and modest disposition, "and he was," says this account, "so possessed with the virtue of charity, that he exercised it towards all, and especially to the weakest and most abject persons. He often visited the sick, when there were any in the place, comforting them, and aiding them with his means as much as he could." One morning it happened that he, together with the other members of his family, ate some poisonous funguses by mistake for mushrooms. They were all taken violently ill, and Letterato, being at the point of death, recommended himself to the Most Holy Madonna of Loreto, and made a vow that he would make a pilgrimage to her Holy House, if she would restore him to health. He soon got well, and in a short time left his little village to go to Naples, in order to take service in the house of Signor Mario Carrafa, that he might earn money enough to pay the expenses of going to and returning from Loreto, in fulfilment of his vow. He had not been long in his new post before Signor Carrafa died, and Letterato, with the money he had already earned, set out for Rome. "Here he visited the Temple of St. Peter and the Seven Churches, and at St. John, Letterato ascended the Holy Stairs with great devotion; and discovering, during his stay in Rome, that he had not money enough to prosecute his journey, he set about finding a master and placing himself in the best way he could, and so was accepted as groom in the household of the Cardinal de' Medici, who was afterwards Grand Duke Ferdinand." In this new service he acquitted himself with such acceptance as to excite the jealousy of one of his fellow-servants, who sought a quarrel with him, in which they both drew their swords, and blood was near being shed. This event led Letterato to reflect that his vow was as yet unfulfilled, and, obtaining a dismissal from service, he set out for Loreto on foot. The journey seems to have been spent in sincere religious exercises, and was not without its effects upon his future life. It was in the winter of 1582, " a most bitter and snowy winter," that he performed his vow, and returned to Rome. On coming back to the city, he saw much poverty, " and especially some poor children deserted and half dead with cold and hunger." This sight touched his heart, and he took, " almost as if by accident," three of these children, who were very famished and weak, and, carrying two of them in his arms, led the other along by the hand, walking very slowly, and by turns, as one grew tired, he took him up, setting down one of the others to walk. So he went through the city, till at length a charitable person gave him a chamber in which to shelter the children, and others furnished him with food and clothing for them. But every day the number of children who needed care and help increased, and Letterato continued his work. Larger rooms had to be procured, and in supplying these with common coarse bedding and other necessary articles of furniture, and in getting clothes for the shivering boys, he spent all the little money that he possessed. But the charity of others, moved by his zeal and devotion, supplied him with fresh means, and, as the number of his boys grew larger, his ability to receive them was increased. "And now he began to teach these little children the Lord's Prayer, the Ave Maria, the Credo, and the Salve Regina, and to sing these and other prayers both morning and evening." And in order that they might not be doing nothing all day, he took them with him, making them walk two by two through the city, singing their prayers and hymns. About this time he laid aside the habit of a layman, and adopted a dark blue coarse dress, and went barefooted, and without any covering on his head, so that, on account of his humble apparel and his troop of boys, Padre Camillo was accustomed to call him "the dumb preacher," as one who made himself understood without speaking. And in order not to seek alms without having deserved them, and in order also still more to humble his pride, (a sin which he distrusted himself for possessing,) he began with his largest boys to sweep the streets, especially where were the most shops and offices; and when the work was finished, and the dirt had been carried away and thrown into the river, he would go and beg an alms from the shopkeepers and others, who willingly gave it to him.

He wished that his boys should behave with modesty not only in the streets, but also when they were together in the house. "As soon as they were out of bed in the morning, he made them all kneel down and thank God who had kept them that night, and before dinner and supper also he made them thank Him." The older boys he used to take with him to the churches, and to talk with them about spiritual things, and of the love of God. And now so much was given to him by those who saw what good he was effecting, that he was able to get new clothes for all his children, and he dressed them in blue stuff, like himself; and when they went to walk in procession, one of them carried before the rest a cross of wood, upon which was cut in large letters the word *Charity*, so that many people gave them alms.

The number of children under his care greatly increased; and not only little boys, but many great boys also, in order not to live like vagabonds about Rome, were glad to be received by Letterato; and as his means for taking care of them had also increased, he secured a piece of ground near the Porta del Popolo, and there erected a building accommodated to the wants of his charge. He had many little beds of brick made in it, one for each of his boys, and supplied them with straw mattresses and sufficient coverlets. There were tables, also, at which they ate in common; and he had made in the house, beside, a chapel, in which there was an altar and a large crucifix of wood, before which he and his boys were accustomed to say their prayers. "And I remember," says the writer of his life, "that, when he showed me this crucifix, pointing toward it with his hand, he said, ' *In eo lætabitur cor nostrum* '; and he said this with so much feeling as plainly showed that he had earnest of eternal happiness."

On one occasion, having been asked how, in the midst

of the temptations with which Rome abounded, he could keep his soul pure and his thoughts fixed on prayer, he replied, "that when a vase was full it could hold nothing more, and that he tried to keep his heart filled with the thoughts of God, and that his aid was the grace of the Lord, who, whenever on our part we do all that we can, never deserts us." "In the care of his poor children," says his friend who describes his life, "he was most devoted, performing the part of father, of mother, and of nurse, entering at once through his compassion into all their affections, and serving them in everything, not as poor castaways, abandoned by their parents and by the world, but as if they were angels, and he were serving the Lord himself, who saith, 'What ye have done for one of the least of these, ye have done for me.'

"He exercised charity also toward many poor strangers, providing them with lodging for at least one night, and giving them what aid he could, that they might return to their homes; and he showed the same care toward the poor whom he found in the city, succoring and aiding them in their greatest needs, and especially if they were old, or feeble, or ill-used, or burdened with incurable diseases, as many are who may be seen every day in the city; and he extended his charity to poor prisoners also, in their great necessities."

But his chief labor was always for his children, whom he taught as well as he was able. He qualified the older boys to teach the younger, especially wishing that they should learn their prayers one from another; but he did not permit the elder to punish the others. This

he did in order that they should love each other more,
and should live in peace and love.

In this course of life, with constantly increasing usefulness, Letterato continued for many years. The children whom he had first taken charge of were succeeded
by others, year after year, and all were served by him
with a thoroughness and fidelity that never failed. At
last, in the autumn of 1594, when he was forty-three years
old, he was taken ill with a fever. Anxious to return to
his children, he did not give sufficient time to the restoration of his health, and having worn himself out with his
renewed exertions, early in 1595 he was again attacked
by illness. He was taken to the house of Cardinal
Federico Borromeo, who had long been one of his
friends, and here his last days were surrounded by all the
comforts and attention that kindness could render. On
the day before his death he sent for his children to come
and see him. When they had gathered about his bed, he
said that he wished they would sing something to him;
and when the little boy whom he loved best of all asked
him what he would like to hear, he answered, that he
should like to have them sing

> " Dico spesso al mio cuore,
> Solo servendo Dio l' alma non muore."

" Often I say to my heart, Only serving God, the
soul does not die."

And when they had sung this, and other spiritual
songs, he joined with them in singing, " I have prepared
to follow thee, Jesus, my hope, through the rough, hard

way, with my cross." When they had finished singing, he said to them, "May God bless you all, my dearest children! Be good and fear the Lord." Then they took leave of him, and went away crying. The next day, the 15th of February, 1595, with words of Christian hope upon his lips, he died.

The writer of his life says, at the close of his narrative, "This is all I have been able to write now of the life and death of Letterato; and from this my little work the pious soul may learn at least something of love, if nothing else."

The usefulness of Letterato did not end with his death. The work begun by him was continued by others, and at the present time an institution for poor children exists in Rome, whose origin may be traced back to the impulse given by his example.

Rome, May 29th, 1856.

Evening schools, similar to those that have been established of late in so many American cities, for the instruction of boys who are at work during the day, were commenced as long ago as 1830 in Rome. They owe their origin to Michele Gigli, an advocate, who devoted his life to good works, and died of cholera in 1837, a victim to exhausting efforts for the poor and sick. The idea of evening schools for the purpose of affording instruction to those who can gain it at no other time seems to have been original with him. There are now thirteen of these schools in different sections of the city, and they are attended by no less than a thousand pupils. Their support depends wholly upon private energy and private means. The government, although it recognizes and controls their existence, does nothing in aid of them. At the head of each school is an ecclesiastic; the teaching is given voluntarily and gratuitously, for the most part, by young men of liberal education, who are willing to devote their evenings to the work. A great difficulty is to find teachers enough; for the schools are open for an hour and a half every evening but Sunday, and there are comparatively few persons who possess sufficient energy and sufficient leisure to attend regularly. One might expect, that, among the priests and friars who overrun Rome, leading inactive lives, enough might be found glad to undertake this duty of teaching. But such is not the case; — many are indifferent to the work, many are too ignorant to perform it. A few there are willing and able, and among these is the Abate Fabiani, to whose good judgment, intelligent liberality, and energy, much of the present success and popularity of these schools is due.

The boys who attend the evening schools are of all ages, from five or six to eighteen or twenty, — from those who are just beginning to learn to read, to those who have made some progress in geometry and in drawing. They advance regularly from the lowest class to the highest, each school being divided into four or more classes. The quickness and intelligence of these boys are very striking to one who has been accustomed to the dulness of intellect that is so often found among the poor children who attend similar schools in our country while the pleasant looks and good manners of the Roman children speak well for their tempers and the common influences by which they are surrounded. Each class in the school is divided into two parties, one called that of the Carthaginians, the other that of the Romans, — and the object of each of these parties is to secure the largest number of the little prizes of pencils, or pens, or boxes of instruments, that are given by the instructor at the end of each term. The first boy of each of the parties is called the Imperator, the next two are Generals, and the fourth the Standard-Bearer, — distinctions that are held by the boys as long as they can keep the first places. Many of the scholars being apprenticed at trades which require a considerable degree of mechanical skill, such as cabinet-making, iron and brass work and jewelry, it has been found of great service to carry them through a course of drawing of more than a mere elementary nature, and the results have been in the highest degree satisfactory. There is a natural aptitude in the Romans for work of this kind, and the talent of the boys exhibits itself greatly in the facility and beauty of their drawings.

The chief difficulty that has to be contended with is the want of good books of instruction. There is no good book, for instance, of reading-lessons for beginners, and no school treatise on geography or history. Such Roman school-literature as there is has, for the most part, been prepared by priests, and is of such a character as to disgust children, not only with learning, but with religion. This difficulty, however, is in the way of being diminished by the preparation of less objectionable books.

During the month of May, which is especially devoted to the worship of the Virgin, a short spiritual exercise in her honor is conducted by the teachers, in which all the children take part. A picture of Mary hangs in the school-room, and candles are lighted before it, and burn during the service.

After the school is over, the boys form a procession, and go through the streets to their homes, accompanied by their teachers. Every care is taken, and every precaution observed, that the schools shall give no reasonable ground of complaint to the large and influential class of bigots, who regard them with suspicion and distrust. Those who are interested in their support are obliged to act with the utmost circumspection, and are checked by continual interference on the part of the ecclesiastical authorities.

On Sundays and on feast-days the Abate Fabiani collects the boys of his school, and walks with them, or takes them to some garden where they may amuse themselves, or visits with them some church. A sincere, devout, and earnest Catholic, he desires to win them through love to good lives, and he exerts the influence he gains over them to make them also sincere Christians in their turn. On the afternoon of Easter Sunday, I met him with his boys at St. Peter's. It was a sight more touching, and a better representation of the spirit of the gospel of Christ, than all the splendid ceremonial of the morning had been, with its pomp, its glitter, its troops of soldiers, the benediction of the Pope, the fans of peacock's feathers, and the multitude kneeling before the church.

ORVIETO.

ORVIETO, March, 1856.

IN the very heart of Italy, midway between Rome and Florence, in the recesses of the Apennines, lies Orvieto, a city of the Middle Ages, — though its name, said to be a corruption of *Urbs Vetus*, tells of an ancient and forgotten origin. It was never very large, never held great power, never played an important part in the drama of Italian politics, — but the arts of two centuries concentrated themselves within its walls to produce a single splendid and complete work, and its Cathedral has long given glory to Orvieto, and still renders it one of the chief cities of pilgrimage in Italy.

Leaving the main road between Rome and Siena at Montefiascone, the way turns north-eastward through the low and desolate hills that lie above the gloomy lake of Bolsena. A slow ascent leads up to a high and bare table-land, over which the March winds, coming out from the hollows of the mountains, sweep fiercely. The plateau suddenly breaks upon a precipitous declivity, and Orvieto, till that moment unseen, appears crowning a rocky height which rises solitary and abrupt from a deep

valley. So narrow is the valley, that, from the point
where the plateau breaks, the city seems almost within
musket-shot. But the perfect isolation of the mountain
upon which it stands, no spur or ridge connecting it with
those that lie nearest to it, makes the approach to the
city slow and difficult, and gives to it a peculiar and striking character of inaccessibility. The truncated oval cone
of an extinct volcano, the height lifts itself with almost
perpendicular sides for more than seven hundred feet,
rising from the valley like a solitary islet of rock. Storms
have washed bare its upper steeps, and have heaped up
their crumbling *débris* upon the plain below, forming
a broad buttress and embankment of stone and earth
around its base. The city with its gray walls set upon
the topmost edge of the scarped reddish cliff, with the
towers of its churches and the gables and pinnacles of its
Cathedral showing clear against the sky, and shining with
various color in the sunlight, looks like a bas-relief cut on
the smooth face of the rock. Near behind it, half encircling it, lies an uneven range of brown and purple mountains, as if to shut it out from the world in a seclusion of
its own. The lower slopes of the height are rich with
vineyards, farms, and wide-spread convents set deep in
trees. The little Paglia winds through the green valley
on its way to the Tiber, and vanishes among the hills.
Before the invention of artillery, a city set on such a hill
was impregnable by assault, and for many centuries Orvieto, always faithful to the Guelphs, was a city of refuge
for Popes driven out from Rome by its turbulent citizens,
or flying at the approach of some foreign enemy. It is a

forcible illustration of the sorrowful history of Italy, that
so many of her towns should have been built upon the
bare tops of hills and mountains.

The city loses something of its apparent beauty as,
after the long ascent to its gates, one enters its dark and
dirty streets. Its walls are too big for it, for it has
shrunk since they were built. Its palaces are mostly deserted, more than one of its old churches is neglected, an
air of decay pervades it, save only in the square on
which its Cathedral stands, where its ancient splendor
remains undiminished, and seems even more brilliant
than of old, from contrast with the surrounding changes
of decline. No city in Italy boasts a more perfect monument of the past munificence and spirit of its people.
The seclusion and the decay of Orvieto have been the
protection of its Duomo, — they have preserved it from
the rifling of invaders, and from the defacing processes
of restorers. Few buildings of the Middle Ages retain
so completely the character of their original design, few
afford so full a record of the lives and works of their
early builders.

With the exception of the Cathedral of Siena, there is
no church in Italy in which the Italian Gothic appears in
freer development of beauty than in this. Architecture,
sculpture, and painting, as represented by mosaic, combined their powers and lavished their wealth in the construction of its three-gabled front. The main lines of
construction are, indeed, somewhat meagre, and the flat
surfaces of the front fail to produce those grand effects
of deep shadow which belong to the carved recesses and

deep-sunk portals of Northern cathedrals; but these defects are compensated by the rich sculpture of its marble piers, by the gold and azure of its pictured gables, and by the host of guardian busts and statues around its central rose-window. It seems like the illuminated page of a marble missal, — the adorned initial letter set at the entrance of the great volume written in stone. As the sunlight falls on the gleaming front, — its glowing colors harmonized by the slow artistic processes of time, — it presents a character of beauty unknown to the more sombre Gothic of the North. Nor is the interior of the church unsuitable to its external richness, though the splendor of the outside is tempered within to an impressive solemnity. The tall, banded marble columns of the nave, the long procession of statues of apostles at their feet, the frescoes on the walls of choir and chapels, the elaborate carvings of wood and gratings of iron, the mingling of patience, labor, and art in every portion of the work, not only give proof of the fervent spirit of the builders of the Cathedral, but suggest many a devout memory and sacred association.

The erection of such a building is no solitary and exceptional fact in the history of the community by whom it was accomplished. It is an illustration of the general spirit of their life, of its strongest faith, its deepest emotions, its most persistent impulses. The building of cathedrals is, in truth, one of the main features of the social history of Europe during the Middle Ages. In England, in Spain, in France, in the Low Countries, in Germany, in Italy, in Sicily, these magnificent monuments of genius and devotion rose in rapid succession during the twelfth and thirteenth centuries. By a great impulse of popular energy, by a long combination of popular effort with trained skill, cathedrals, each requiring almost the revenues of a kingdom for its construction, sprang up from the soil in the hearts of scores of rival cities. There have been no works of architecture in later times comparable with them in grandeur of design, in elaborateness of detail, in that broad unity of conception which, while leaving the largest scope for the play of fancy and the exercise of special ability by every workman, subordinated the multifarious differences of parts into one harmonious whole. The true cathedral architecture partook of the qualities which Nature displays in her noblest works, — out of infinite varieties of generally resembling, but intrinsically differing parts, creating a perfect and concordant result.

But the period during which the great cathedrals were built was comparatively short. After the fourteenth century, the practice of cathedral architecture of the old kind fell fast into desuetude. In the fifteenth century, canons of taste were established, and modes of judgment introduced, which, symptomatic as they were of a general change in the spiritual condition of society, debased the standard of an art whose capacities of execution were daily growing more limited. The traditional knowledge of the methods of the unrivalled masters of two centuries before, such masters as Erwin von Steinbach, Arnolfo di Lapo, and Lorenzo Maitani, rapidly died out. The Renaissance — the birth of a pseudo-classi cism — was the destruction of Gothic architecture. The rules of Vitruvius were studied as the only rules of desirable and excellent building. The original works of the time between the fall of the Roman Empire and the irruption of Roman literature were esteemed barbarous and unworthy of admiration. Architecture was henceforth to be imitative. It is a curious fact, that at Rome itself there is not one truly Gothic church. Whatever may be the architectural merit of St. Peter's, it is not to be compared, in originality of conception or in thoughtfulness of detail, with any of the great Gothic buildings. It belongs to the architecture of the intellect, — not to that of the imagination. Its chief feature is its size, not its design. St. Peter's is contemporaneous with the Reformation, and the character of the religion of the Papal court at that time is well perpetuated in a church, built less as a place of worship than as a magnificent theatre for the splendid displays of Papal ceremonials. Protestantism failed to protest against the style of ecclesiastical architecture characteristic of Rome, but, on the contrary, often strangely adopted it for its own churches, and not infrequently turned its iconoclastic zeal against the more ancient style, which, though sometimes embodying the extremest superstitions, embodied also the expression of a real, if a mistaken, piety.

The best Gothic architecture, indeed, wherever it may be found, affords evidence that the men who executed it were moved by a true fervor of religious faith. In building a church, they did not forget that it was to be the house of God. No portion of their building was too minute, no portion too obscure, to be perfected with thorough and careful labor. The work was not let out by contract, or taken up as a profitable job. The architect of a cathedral might live all his life within the shadow of its rising walls, and die no richer than when he gave the sketch; but he was well repaid by the delight of seeing his design grow from an imagination to a reality, and by spending his days in the accepted service of the Lord.

For the building of a cathedral, however, there needs not only a spirit of religious zeal among the workmen, but a faith no less ardent among the people for whom the church is designed. The enormous expense of construction, an expense which for generations must be continued without intermission, is not to be met except by liberal and willing general contributions. Papal indulgences and the offerings of pilgrims may add something to the revenues, but the main cost of building must be borne by the community over whose house-tops the cathedral is to rise and to extend its benign protection.

Cathedrals were essentially expressions of the popular will and the popular faith. They were the work neither of ecclesiastics nor of feudal barons. They represent, in a measure, the decline of feudalism, and the prevalence of the democratic element in society. No sooner did a city achieve its freedom than its people began to take thought for a cathedral. Of all the arts, architecture is the most quickly responsive to the instincts and the desires of a people. And in the cathedrals, the popular beliefs, hopes, fears, fancies, and aspirations found expression, and were perpetuated in a language intelligible to all.   The life of the Middle Ages is recorded on their walls.   When the democratic element was subdued, as in Cologne by a Prince Bishop, or in Milan by a succession of tyrants, the cathedral was left unfinished.   When, in the fifteenth century, all over Europe, the turbulent, but energetic liberties of the people were suppressed, the building of cathedrals ceased.

The grandeur, beauty, and lavish costliness of the Duomo at Orvieto, or of any other of the greater cathedrals, implies a persistency and strength of purpose which could be the result only of the influence over the souls of men of a deep and abiding emotion.   Minor motives may often have borne a part in the excitement of feeling, — motives of personal ambition, civic pride, boastfulness, and rivalry; but a work that requires the combined and voluntary offerings and labor of successive generations presupposes a condition of the higher spiritual nature which no motives but those connected with religion are sufficient to support.   It becomes, then, a question of more than merely historic interest, a question, indeed, touching the very foundation of the spiritual development and civilization of modern Europe, to investigate the nature and origin of that wide-spread impulse which, for two centuries, led the people of different races and widely diverse habits of life and thought, to the construction of cathedrals, — buildings such as our own age, no less than those which have immediately preceded it, seems incompetent to execute, and indifferent to attempt.

It is impossible to fix a precise date for the first signs of vigorous and vital consciousness which gave token of the birth of a new life out of the dead remains of the ancient world. The tenth century is often spoken of as the darkest period of the Dark Ages; but even in its dull sky there were some breaks of light, and, very soon after it had passed, the dawn began to brighten. The epoch of the completion of a thousand years from the birth of Christ, which had, almost from the first preaching of Christianity, been looked forward to as the time for the destruction of the world and the advent of the Lord to judge the earth, had passed without the fulfilment of these ecclesiastical prophecies and popular anticipations. There can be little doubt that among the mass of men there was a sense of relief, naturally followed by a certain invigoration of spirit. The eleventh century was one of comparative intellectual vigor. The twelfth was still more marked by mental activity and force. The world was fairly awake. Civilization was taking the first steps of its modern course. The relations of the various classes of society were changing. A wider liberty of thought and action was established; and while this led to a fresh exercise of individual power and character, it conduced also to combine men together in new forms of united effort for the attainment of common objects and in the pursuit of common interests.

Corresponding with, but perhaps subsequent by a short interval to the pervading intellectual movement, was a strong and quickening development of the moral sense among men. The periods distinguished in modern history by a condition of intellectual excitement and fervor have been usually, perhaps always, followed at a short interval by epochs of more or less intense moral energy, which has borne a near relation to the nature of the moral elements in the previous intellectual movement. The Renaissance, an intellectual period of pure immorality, was followed close by the Reformation, whose first characteristic was that of protest.   The Elizabethan age in which the minds of men were full of large thoughts, and their imaginations rose to the highest flights, led in the noble sacrifices, the great achievements, the wild vagaries of Puritanism.   The age of Voltaire and the infidels was followed by the fierce energy, the infidel morality of the French Revolution.   And so at this earlier period, the general intellectual awakening, characterized as it was by simple impulses, and regulated in great measure by the teachings of the Church, produced a strong outbreak of moral earnestness which exhibited itself in curiously similar forms through the whole of Europe.

The distinguishing feature of this moral revolution was the purely religious direction which it took.   For a time it seemed that the moral sense of men had become one with their religious instincts and emotions.   Religion lost its formality, and the religious creed of the times possessed itself thoroughly of the spirits of men.   The separation which commonly exists between the professed faith of the masses of men and their intimate moral convictions, the separation between faith expressed in words and faith expressed in actions, was in large meas-

are closed over. The creed even of the most intelligent was very imperfect. It was based on material conceptions, and was far from corresponding with the higher spiritual truths of Christianity. The creed of the ignorant was, for the most part, a system of irrational and contradictory opinions, in which a few simple notions of a material heaven and hell held the first rank. But these notions were believed in as realities. And, moreover, in accordance with a general law of human nature, the very materialism of the common creed afforded nourishment to religious mysticism and the ecstasies of devotion.

It is at such times as this, when moral energy corresponds with and supports a condition of spiritual enthusiasm, that the powers of men rise to their highest level. Personal interests are absorbed in devotion to great spiritual ideas. Enthusiasm neither submits to the common laws of reason, nor is bound by the established customs of society. It makes its abode in the New Jerusalem, and builds for itself mystical mansions of the spirit. But it must find external expression, and must relieve itself in action; for, when the full tide of faith floods the heart, it brings to the soul a sense of strength above its own, and compels it to its exercise. Thus, at this period, the religious excitement found vent in two extraordinary and utterly unparalleled expressions, — the Crusades and the Cathedrals. And the depth of the inward feeling was marvellously manifested by the long succession of exhausting efforts, by the persistence of hope, and by the actual accomplishment of works of the grandest design, during a course of more than two hundred years. Energy and enthusiasm had become, as it were, hereditary among men. A real faith in the Divine government of the earth, trust in the Divine power, zeal in the service of God, combined with selfish hopes and fears, and with heathen notions of propitiation, to inspire the various people of Europe with strength for the most arduous undertakings. *Deus vult* was the animating watchword of the times; the cross was the universal symbol, — a symbol not merely of sacrifice, but of victory.

Such spiritual conditions as were then exhibited are possible only during periods of mental twilight, when the imagination is stronger than the reason, and shows the objects of this world in fanciful and untrue proportion. With the advance of civilization and enlightenment, popular enthusiasm becomes more and more rare, and, as a stimulus to combined and long-continued action, almost wholly ceases. Principles of one sort or another occupy, but do not supply its place. The works which it has produced cannot be repeated; for in their production it counts no cost extravagant, no labor vain, which makes them worthier offerings of faith, and more perfect expressions of devotion.

The general features of the religious excitement which began in the eleventh century are thus broadly marked and easily stated. The chief historic facts of the time are sufficiently clear. The details of the Crusades are, for the most part, well known; but much obscurity still rests over the manner in which the popular impulses took form in the building of cathedrals. The old chronicles, full of battles and sieges, have little space for accounts of the great works which were going on within the walls of quiet towns, and in the chief squares of busy cities. The records of building, with all the illustration they might afford of the thoughts, feelings, and ways of life of the people, have in great part perished. Here and there something more than the mere name of the architect and the date of construction has been preserved; but the lives and labors of the builders, the modes of work, the zeal of the community, are, for the most part, only to be inferred from the character of the building itself.

Fortunately, the position and the circumstances of Orvieto, and the fact that its cathedral was not begun till a comparatively late date, have been favorable to the preservation of a mass of records which throw a vivid light, not only on the methods of construction, but also on the character and customs of the builders and the people of the town, during the thirteenth, fourteenth, and even the fifteenth centuries.*

The immediate motive for the erection of this cathedral is to be found in one of the most famous events of the dogmatic history of the Middle Ages, and by this

* The subsequent narrative is derived, in great measure, from the *Storia del Duomo di Orvieto.* [Dal Padre G. della Valle.] 4to. Roma, 790. The most valuable part of the volume is the long appendix of Documents, taken mostly from the manuscript records of the Duomo. The volume of plates in folio, which accompanies the Padre della Valle's work, contains representations of some of the most important works of Art in the Cathedral, and is of much value as illustrating the history of Italian Art. There is no other building in Italy which surpasses the Duomo of Orvieto as a storehouse of precious works

circumstance the building is connected in close association with one of the most wide-spread and splendid ceremonials of the Roman Church. This event was the Miracle of Bolsena, from which the festival of the Corpus Domini, celebrated wherever the Roman Church extends, takes its date. It is one of the chief glories of the Church Triumphant.

In the year 1263, Pope Urban IV., flying from dangers that surrounded him in Rome, "*poco fidandosi di quell' istabile cittadinanza,*" retired to the safe refuge of Orvieto. All Italy was in a wretched state of turbulence and war. But on this solitary and inaccessible rock there was quiet, and within the shelter of its friendly walls the Pope might dwell securely. And here also, at this time, Thomas Aquinas, the most famous man of his age, who was even then stamping the impress of his thought upon the whole system of Romanist doctrine, had taken up his abode, and was giving public instruction in a course of lectures on theology. One day, in the summer of the next year, according to the tradition, the Pope was surprised at the sudden appearance of a strange priest, who, in great agitation, threw himself at his feet, and with tears, confessing his past want of faith, and praying for absolution from his sin, related the following story. He said that he was a German priest, that he had long been troubled with doubts as to the Real Presence in the Holy Sacrifice of the Mass, and that, in hope of removing such pernicious questionings from his soul, he had undertaken a pilgrimage to Rome for the purpose of strengthening his faith at the tombs of the Apostles.   He had reached the little town of Bolsena, which lies just on the border of the lake to which it has given its name, and within the diocese of Orvieto, and there had engaged in the celebration of the Mass.   But in the very midst of the service he was assailed by his old doubts, when, to his wonder and dismay, as he raised the consecrated wafer and broke it, he beheld drops of blood falling from it upon the sacred napkin laid under the chalice, and, as they touched the linen cloth, spreading out upon it into the likeness of the Saviour's countenance.*

* One of the series of Raphael's pictures of the Church Triumphant in the Stanze of the Vatican has made the scene of this miracle familiar. His imagination does not seem to have been touched by the subject, and the picture is a mere fancy piece, cold in feeling and devoid of any expression of faith.

A miracle of similar character to that of Bolsena is reported to have occurred at Canterbury, in the time of St. Odo, about the middle of the tenth century. Some of the priests of Canterbury were troubled with doubts like those by which the German priest was possessed. The Saint prayed that these doubts might be removed, and during the performance of the Mass, at the breaking of the Host, blood dropped from it into the chalice. By this miracle the doubters were brought into the true faith. — See Butler's *Lives of the Saints: St. Odo* — Many similar miracles are reported as having taken place in Spain. "No Christian country," says Mr. Ford, "has offered more wonderful evidences of the fact" of a corporeal presence in the Host. At Ivorra, a portion of a consecrated wafer is preserved, called *Lo Sant Dupte*, "the Holy Doubt," from which blood gushed out, to confound a doubting priest; — at Daroca, in New Castile, is the tradition of *Los Santos Corporales*, — six Hosts, which, in 1289, being hidden from the Moors, turned to bleeding flesh.

Thus has the Roman Church corporealized a spiritual symbol, — disregarding both the meaning and the letter of its institution. A

8

The miracle occurred at a fortunate time, not only for the removal of the doubts of the German priests, but for the interests of the Roman Church, by affording a decisive argument against the heretical doctrines in regard to the Real Presence, which had spread widely among the ranks of the clergy, and had excited much alarm in the minds of the ecclesiastical authorities. Urban, rejoicing at so signal a display of the divine grace, at once dispatched the Bishop of Orvieto to Bolsena to bring back the sacred *corporale* or napkin, for safe-keeping in his immediate possession. The next day the Holy Father himself descended to the valley, attended by his Cardinals, the officers of his court, the chief citizens, and many of the common people, to meet the Bishop on his return. The two processions, — for the Bishop came accompanied by great numbers of the people of Bolsena and the neighboring towns, filled with excitement at the news of the prodigy, — the two processions met at the bridge of Riochiaro. The Pope fell upon his knees in adoration of the sacred cloth, and, taking it in his hands, bore it up the hill to a place of secure deposit in the episcopal church of Orvieto. It is said that for use on this solemn and memorable occasion, Thomas Aquinas composed the service which is still employed on the recurring anniversaries of the day in the Roman churches the world over. Urban published a bull, in which he appointed Thursday

natural explanation has been suggested for these miracles, in the fact that under certain conditions blood-red animalcula are found in some sorts of flour, and in the bread made from it, in quantities suffi sient to produce the effects supposed to be miraculous.

of the week after Pentecost as the day on which, in each
year, the festival of Corpus Christi should be celebrated,
and a new dogma was added, by authority, to the creed
of the Church.

> " Tantum ergo sacramentum
> Veneremur cernui;
> Et antiquum documentum
> Novo cedat ritui;
> Præstat fides supplementum
> Sensuum defectui."

Whatever opinion may be held as to the reality of the
asserted miracle, there is a concurrence of authorities as
to the fact of the popular belief in it, and of the religious enthusiasm that followed on this belief among the
citizens of Orvieto and the neighboring districts.   Some
time, however, elapsed before this enthusiasm exhibited
itself in any permanent external manifestation.   By degrees, the idea of a new and splendid church, in which
the miraculous *corporale* should be preserved for all
future time, and which should serve not only as a fitting
memorial of the miracle, but also as a proof of the devotion of the citizens to the Virgin Mother of God, seems
to have taken root in the minds of the people, and perhaps the more easily from a feeling of rivalry between
Orvieto and its neighbor, Siena, in which latter city a
splendid cathedral had been begun half a century before, and was now approaching its superb, though imperfect completion.

The first document that has been found relating to the
proposed building bears date the 22d day of June, 1284,

and in this the project "of erecting a new and honorable church in honor of God and the Blessed Virgin Mary" is spoken of as one that has been for a long time entertained. It is amusing, as an illustration of the persistency of one of the minor traits of human nature, that the earliest records of the Cathedral should relate to a quarrel between the members of a sort of preliminary building-committee — the Bishop and his chapter — concerning the arrangement to be made between them in regard to the ground, in which they had joint interest upon which the new church was to stand. The difficulty was not settled without the intervention of the Papa authority, and it was not until the year 1290 that the work of construction was actually begun.

The 13th of November, the day of San Brizio, the patron saint of the city, was chosen as the day for laying the corner-stone of the great edifice. "And so," says one of the chroniclers, "the Pope, Nicholas IV., being in Orvieto, with the Court of Cardinals and other Prelates, there was a solemn procession, with His Holiness at its head, followed by Cardinals, Archbishops, Bishops, and other Prelates, by the Clergy of the city, with the Magistrates, the Podestà, the Captain, the Seniors, and all the Council, with infinite numbers of gentlemen and citizens, women and children. And the Pope went down to the foundations, and with his own hand placed the first stone in the mortar, and with many other ceremonies blessed the future temple *in secula seculorum.*"

Lorenzo Maitani of Siena had given the design for the church, and had been appointed the chief architect.

A better choice could not have been made. Already the
means for carrying forward the work had been provided
by free-will offerings, by lands given in fee by their proprietors, by taxes imposed by the magistracy, by annual
tributes laid upon territory subject to the city, as well as
by the offerings of many churches far and near, and of
the pilgrims who were annually attracted to Orvieto by
the fame of a miracle-working picture of the Madonna,
which had been given to the city, according to tradition,
by its patron saint.

Nor was the work left to depend simply on the general interest and zeal, unwarmed by special incitements.
The Pope bestowed liberal indulgences on those who took
part in forwarding it by contributions or by labor, and his
example in this respect was followed in after times by
his successors. The list of contributions to the building
during the first year gives a curious glimpse of the char
acter of the times, and of the means used for the execu
tion of such a work. It begins thus : —

MCCLXXXX.
Urbevetellum solvit Cereum librarum XV Marcus II. Bra
vium aureorum VIII.,*

---

* The word *bravium*, or *blavium*, seems to be a corruption of *pal-
lium*. Thus, in an extract from the Florentine Archives, (Gaye, *Carteggio*, I. 449,) we read, "60 *floreni auri et sol.* 12 *pro pretio blavii
seu pali duarum petiarum samiti pilosi* " It was used to designate
rich cloth of various sorts for tapestry, hangings of churches, prizes
at games and races, and must have borne a ready marketable value
" *Il drappo verde* " of Verona (*Inferno*, XV. 122) was, no doubt, a
bravium. Probably part of the *bravia*, as well as of the wax contrib-
uted to the church, was used in church ceremonies, and part was
sold.

which may be translated, " Orvieto paid fifteen pounds of wax, two [silver] marks, and cloth of the value of eight gold pieces." The town of Clusium, more liberal than Orvieto itself, sent thirty pounds of wax, two marks, four horses, and five hundred loads of grain. Little Montepulciano even, from the small resources of her vine-growing hill, sent fifteen pounds of wax, two marks, and two horses. The abbey Sancti Salvatoris made a liberal offering. Aquapendente, San Lorenzo, Bolsena, which appears on the list as Volsinium, recalling its ancient fame, Radicofani, and many other towns near and far, gave contributions according to their zeal or means. The Lord of Farnese, Count Guido of Santa Flora, the Lord of the Sons of the Bear [Orsini] of Mugnano, and numerous feudal barons beside, gave horses, wax, and grain to the new church. Altogether, the contributions recorded for this year from towns and barons amount to 731 pounds of wax, 24 marks, 29 horses, 3,858 loads of grain, and *bravia* worth 84 gold pieces. Nor does this list include the more numerous minor offerings of pilgrims and citizens to the treasury of the works. The gifts of horses must have been of especial value, from the fact that the materials for building were all to be brought from a distance, and to be carried up the difficult ascent to the very crest of the mountain of Orvieto. The labor of transportation added vastly to the costliness of the edifice, but the spirit in which it was undertaken was sufficient to overcome whatever obstacles opposed themselves to its progress.

The great foundations were scarcely laid, *fundamenta*

quæ fuerunt terribilia ad videndum, before a Board of Works was established by the popular authorities of the city, to superintend and direct the erection of the Cathedral. It was, in fact, a special magistracy with full powers, so far as their charge extended, but bound to render, from time to time, an account of the income and the expenses to the representatives of the people. The constitution of the government of Orvieto seems to have been democratic, except in so far as the powers of the elective magistracy were subordinate to the authority of the Pope, or of his delegates. That there was rarely any collision between the Papal and the popular will may be inferred from the fact, that, after the twelfth century, during some part of which Orvieto was troubled by heresy, through the most violent and divided times, the city remained attached and faithful to the interests and the party of the Papacy.

For some years the Cathedral advanced rapidly. Indeed, so speedy was its progress, that in the year 1298, Boniface VIII., a Pope familiar to the readers of Dante, celebrated a pontifical service within its unfinished inclosure, on the festival of the Assumption of the Virgin. The work of laying the foundation and the lower walls not demanding the continual presence of the architect, Maitani remained at his native Siena, coming to Orvieto only as occasion might require. But in the year 1310, twenty years after the laying of the corner-stone, the building having risen so far that his constant oversight was needed, and some portions of the completed work showing symptoms of weakness, Maitani was invited to become a citizen of Orvieto, with promise of a monthly salary " of twelve florins of good and pure gold, and of just weight," with leave to bring such scholars as he might wish, who should be employed upon the building, with the provision that he and his family should be exempt from every tax and burden, and with permission to himself to wear whatever arms he might choose. Upon these terms he came, and from his coming may be dated the second, and, in relation to Art, the most important period in the building of the Cathedral. The *façade* had already reached a considerable height, and now began to exhibit that lavish display of works of the various arts which still makes it one of the chief glories of Italy.

The immense amount of labor employed in the construction, and of labor of the most diverse description, from the highest efforts of the inventive imagination, to the simplest mechanical hammering of blocks of stone, led to a careful organization of the whole body of workmen, and to the setting aside of a special building, the *Loggia*, on the Cathedral square, for the use of the masters in the different arts. Each art had its chief, and over all presided " the Master of the Masters," skilled no less in painting, mosaic, and sculpture, than in architecture. The larger number of the most accomplished artists came at this time from Siena and Pisa, where the growth of the arts had a little earlier spring than in Florence.*

---

* The following passage from a letter of the Heads of the People, *I Presidi del Popolo,* to the Signiory of Siena, dated 12th May, 1409 shows the high place which the master-workmen of the latter city

Whatever designs and models were required for any portion of the work were first submitted for approval to the head of the special art to which they belonged, and, if approved by him, were then laid before the Master of the Masters, and the Board of Superintendents of the Work. These officers occupied a house opposite the front of the Duomo, in which they assembled for deliberation, and where the records of their proceedings were kept in due form by a notary, who every week registered the works accomplished, the cost of materials, and the wages of those employed on the building.*

Beside the masters and men at work at Orvieto, many others were distributed in various parts of Italy, employed in obtaining materials, and especially in quarrying and cutting marble for the Cathedral.† Black marble

had held for more than a century at Orvieto: — " Vestrique cives in honore eximio magistratus tam incliti operis obtineant principatum a primordio fundamenti " Gaye, *Carteggio*, I. 89.

* This office was established in 1321, and the Padre della Valle, writing at the end of the last century, says, " It has lasted even to the present day." A delightful instance of permanence.

† In the summer of 1821 more than fifty masters of the various arts were receiving pay in the service of the *Fabbrica*. Not quite half of this number were employed at Orvieto itself ; the others were elsewhere overseeing the preparation of materials. A great part of the shaping of the marbles and timber for use in the building was performed at the places from which they were obtained, in order to diminish the cost of carriage. The preparation of working drawings to send to the different stations of work must have been one of the most important occupations of the masters who remained at Orvieto. Of the number of workmen not yet inscribed as masters in their respective arts there seems to be no record; but it must have been very large.

was got from the quarries near Siena, alabaster from
Sant' Antimo, near Radicofani, and white marble from
the mountains of Carrara. But the supply of the richest and rarest marbles came from Rome, the ruins of
whose ancient magnificence afforded ample stores of cost-
liest material to the builders not only of the Papal city
itself, but of Naples, of Orvieto, and of many another
Italian town. The Greek statuary marble, which had
once formed part of some ancient temple, was transferred to the hands of the new sculptors, to be worked
into forms far different in character and in execution
from those of Grecian Art. The accumulated riches
of Pagan Rome were distributed for the adornment of
Christian churches.

To destroy the remains of Paganism was regarded as
a scarcely less acceptable service than to erect new buildings for Christian worship. Petrarch had not yet begun
to lament the barbarism of such destruction. The beauty
of the ancient world was recognized as yet only by a few
artists, powerless to save its vanishing remains. Not yet
had the intoxicating sense of this beauty begun to re-
corrupt and reëffeminate Italy. A century later, Rome
began to preserve in part the few remaining memorials
of her ancient splendor; and not many years after, the
Renaissance, with its degraded taste and debasing principles, set in, and the influence of ancient Art on modern morals was displayed.

The workmen who labored in quarrying at Rome dur
ing the winter retired in summer to the healthy heights
of the Alban mountains, and there, among the ruins

of ancient villas, continued their work, and thence dispatched the blocks, on wagons drawn by buffaloes, to their distant destination. The entries in the book of the records of the *Fabbrica* show with what a network of laborers, in the service of the Cathedral, the neighboring provinces were overspread. Thus, under date of the 13th of September, 1321, there is an entry of the expense of the transport of marbles, and of travertine for coarse work, from Valle del Cero, from Barontoli, from Tivoli, and from Rigo on the Tiber ; and on the 11th of the same month, sixty florins of gold and fourteen *lire* in silver were paid for the transport, with sixteen pairs of buffaloes, from the forest of Aspretolo, of sixteen loads of fir timber for the soffit of the Cathedral, and one beam of the largest size. Again, there is an entry of the payment for bringing four great pieces of marble, of the weight of 8,100 pounds, from the quarter of St. Paul at Rome, and a little later another for 14,250 pounds of marble, also from Rome. On the 21st of June, nine *lire* and eleven *soldi* had been spent in the purchase of an ass, — " *quem somarium Mag. Laurentius caput Magistrorum operis et Camerarius emerunt pro portandis ferris et rebus Magistrorum operis Romam.*" From the quarry of Montepisi came loads of marble for the main portal and for the side-doors ; and from Arezzo, famous of old for its red vases, was brought clay for the glass-furnace for the making of mosaics. On the 3d of August, a messenger was dispatched with letters from the architect to the workmen at Albano, " *Magistris operis qui laborant marmora apud Castrum Albani, prope Urbem.*" Such

entries as these extend over many years, and show, not
only the activity displayed in the building, but also its
enormous costliness, and the long foresight and wide
knowledge of means required in its architect.

Trains of wagons, loaded with material for the Cathedral, made their slow progress toward the city from the
north and the south, from the shores of the Adriatic
and of the Mediterranean. The heavy carts which had
creaked under their burdens along the solitudes of the
Campagna or the Maremma, which had toiled up the for-
est-covered heights that overhang Viterbo, through the
wild passes of Monte Cimino, or whose shouting team-
sters had held back their straining buffaloes down the
bare sides of the mountains of Radicofani, arrived in unending succession in the valley of the Paglia. The worst
part of the way, however, still lay before them in the
steep ascent to the uplifted city. But here the zeal of
voluntary labor came in to lighten the work of the tug-
ging buffaloes. Bands of citizens enrolled themselves to
drag the carts up the rise of the mountain, — and on feast-
days the people of the neighboring towns flocked in to
take their share in the work, and to gain the indulgences
offered to those who should give a helping hand. We
may imagine these processions of laborers in the service
of the house of the Lord advancing to the sound of the
singing of hymns or the chanting of penitential psalms;
but of these scenes no formal description has been left.
The enthusiasm which was displayed was of the same
order as that which, a century before, had been shown a.
the building of the magnificent Cathedral of Chartres,

but probably less intense in its expression, owing to the change in the spirit of the times. Then men and women, sometimes to the number of a thousand, of all ranks and conditions, harnessed themselves to the wagons loaded with materials for building, or with supplies for the workmen. No one was admitted into the company who did not first make confession of his sins, " and lay down at the foot of the altar all hatred and anger." As cart after cart was dragged in by its band of devotees, it was set in its place in a circle of wagons around the church. Candles were lighted upon them all, as upon so many altars. At. night the people watched, singing hymns and songs of praise, or inflicting discipline upon themselves, with prayers for the forgiveness of their sins.

Processions of Juggernaut, camp-meetings, the excitements of a revival, are exhibitions, under another form, of the spirit shown in these enrolments of the people as beasts of burden. Such excitements rarely leave any noble or permanent result. But it was the distinctive characteristic of this period of religious enthusiasm that there were men honestly partaking in the general emotion, yet of such strong individuality of genius, that, instead of being carried away by the wasteful current of feeling, they were able to guide and control to great and noble purposes the impulsive activity and bursting energies of the time. Religious excitements, so called, of whatever kind, imply one of two things, — either a morbid state of the physical or mental system, or a low and materialistic conception of the truths of the spiritual life. They belong as much to the body as to the soul, and they

seek vent for the energies they arouse in physical manifestations.   Between the groaning of a set of miserable
sinners on the anxious seats, and the toiling of men and
women at the ropes of carts laden with stone for a church,
there is a close relation.   The cause and nature of the
emotion which influences them are the same.   The difference of its mode of exhibition arises from original
differences of character, from changes in religious creeds,
from the varied circumstances of different ages.   It is
a difference exhibited in the contrast between the bare
boards of a Methodist meeting-house and the carved
walls of a Catholic cathedral.

It was the fear of hell, rather than the hope of heav-
en, which, working in men's minds, lay at the foundation
of these mediæval achievements.   Unless the conception
of heaven be lowered to that of a Mahometan paradise, unless heaven be made the scene of merely sensual delights, it is more difficult for the imagination to
behold its promised joys as realities than to picture to
itself the actual existence of the coarse and earthy torments of the vulgar notion of hell.   The Church has
found its power easily increased by strengthening the
force and domination of the dread of future punishment.
For the God of love it substituted the God of vengeance.
The popular fancy dwelt continually on the danger of
damnation, on the variety of the punishments of hell.
The scenes of the Inferno were represented even at festi-
vals.   In 1304, in the month of May, the gay time of the
year, one of the Florentine companies of revellers gave
notice to the citizens, that whoever would hear news of the

other world should assemble on a certain morning on the bridge *alla Carraia* across the Arno. Boats and rafts were moored on the river below, and there this joyous company represented the scenes and sufferings of hell with fires and torments, some of the band counterfeiting horrible demons, and others appearing as naked souls in woe, with great howling and uproar, frightful to hear and to see. In the midst of the scene, the bridge, overladen with the mass of spectators, suddenly broke down; so that, says the chronicler, "the game changed to earnest, and many went in reality to learn news of the other world." *

To this pervading sentiment of fear, combined often with nobler emotions and with high spiritual conceptions, Gothic architecture gave expression in many of its most characteristic features. The grotesque, which enters so largely into its details, was an expression of a natural rebound of the spirit from the constraint of a severe and compulsive creed. There is a fear which is simply oppressive, which crushes out the principle of life, — and also a fear which, while it impedes the development of some portion of the spiritual faculties, vitalizes and stimulates, in combination with other principles, the general powers of the soul. The one finds its expression in the dead gloom of low-browed Hindu temples, — the other, in the solemn, but aspiring grandeur of Gothic cathedrals. On the *façade* of the Duomo of Orvieto, upon one of the piers at the side of its doors of entrance, were sculptured representations of the Last Judgment and of Hell.

* Giov. Villani, Lib. viii. Cap. lxx.

As years went on, the beautiful church, "the palace of God," advanced rapidly toward completion. Already, as we have seen, in 1321, the timbers for its roof were brought from the forest where they had been hewn. The sculptures and mosaics upon its gorgeous *façade*, displaying "doctrine and life, colors and light in one," were actively carried forward. The great windows were filled with slabs of translucent alabaster, through which a mellow light fell into its marble aisles. The bronze figure of the Virgin to surmount the main portal was cast, and set in the place which it still holds, looking down upon the worshippers who enter the church dedicated to her honor. The beauty and lavish magnificence of the building had taken visible form in the thirty years that had passed since its "foundations, terrible to behold," were laid, and that which had been only a vision in the imagination of the architect was now a reality plain to the sight of all men. The Duomo already ministered to the civic pride of the people of Orvieto, and the recorded contributions for its support for the year 1323 amount to nearly 8,000 *lire*, — a large sum in those times, when the chief architect received but forty-eight *lire* a month, and the monthly pay of the masters in the different arts varied from ten to six *lire*, according to their abilities or reputation. In addition to this sum received from voluntary contributions, large revenues were derived from legacies, as well as from the tribute exacted by authority of the state from the towns and feudal proprietors subject to the dominion of Orvieto.

The genius and comprehensive ability of Maitani had

been displayed, not only in the original plan of the building and in a general oversight of its construction, but also in his practical acquaintance with the processes of the various subsidiary arts, and in the superintendence and combination of the labors of the parties of workmen scattered over the country. The Cathedral was moulded in all its portions by his hands, and upon him, in great measure, its steady progress had depended. In the year 1330, after forty years devoted to its service, he died. He had lived long enough to see his great design complete in all its main features, and rivalling in its splendid adornments the finest churches of Italy. The Duomo at Florence, — Santa Maria de' Fiori, — begun about the same time, and on a scale of superior grandeur, befitting the greater size, the wider power, and the more abundant wealth of the city of which it is still the chief ornament, had not advanced so rapidly, had not been the object of so fond and liberal a regard, as the mountain Cathedral of Orvieto. Rare fortune for an artist, to embody his life and imagination in one work, and to live to see his work accomplished !

The history of the church loses interest after Maitani's death. It relates thereafter not so much to the larger processes and methods of construction as to the details of ornamentation, — to the mosaics, the paintings in chapels, the elaborate wood-inlaying of the choir stalls, the making of the costly reliquary, — all of which show the zeal of the Orvietans in the decoration of the building, and illustrate the history of the minor arts, but fail in exhibiting any of the grander features of social life and religious emotions. The race of men to which Maitani belonged was fast disappearing in Italy, and it would have been difficult, had there been need, to find a successor able to occupy the place he had filled. After the death of Arnolfo, the Duomo of Florence was left to stand incomplete for nearly a century, and was then partially finished, on a plan inferior to, and discordant with, the original design. The grandest part of the plan for the Cathedral of Siena was never carried out. The Cathedral of Milan remained unfinished till the present century. The Campanile at Florence is one of the few great works of architecture in the North of Italy begun and finished in the fourteenth century, and Giotto was almost the last of the long line of complete artists who comprehended architecture, sculpture, and painting in the full circle of their acquirements. Before the end of that century Gothic architecture was lost to Italy, not more through the inability of her artists than through the change in the spirit and the decline in the temper of her people, of which this inability was one of the marked consequences and indications.

Of all the work that had been accomplished on the Duomo during the lifetime of Maitani, the most important in the history of Art, and the most intrinsically precious, were the sculptures which still hold their place upon the four piers at the sides of the doors of entrance. Neither the exact date at which they were carved, nor the names of the artists who executed them, are known with certainty. Vasari, in his life of Niccola Pisano, attributes them to this master; but Niccola died before the Cathedral of Orvieto was begun, and these works show a consummate power and skill, such as even this great artist rarely exhibited. It is a circumstance that marks the temper of the men who created these and most other of the best works of Art down to this period, that they left no record of their names upon the marble which they carved or the walls which they painted. In his life of Arnolfo di Lapo, Vasari complains of many works, that he was not able to find out in what century they were executed, so that, as he says, "I cannot but wonder at the stupidity and the little desire for glory of the men of those times." This wonder was natural at a period when artists cared more for distinction than for excellence. It was, however, neither stupidity nor carelessness of fame that had led the earlier masters to the neglect of the preservation of their names; but their chief desire was to produce works that should deserve to last in the service of religion, and not as memorials of themselves. All Art was sanctified by its religious character. As the priest at the altar forgot himself in the presence and service of the Almighty, so they who painted the sacred picture or carved the altar-steps thought little of human praise and acceptance in the performance of their works. They shared in the exalted religious feeling of the period. Glory to God, fear of His judgments, joy in the works of His hand, filled their hearts and warmed their imaginations. In the heated air of devout enthusiasm, personal ambitions and vain exultations were scorched and withered up. But as the spiritual conditions that produced such results passed away, as the religious motives of Art grew weak, the desire of fame took the place of purer desires, and artists inscribed their names even upon works professedly sacred, for the direction of admirers and the information of posterity.

These Orvietan sculptures, although not the work of Niccola Pisano, proceeded from the school which he founded, and which was carried forward by his son, Giovanni. Their style connects them with other works known to be from the hand of Giovanni or his immediate disciples; and though no direct evidence remains of his being at Orvieto, yet, as he labored long both at Perugia and at Siena, there is every likelihood that he, as the most famous sculptor of the times, would have been called on to take charge of the most important work in marble of the century. It may well be that other sculptors had part in it, and some apparent differences in style are to be traced under a general similarity in the execution. But

> " Qual di pennel fu maestro e di stile,
>   Chi ritraesse l' ombre e i tratti ch' ivi
>   Mirar farieno un ingegno sottile,"

will, perhaps, never be certainly known.

In poetical conception, in imaginative mingling of symbolism and realism, in the combination of mystic fulness of allegory and suggestion with a simple, straightforward, and natural development of the leading ideas, in play of fancy, in truth and tenderness of feeling, and in the exhibition of a sincere and ardent faith, these sculptures take rank among the noblest works of mediæval genius.

Nor is it only in their intrinsic qualities that they deserve admiration.   The imagination and feeling manifest
in the works of the early masters are often superior to
their powers of execution.   They succeed in expressing
themselves only in part and imperfectly, owing to the
want of technical skill, and the failure of the hand to
give due form to the conceptions of the brain.   The unsuccessful result of efforts to break loose from inherited
and conventional methods of representation, the baffled
attempts to express the new thoughts and feelings which
were stirring in the minds and hearts of men, often give
a curious pathos to the works of the first centuries of the
Revival.   Giotto himself rarely drew with entire correct-
ness, so far as mere physical rendering was concerned.
The progress of the hand was far slower than that of the
spirit.   Knowledge is of later birth than feeling.   But
in these bas-reliefs, which Vasari qualifies as " respec-
table works for the time," there is less imperfection of
rendering, less deficiency in knowledge of anatomy, of the
figure in motion, and of perspective, than in most other
contemporary works.   They show not only study of the
ancient models, from which the Pisans had learned much
in their own city, but also careful study from life, of the
human figure, and of draperies.   They show, indeed, that
there was still much to learn, but, in spite of many defects, the forms have animation, and the faces have natural
expression.   Modern sculpture can show nothing which,
in variety of imagination and liveliness of rendering, ex-
cels these works executed five centuries and a half ago.

On the four piers, each of which is about twenty-five

feet high by sixteen feet in width, the spiritual history of the human race, according to the Scriptural view, is sculptured in direct or typical representations. The first is occupied with bas-reliefs which set forth the Creation and the Fall of Man, and the two great consequences of the fall, Sin and Labor. On the next pier are sculptured with great fulness and variety, and not always with plain meaning, some of the prophetic visions and historic events in which the Future Redemption of the world was seen or prefigured by the eye of faith, or which awakened longings for the coming of the Messiah. On the third is represented the Advent, the Life and Death of the Saviour, at once the reconciling of God and man and the fulfilment of prophecy. And on the fourth is the completion of the things of the spirit, in the Resurrection, the Last Judgment, Heaven and Hell.*

Thus were the great facts of his religious creed set before the eyes of him who approached the church, about to pass over its threshold from the outer world. Every eye could read the story on the wall; and though few might comprehend the full extent of its meaning, and few enter into sympathy with the imagination of the artist, yet the inspiration of faith had given such power to the work, that no one could behold it without receiving some measure of its spirit, and being influenced by its devout and serious teachings.

---

* Engravings of the sculptures on these piers are to be found in *Die Basreliefs an der Vorderseite des Doms zu Orvieto.* . . . *Mit erläuterndem Texte von* EMIL BRAUN. *Herausgegeben von* LUDWIG GRUNER. Leipzig 1858. A volume of great beauty and interest.

The series of bas-reliefs on the first pier begins at the lower corner on the left hand, with a representation of the work of the fifth day of Creation. The three persons of the Trinity take part in the act; but the Father is represented only by a hand in the act of blessing, from which rays proceed, appearing in the heavens amid the sun, moon, and stars. The Holy Spirit hovers as a dove above the head of the Saviour, who, as the chief agent of the creation,* stands with his right hand outstretched toward a stream of water filled with fishes, and toward a flock of birds gathered on the farther bank of the stream. The figure of the Saviour is that of a young man, his bearded face has a Grecian type of beauty, and the drapery of his garment exhibits in its breadth and dignity the influence of classical models. The fowl that may fly above the earth are so treated as to show the artist's careful fidelity to Nature. There are at least sixteen birds in the group, massed together, but in most instances distinguished by some special characteristic. In front stands the eagle, with flat head, curved beak, and sharp talon, as if in his very form foretelling the starvation that would await him in Paradise, according to the common notion of that place, were man not soon to fall. On a shrub near by sits a little bird, seemingly a dove, which,

---

* The wide-spread idea, that the creation was effected through the agency of the Son, was derived from a false interpretation of the words, " All things were made by him," John i. 3, that is, by the Logos or Word of God. See Didron's *Christian Iconography*, translated by Millington, I. 170–196. Thus, in the Nicene Creed, repeated daily in the Mass, occur the words, " *Iesum Christum, filium Dei unigenitum, ... per quem omnia facta sunt.*"

with wings upraised and neck stretched forward, appears to exult in its new-created life. It is a figure small, but full of delight, carved by a lover of Nature. Behind the Saviour are two wide-winged and beautiful angels, one looking upward, the other watching the process of creation.

The next bas-relief is occupied by the representation of the sixth day's work. The third shows the Creation of Man. The significance of the words, " The Lord God formed man of the dust of the ground," is conveyed by the figure of a man stretched in lifeless listlessness upon the earth. This figure is one of the marvels of sculpture. It lies neither dead nor sleeping, but simply without animation. Life has not heaved the chest nor moved the countenance. Above the form stands the Creating Saviour, bending a little forward, as if in contemplative interest, his right hand stretched out with extended forefinger, as if guiding the obedient dust, and shaping it to perfect man. The attendant angels are not now side by side, but opposite each other. The one that floats at the head of the man is unsurpassed in lightness and composure of poise and motion, in sweetness of aspect and of attitude. The band of angels in these sculptures and in those of the third pier take their place in the memory with Fra Angelico's portraits of the heavenly host. The serenity, the sweetness, and the intensity of their expressions, the piety and various emotion manifest in their gestures and attitudes, the sweeping curves of their balanced white wings, the self-support of their floating forms, the simple lines of the drapery that clothes them, their diversity and their similarity, all give to them a place in sculpture exclusively their own.

Take them, for instance, in the next sculptured picture of the series, where they hover side by side, watching the final work of Creation, beholding the Lord with his left hand resting upon the head of man, and with his right hand, in the act of blessing, brought close to the face that he had formed out of the dust, breathing into its nostrils the breath of life. The one with hands folded across the bosom seems wrapt in wondering and reverent contemplation, — while the other, with one hand pointing to earth and one to heaven, seems as if marking the union of earth and heaven in the body and the spirit of man. Man erect, but not yet alive, life seems to be quivering through his limbs in the first throb of consciousness, — the eyes are unclosing, the hand starting into motion, the legs becoming firm for support. A moment more, and man will be a living soul.

To the imagination that conceived of the presence of these spiritual witnesses at the miracle of Creation, the reality of the angels of the Lord was a fact as literal as the reality of men. With inward vision the artist beheld the heavenly messengers, and he carved each successive figure as he beheld it passing in the beauty of holiness before his purified eyes.

> " A lui venia la creatura bella
> Bianco vestita, e nella faccia quale
> Par tremolando mattutina stella."

The series of sculptures on the first pier, advancing

from the Creation of Man to the Creation of Woman, then to the scenes in the Garden, and to the Fall, the Expulsion from Paradise, and the Murder of Abel, ends with two tablets which seem intended for typical representations of the fulfilment of the doom of labor which had been pronounced against man. The labors in which he engaged ended in weariness of soul and vexation of spirit. Parted from God, he found the earth full of thorns and thistles. The present was sorrowful, the future dark, and only in his visions, in prophetic foregleams of joy, did he behold the promise of a brighter day.

This spiritual forecasting of a reunion between the Almighty and the children of men occupies the second pier in a long series of involved sculptures. The separate compositions exhibit different passages of the obscure prophetic and poetic history of the children of Israel, — displaying the pride, the desolation, the sorrows, and the hopes of the race.

Along the middle of the pier, in an ascending line of ovals, formed by an intricate and fanciful arabesque which divides the carved scenes one from another, are seen six of the kings of the house of David, beginning with David himself, holding his harp. In the seventh oval appears Mary, the mother of Jesus; and in the eighth and last, crowning and fulfilling all, sits the Messiah himself, his right hand raised to bless, his left holding the Book of the New Covenant.

Two lines of prophets cross the pier horizontally at its base. One among them is distinguished from his companions by a garland of leaves upon his head. Possibly

under this figure thus distinguished, the artist intended to
represent Virgil, who, throughout the Middle Ages, bore
a semi-prophetic character, and was supposed to have
foretold the coming of Christ. A female figure upon
the opposite side suggests also an intention on the part
of the sculptor to represent one of the Sibyls, who,
in popular credence, no less than the prophets, — " *Teste
David cum Sibylla,*" — had foretold the birth of the
Redeemer.

Among the scenes represented on either side of the
line of kings, are the Anointing of David, the Vision of
Ezekiel, the Birth of Immanuel, (Isaiah vii. 14,) the
Mourning of Jerusalem, and the Weighing of Souls or of
the actions of men (1 Samuel ii. 3). The final scene is
that of the Crucifixion, not displayed as a literal event,
but as foreshadowed in dim words and obscure hints in
the ancient prophecies. In the death of Him who taketh
away the sins of the world the cycle of prophecy was
closed. But above the Crucifixion sits the Virgin, and
above her appears her Son in glory. On one side an
angel, flying toward Mary, seems to speak the sweet
words of the Annunciation, while on the other a prophet,
looking up to the Saviour, displays his open roll of
prophecy, the meaning of which is now clear, and the
service of which is ended.

On either side of the main compositions on this pier,
almost from bottom to top, is a line of prophets and aged
men engaged in instructing the successive generations of
mankind, who are represented in half-figures. In these
groups it was, perhaps, the intention of the sculptor to

exhibit those men, and the followers of them, who " all
died in faith, not having received the promises, but having seen them afar off, and were persuaded of them, and
embraced them, and confessed that they were strangers
and pilgrims on the earth."

Thus this pillar of prophecy leads on to the pillar of
fulfilment, which stands on the opposite side of the central door.   Again, a tree of arabesque rises up through
it, forming in graceful curves a series of seven central
ovals inclosing figures of prophets, and on either side a
corresponding series of eight circles, in which scenes from
the life of the Saviour are sculptured, and finishing at
the edges of the pier with smaller circles, which inclose
half-figures of angels.   The arrangement separates scene
from scene, but leads the eye easily from one to another.
The passages of the gospel narrative which are illustrated form a series such as was often developed by the
mediæval artists, with such variations as special circumstances or individual feeling might induce.   First is the
Annunciation, — " the angel who came to announce the
peace wept for for many years " kneeling before Mary,
who stands with half-troubled look hearing the words of
his message.   The angel in half-figure in the outer circle,
with hands crossed upon the breast, listens with apparent
tranquillity of joy to the words from the lips of Gabriel.
The Annunciation is followed by the Salutation, — in
which the figures are of extraordinary excellence, especially that of an old woman who seems to be the attendant of Mary, and whose air and expression are copied
from nature, from a model such as the streets of Orvieto

might easily afford. The next scene represents the Birth of Christ. Mary is lying upon a couch; her figure and the drapery have a freedom and beauty which recall Grecian sculptures; while the fact that the Saviour is represented as lying in a sarcophagus, which serves as a cradle, shows the direct influence of the remains of ancient Art. But though this sculpture exhibits the readiness of the Pisan artist to take lessons from the work of former masters, it gives evidence of the entrance of new ideas within the range of Art, and of the existence of conceptions unknown to the ancient schools. In the attitude of the Virgin, as she raises herself, leaning on her right arm, to lift the veil that hung over the cradle of her divine Son, and to look with earnest gaze into his face, there is a tenderness of expression and a simple rendering of natural maternal feeling which betoken some of the peculiar characteristics of Christian as distinguished from classic Art. The attendant angel, with face upturned and hands clasped and raised toward heaven as in prayer, seems to partake in the mingled emotions of the scene.

Passing over the intermediate bas-reliefs, we come, near the close of the history, to a *naïve* and forcible composition representing the Betrayal in the Garden. Judas, with his hand resting upon the arm of Jesus, draws the Saviour toward him to receive the treacherous kiss. The multitude, with swords and staves, appear behind. One of the attendants raises his hand to strike the unresisting Jesus. In the corner, Peter has thrown down the servant of the high-priest with his face toward the ground, and, with an amusing appearance of deliberate malice, is engaged in cutting off his ear.

The Scourging follows the Betrayal. The angel of this sculpture no longer appears watching the scene before him, but, with head bowed, and hands crossed, and fingers clenched, expresses in his attitude a shrinking horror at the sight. After the Scourging comes the Crucifixion. It is represented in a manner at once conventional and painful, but again the angel exhibits the imagination of the artist, in the force and pathos of his passionate attitude, in his hands pressed closely upon his eyes. But in the representation that follows, of the Three Marys at the Sepulchre, where the three women are seen listening with imperfect comprehension to the angel, who, sitting upon the tomb, and pointing upwards, says to them, "He is not here, for he is risen," the angel at the side, with full understanding of the marvellous words, and of the joy of the resurrection, lifts face and hands to heaven in exulting thanksgiving. In the last scene, Mary Magdalene is casting herself at the feet of him whom she had supposed to be the gardener. The dramatic conception is striking, but the execution is feeble and defective.

It was thus that the artist told the life of the Lord. The pictures and sculptures of the Church were the Bibles of the poor; they served to give shape to vague ideas, to confirm faith by giving reality to its objects, to quicken devotion by awakening slumbering affections and imaginations. The artist became a preacher of the Word. He might behold in his own day the influance of his works. He saw them studied, not by the cold and critical eye of connoisseurship, but by the tender heart of faith ; their meaning was spelt out by rustics and told to the little children. He saw them serve, not as the mere ornament of, but as a spiritual introduction to the House of God. Inspired by faith in the truths of his religion, by a sense of the power of his art, by a recognition of his opportunities as a teacher, — what wonder, if his heart burned within him, and his hand found means to answer to the desire of his heart to make his work worthy, in spirit and in execution, of the place it was to hold, of the affections it was to promote ?

But the chief strength of the maker of these sculptures, and the highest exercise of his imagination, were reserved for the bas-reliefs of the fourth and last pier. It was here that he showed the consummation in eternity of the lives of men upon earth, exhibiting the judgment and the life to come in typical representations, which were regarded by the common people as depicting absolute realities. The very forms and manner of the resurrection and the future world being conceived of with material distinctness, and with what was supposed to be even more than a mere general exactness, the work of the artist was not so much to embody his individual imaginations in independent and original designs, as to give to the common and accepted types such elevation, such power and beauty, as lay within the compass of his genius to conceive and to exhibit. The same subjects appeared on cathedral walls all over Europe, under the same general forms, though with every variety of accessory and difference of detail. But among all the representations of them, there are few that equal those of this pier in vividness of conception, in poetic spirit, in skill of composition.

From the middle of the foot of the pier springs a grape-vine, which, rich in tendrils, clustering leaves, and abundant bunches of fruit, — rich, too, in the suggestions of ancient symbolism, — divides the sculptured surface with its main trunk and branches into ten compartments. At the lower left-hand side is the Resurrection. Men and women are seen rising hastily from their graves, with energetic action pushing off the heavy covers of the sarcophagi in which they had lain, and with various aspects hearing the long-awaited and awful summons. The composition is full of life. The actions and the forms of the souls rising for judgment display a power of invention, a knowledge of anatomy, and a variety of expression, surpassing those shown in any of the previous works of the *façade*, and, so far as I am aware, unequalled by any other work of Italian sculpture of the period. Michel Angelo himself did not design more vigorous muscular action or more eager effort than are here shown. The figures of the dead coming from their graves in his Last Judgment exhibit no more nature, though much more that is painful and revolting, than those in this work of the earlier and simpler master. The joy of those whose names are written in the Book of Life appears on the uplifted faces of some, who, with clasped hands, look toward heaven, where Christ is seated. The horror of condemnation is already on the faces of others. A monk, who is trying to climb up by the grape-vine, the vine of the Lord, to seize the fruit to which he is not entitled, has upon his face a look of disappointment and alarm at once pathetic and amusing, from the simplicity with which it is rendered, and the satire which it implies. Immediately above this scene of the Resurrection is a group of the redeemed, who, with faces full of peace, are led heavenward by angels, whose attitudes overrun with tenderness. One has his hand upon the shoulder of a youth, pressing him forward; another clasps the figure of a worthy priest; another, with his hand supporting the head of a young man, points upward, as if directing his eyes to the Source of life. In its suggestions of beauty and love, in the sweetness of its pervading sentiment, this bas-relief is one of the finest of the *façade*. It is the work of a man who entered through sympathy into the delight of the blessed, and the happiness of the ministering angels whom he ventured to depict.

Corresponding with this, on the other side is a composition of equal power, but power of another kind, in which the damned souls are seen drawn down to the mouth of hell. An angel, driving them in, stands under the vine; while horrible demons receive them at the other side, one of whom is dragging them in by cords fastened around their necks. A serpent is winding along the ground near the angel's foot. The attitudes and expressions of despair are rendered with marvellous force, and with little offensive exaggeration. One figure stands in the memory as the very statue of Dismay; bent over, with hands resting against his knees, a lock of his long

10

curling hair is seized by a grisly demon, who lashes his broad bowed back with a writhing snake.   Beneath, opposite the sculpture of the Resurrection, is Hell itself, — a horrid confusion of fierce, bat-winged, long-clawed devils, of biting and venomous serpents, of flames, of tormented souls.

It is by no means unlikely that the descriptions of Dante may have been in the mind of the Orvietan artist, so great is the similarity in some points of his work to passages of the *Inferno*.   The coincidences between the work of the poet and that of the sculptor are interesting, if not as proofs of the direct and early influence of the *Divina Commedia*, yet as illustrations of the similarity of contemporary conceptions, derived more or less remotely from the popular beliefs.   Thus, Dante gives to Lucifer wings, not of birds, but of bats, (*Inferno*, xxxiv. 49,) and his description of the serpents of the seventh *bolgia* serves for a description of those of this sculptured Hell.   "And I saw there a terrible throng of serpents, and of such fearful look that the remembrance still freezes my blood. . . . . In this cruel and most dismal swarm were running people naked and terrified, without hope of escape or concealment."   (*Inferno*, xxiv. 82–93.)   Other resemblances are apparent in the figure of Lucifer, and in the tortures of the wicked.   Throughout this sculpture there is a masterly power of execution, which perhaps raises it in technical merit above any of the other bas-reliefs.   The composition is crowded, but not confused ; the actions of the separate figures are of astonishing variety and intensity of expression.   There is one figure in which the depth of misery from physical and moral torture is rendered with a power unequalled in sculpture. One of the dragons that coil round Lucifer has seized the arm of this wretched man in his teeth, and is dragging it from its socket. The head of the sinner falls forward fainting, his whole body droops, his knees bend, his other arm hangs stiffly down, and yet in this act of swooning there is no suggestion that the sensibility to torment becomes less, or that the swoon reaches farther than the muscles. As a mere study of human action, this figure is wonderful, for the time at which it was produced; as a piece of imaginative realism, it is still more remarkable.

It may seem that such representations as these are simply shocking in their display of barbarous horrors; but it is to be considered that they are triumphs of Art in respect to the end to which they were directed, — that end being to affect the imaginations of those who depended on the means of salvation held out to them by the Church, by awakening in them a positive alarm in regard to their future condition. To render the torments of hell real to the fancies of men has been one of the most constant efforts of the Roman Church, as well as of other churches and other sects of diverse origin and name. The sermons of Jonathan Edwards are not less horrible in their revolting pictures of the material sufferings of the damned, and show no more spiritual conceptions of the future life, than the common Romanist representations of hell. Both belong to a perverted system of heathenism raised upon a professedly Christian founda tion.

The next two sculptures, forming a band across the pier, divided only by the stem of the ascending vine, are filled with the figures of the blessed, attended by their guardian angels. Above, forming the next band, appear on one side confessors, bishops, priests, and other servants of God, and on the other the virgins who sealed with their blood the bond which bound them to the Lord. The central figure of the first group is that of a Pope, which may be intended for a likeness of Nicholas IV., who laid the corner-stone of the Cathedral; he stands between St. Francis and St. Dominick. In the background is seen the figure of a master-builder, with an architect's square upon his shoulder and a workman's cap on his head. It is pleasant to believe that in this figure we see Lorenzo Maitani, the great architect of the Duomo.

Still again, above the churchmen and the virgins, sit, in opposite ranks, the prophets and the apostles, on either side of the Lord, who appears seated within an aureole held up by the angels around the throne. Just without the aureole stands Mary, and opposite to her John the Baptist. Higher up are the instruments of the passion, and from the clouds on each side two angels are seen to issue, blowing the trumpets of judgment. The figure of the Saviour, different in this respect from later and more famous representations, has nothing terrible or vindictive in look or action. His face is calm and mild; his hands are so held as to display the wounds upon them, and the aureole within which he sits is formed out of the bars of the cross.

Thus were heaven and hell displayed, with their separate companies of spirits, — and thus was the final composition completed, opening to sight that future world, to prepare for which was the great duty of life. The expectation of the speedy second coming of the Saviour was still a common one, and these representations appealed with peculiar force to men who fancied, that, even in their generation, they might see " the angel fly in the midst of heaven, having the everlasting gospel to preach unto them that dwell on the earth, saying with a loud voice, Fear God, and give glory to Him, for the hour of His judgment is come, and worship Him that made heaven and earth." *

Although the faith of men has in the progress of years grown less ardent, and the conceptions on which that faith is based have in great part changed, and though these sculptures consequently have lost something of their original power in the service of religion, yet in looking at them now, worn by the beatings of storms, yellowed by sun and rain, here and there scratched and broken by carelessness or wantonness, but even thus giving evidence of long existence, — in so seeing them, one cannot but feel that the centuries, while taking from them one source of effect upon the imagination, have given them another in its place.

For more than five hundred years no day has passed that many eyes have not rested upon them, and from their sight gained some impression of the significance of the scenes which they represent, some refreshment of

* Revelation xiv. 6, 7.

moral energies, some quickening of religious emotions, some awakening of spiritual hopes and aspirations. Pilgrims on their way to Rome and the shrines of the Apostles have rested under the shelter of the sunny Cathedral front, and have here renewed their vows in presence of the figure of their Lord. Artists have come to study from these marbles,* and have sought in vain from them the secret of their inspiration. Popes have bowed before them. Boys have flung willing stones against the sculptured and unmindful devil. The common worshippers, in all the different moods of life in which they have sought the church, have seen a story wrought here as if in counterpart to their own inmost experiences, as if in answer to their longings for sight of the invisible. Generation after generation has passed along between the sculptured piers through the wide doors, first for baptism into the Church, then for its successive holy sacraments, till at length the priest in sacred vestments has at the appointed time gone out from between the same sculptures to carry to the dying sons of men the last gifts which the Church can bestow upon her children. Here

* Vasari relates, in his Life of Brunelleschi, that one morning, soon after his return from Rome, in the year 1407, that great architect fell into talk with the sculptor Donatello, and other artists, in the square of Santa Maria del Fiore, about the ancient works of sculpture, and that Donatello said, "that, when he returned from Rome, he went by the way of Orvieto, in order to see the celebrated marble *façade* of the Duomo, sculptured by the hands of divers masters, and esteemed a notable thing in those days." In 1428, Donatello, then the chief sculptor of his time, was employed to make a figure in bronze gilt of St. John the Baptist, to place upon the font in the Cathedral.

were birth and baptism, sin and sorrow, repentance and consolation, joy and grief, death and resurrection, all displayed, prefiguring the events that each successive generation should know as its own. And thus, year after year, as the mellowing marble has gained a deeper tint of age, has it also gained a fuller tone of meaning, a richer depth of association.

While these works were accomplishing, labor upon other portions of the Cathedral was not interrupted; and after the sculptures were finished, their excellence acted as an incitement to make the remaining works of decoration worthy of being associated with them. Skilful workmen and fine materials were sought, as before, from all the neighboring districts. The records of the works continue full of information in regard to the processes, the materials, the cost of the different branches of Art. Great pains were taken by the superintendents of the building that nothing should be done in a slovenly or imperfect manner. At one time they sought for "a good and honorable picture for the great altar; and as none could be found, it was determined to have one painted as beautiful as possible." At another, they sought for "a good head master, expert, and of good life, diligent and steady, who should carry on the works in the best manner." Toward the end of the century, it was determined to obtain an organ that should be suited to the grandeur of the Cathedral; and to this end a decree was passed that "an organ greater than any other in the world should be made," — *fiat organum majus de toto mundo.* In 1354 there is a record of marble brought from Rome, from the ruins of the temple of Jupiter, — showing that the Roman quarries were still worked to advantage by these new builders. Already a reliquary of the most elaborate workmanship had been made to contain the sacred *corporale*. It is of pure silver, ornamented with rich and brilliant enamels, and weighing no less than four hundred pounds. But the beauty of its execution surpasses the costliness of its material. Representing on one side the *façade* of the Cathedral, its architectural structure is adorned with statues of saints and angels, and with enamelled pictures of sacred subjects, and illustrations of the history of the precious relic within it. Fortunate is the position of Orvieto, which has saved such a treasure from being seized and melted down !

Amid all the vicissitudes of sad seasons, amid all the excitements and troubles of Italy, the building was carried forward with more or less steadiness, but with little diminution of the interest of the citizens in its progress. The Popes continued to favor it, and its own beauty stimulated contributions for its increase. One generation had seen the Duomo begun; another had watched its rapid advance, and taken delight in the splendor of its construction; a third had continued to lavish labor and treasure in its adornment; and at the beginning of the fifteenth century, a fourth was taking part in a work which was no less the object of its pride than of its devotion.* The ablest artists were still sent for; and through

* Among the entries in the records near the beginning of this century is one which contains an exhibition of simple and natural feel-

the course of this century the names of many of the most famous of their time are enrolled on the Orvietan lists.

The most interesting and important works in the Cathedral during this period were the paintings executed by Fra Angelico and Luca Signorelli in the chapel of the Virgin. It was in the spring of 1447 that the first of these great artists, being in Rome, and desirous, perhaps, to escape from the unhealthy air of the city during the summer, sent to the Board of Works an offer of his services for three months. The offer was gladly accepted, and liberal terms were made, so that, on the 14th of June, Fra Angelico signed the contract at Orvieto, whither he had come, accompanied by his favorite pupil, Benozzo Gozzoli, and by two apprentices.* It was de-

ing. In the year 1411, one Agostino Catalini represents to the Board of Works that he has been from a child employed on the building, "et ibidem didicerit a pueritia sua," and now desires to give proof of his ability in sculpture, "ad sculpendum lapides cujuscumque generis"; whereupon he was engaged as sculptor for a year, at the rate of sixteen *lire* a month.

* There is an amusing quaintness in some of the terms of this contract. "In Dei nōe. Amen. Congregatis [Conservatoribus] .... et habitis inter eos et pictorem multis colloquiis super omnibus et singulis .... unanimiter .... Camerarius .... conduxit ad pingendam capellam novam .... religiosum virum frēm Johēm Petri Magrūm pictorem Ord. Predicatorum Observantie Scī Dominici ibid. presentam et acceptantem et picturas totius dicte capelle locavit d. Mag. fratri Johī cum pactis quod d. frater Johēs .... serviret ad picturas pred. cum persona sua. Item cum persona Benotii Cesi de Florentia. Item cum persona Johīs Antonii de Florentia. Item cum persona Jacobi de Poli bene et diligenter et cum ea que decet solertia et solecitudine.

termined that he should paint a Last Judgment; and in honor of his recognized merit, the title of *Maestro dei Maestri* was conferred upon him. The work was soon begun; and in the course of the summer the painter had finished the figure of the Saviour, and a noble band of prophets. He worked with zeal, and his figures were in truth "beautiful and praiseworthy," — for they possess those characteristics which give to the paintings of this devout master a place by themselves among the most precious productions of Art. The figure of Christ, with his right hand raised, in the act, as it were, of denouncing a revengeful judgment upon the world, is, indeed, one such as rarely proceeded from the mild pencil of Angel- ico. The force of expression in some degree makes up for the painful nature of the conception; and so similar is it in design to the figure of Christ in Michel Angelo's more famous picture, that the assertion has often been made that it is the original from which Michel Angelo drew. In September, Fra Angelico returned to Rome, and, from some unexplained cause, never again, during the seven remaining years of his life, visited Orvieto. At the time of his death, the work which he had be- gun there was still unfinished.

"Item quod faciet et curabit quod d. figure dd. picturar. erunt pulchre et laudabiles.

.   .   .   .

"Item quod omnia faciet . . . . sine fraude, dolo, ad commendatio- sem cujuslibet boni Mag. pictoris.

.   .   .   .

"Item pro eorum expensis ultra salaria panem et vinum quantum sufficiet eis."

Years passed, and no one was found worthy to complete the work, until, in 1498, Luca Signorelli, then "*famosissimus pictor in tota Italia*," was engaged to go on with the paintings in the chapel.* Signorelli at once began, and labored steadily for four years, till the whole chapel was finished, and till he had accomplished a work which secured his fame for all time, and which was a source from which both Michel Angelo and Raffaelle drew instruction and inspiration. The walls of the chapel are, in the greater part of their surface, covered with a series of subjects that, in connection with the previous work of Fra Angelico, form a continuous painted drama of the end of this world and the beginning of the world to come. First is seen the preaching of Antichrist, tempting the people with gold and jewels and the promise of power; many groups in various attitudes and expressions of conflicting passions show the confusion of the times. The followers of Christ are persecuted. Antichrist is beheld borne on high by demons, as if to give to his followers belief in his ascent to heaven; but the Archangel Michael descends with drawn sword against him, and casts him overpowered into hell. As witnesses of the fall of the deceiver of men, Luca has introduced the portraits of himself and his beatified predecessor. Then comes the Resurrection, a work displaying the most fer-

---

* The entries in the records concerning this agreement with Signorelli are long and interesting, and written in most amusingly bad Latin; for instance: "Spectabilis vir Jo. Lud. Benincasa surgens pedibus .... consulendo dixit qd. mittatur iterum pro d. Mag. Luca, et cum eo habeatur conventio .... et fiat eidem unum instrumentum prout est instrumentum Magri Petri Perusini."

tile imagination, and most thorough knowledge of anatomy and of expression. The awakening of the dead at the sound of the trumpets of judgment is rendered with such fulness of detail, such power of composition, such strength of feeling, as to surpass any other similar representation by later or earlier painters. The same praise belongs to the scenes of Hell and of Heaven, with which the grand representation closes. On the one hand are those who " drink of the wine of the wrath of God, which is poured out without mixture into the cup of his indignation, and who are tormented with fire." On the other are " they who kept the commandments of God and the faith of Jesus." In the contrast between these two scenes, — between the horrible demons, the tormented spirits, and the utter frightfulness of the one, with the blessed angels, the spirits in peace, and the complete beauty of the other, — Luca exhibited his highest power, and showed himself one of the most imaginative and noble artists that have ever lived. One group of the picture of Hell deserves special notice, from the tradition which is connected with it. It represents a powerful demon flying through the air, dragging a beautiful woman to the tortures of the pit. It is said that the figure of the woman was the portrait of one who had given herself *al bel tempo* while Luca was painting at Orvieto, and who, having through curiosity come to see the pictures in the chapel, recognized herself in the figure on the wall. Struck with confusion and dismay, she left the chapel contrite and repentant, and thenceforth led a pure and holy life. The angels, the archangels, and the seraphim of heaven have a beauty and grace which render them the worthy companions of Fra Angelico's heavenly groups, and of the angels of the Pisan sculptors. In vigor of form, in strength of action, in variety of character, they surpass those of the earlier masters, nor do they fall short in sweetness of expression and the beauty of holiness. Besides these main compositions, there is a series of minor subjects, on the lower part of the walls, taken from the classic mythology and history, chiefly relating to the ancient conceptions and stories of a future life; among them, the Descent of Æneas, the Rape of Proserpine, Orpheus and Eurydice, — and connected with these, a series of the heads of famous poets, Virgil, Claudian, Statius, Dante, and others. The task would be too long to describe in full the many minor scenes and passages which are here represented, and to attempt to convey any just idea of the wealth of arabesque and ornament with which the chapel is adorned. The work, taken as a whole, is one of the greatest masterpieces of Art, one of the chief works of painting to which Italy has given birth. While retaining much of the simple straightforwardness and the strong impress of faith which distinguished the productions of the early masters, it exhibits also the refined graces and the complicate power of the works of later times. Luca Signorelli closed the line which began with Giotto, and opened that which reached its height in Michel Angelo and Raffaelle. "He roused by this work," says Vasari, "the spirit of all those who came after him, and they have since found easy the difficulties of this manner.

Wherefore I do not wonder that the works of Luca were always praised in the highest degree by Michel Angelo, nor that many things in his divine Last Judgment were in a noble way taken by him from the inventions of Luca." *

With the account of these great works the history in detail of the Duomo may well be concluded. The sixteenth century was one of decline at Orvieto. Its chief nobility and its richest citizens were drawn away to Rome, or to the courts of neighboring princes; its revenues were diminished in the civil wars of Central Italy, and the works on its Cathedral languished. Still, however, from time to time, some new work of painting or

---

* Vasari's biography of this great painter is one of the best of his pleasant series of Lives. When a boy, he had seen him in his old age, and Luca had kindly encouraged him in his love of drawing. "Turning to me, who was standing straight up before him, he said, 'Learn, my dear little cousin.' And he said much else to me, which I will not repeat, for I know that I have come far short of confirming the opinion which that good old man had of me." The whole account gives a delightful impression of the sweetness and nobility of Luca's disposition and the excellence of his long life.

In 1845, two German artists undertook to restore the frescoes in the chapel at Orvieto. They removed some whitewash with which portions of Luca's work had been concealed, and they retouched and repainted other portions. Their work was so highly esteemed by the Orvietans that they were made honorary citizens of Orvieto. But in this, as in so many instances in Italy, one is forced to repeat the words of Vasari, — "In truth, it would be better sometimes to keep the things done by excellent men half spoiled, than to have them retouched by those who know less."

Among the records of the time when Luca was painting at Orvieto is one, in 1500, of a payment to him of ninety ducats, "de quibus dictus magister vocavit se bene solutum."

of sculpture was added to it, and the older adornments
of the building were repaired as they were menaced by
decay. But the chief interest of its history ended with
the departure of Signorelli. The later period of the
Renaissance and of the Reformation could bring to it no
new glory. The age of such faith as had directed its
foundation was gone by, the sources of such lavishness
of wealth as had brought to its construction all that was
most costly in material and most precious in workmanship were almost exhausted. It was henceforth to be
rather a monument of the past than a work of present
times. Yet the labor upon it has never ceased; and,
in the spring of 1856, workmen were engaged in restoring one of the mosaics of its *façade*.

ROME. NAPLES. VENICE.

Rome, 30th March, 1856.

" *Rara temporum felicitas, ubi sentire quæ velis et quæ sentias dicere licet,*" says Tacitus. It is a felicity rare at Rome. To feel and to speak, to think and to act, independently, are privileges denied to Romans. They are privileges too dangerous to the Church, to be allowed by the ecclesiastical masters of the State. The less feeling and the less thought there are at Rome, the better for its rulers. The system of the Church cannot coexist with freedom in any direction. The claim of infallibility does not recognize that of individual opinion. No theories of government and of religion can be more diametrically in opposition than those prevalent at Rome and in America. As an American, born into the most unlimited freedom consistent with the existence of society, — trusting to the results of the prevalence of general freedom, as affording a moral check upon the excesses of individuals, — believing in freedom in the fullest extent, as the divine rule for individual development, — regarding feeling, thought, and speech as having a natural privilege of liberty, — honoring the right of private judgment in all matters, — it is difficult, even at a distance, to regard the system of the Roman Church as being other than a skilful perversion of the eternal laws of right ; and it is impossible to regard it, after familiar acquaintance with its workings at its source, save with a continually deepening sense of its direct opposition to the most precious of human rights, to the most sacred of human hopes.

Society, which in a condition of freedom knits its bonds continually closer and stronger, becomes disintegrated under the influence of a government which undertakes the control, not only of public, but also of private affairs, and which claims to exercise its authority as well over the consciences and the thoughts of its subjects as over their actions.   Such a government can be carried on only by secret and corrupt means.   The confessional becomes an instrument of the State, the secret police an instrument of the Church.   Suspicion is universal.   " We never talk openly together, we cannot trust each other," is the common confession of Romans.   My Italian servant is afraid of my Italian friend, and my friend fears lest my servant should overhear his talk.   " I cannot venture to have friends, except those of science," says a Professor of the Collegio Romano.   The nephew of one of the exiles of 1849 brings me a letter for his uncle, to send under an inclosure of mine, for he does not think it pru dent to let it pass openly through the post-office. *Fidati era un buon uomo, Nontifidare era meglio*, says the Roman proverb.*

Divide et impera, is the standing method of Rome.

* Trust was a good man, Distrust was a better.

The government relies upon the mutual distrust of the citizens as a source of strength. But such strength is mere weakness in disguise. Every man is taught to distrust his neighbors, but all men learn to distrust their rulers. The government which undertakes to control everything, and which seeks to know everything of its subjects' affairs, is necessarily baffled, finding the work, however skilfully it may be planned, beyond its powers. The aphorism of Domitius Afer, " Princeps, qui vult omnia scire, necesse habet multa ignoscere," has a closer application to Papal than to Imperial rule. As persecutors breed heretics, so spies breed liars. In vain is the truth sought from those whom the instinct of self-preservation has taught to deceive.

In only one view can the Roman ecclesiastical system of government be called successful. It has succeeded in enlisting on its side the fears of its subjects.

ROME, 2d April, 1866.

It is in Rome, and on the Campagna around it, that the bitterness of the Italian poets becomes intelligible. *Ahi, serva Italia! di dolore ostello,"* seems the natural language of patriotic emotion. Grief for the desolation of the country and the degradation of the people is made sharper by the beauty of the land and the excellent qualities of the popular character, and vents itself in the exclamation, *"Deh, fossi tu men bella!"* Petrarch's denunciation of the modern Babylon, Alfieri's tremendous invective against Rome, are no mere outbursts of passion, but the literal statement of undisguised truth. From the earliest to the latest of the real poets, the same indignant sadness embitters their verse, and the strain begun by Dante is closed by Leopardi, with the line, —

" Piangi, chè ben hai donde, Italia mia!"

Rome, 8th April, 1856.

There are few stories of the old Romans in which much tenderness of feeling or sentiment of character is manifested.   Such qualities as these were not valued in classic times in proportion to the manlier virtues.   Their true relation to those virtues was not understood.   The philosophers excluded them, for the most part, from regard, and there was little in heathen modes of life to develop the growth of these refined and softer elements of character.

Among all Plutarch's stories, there is, perhaps, none more touching, as an exhibition of sentiment, than that which he tells of the love of Sertorius for Rome.   " In the height of his power in Spain, he sent word to Metellus and Pompey that he was ready to lay down his arms and live a private life, if he were allowed to return home ; declaring that he would rather live as the meanest citizen in Rome, than, exiled from it, be supreme commander of all other cities together."

Naples, 14th April, 1856.

" *Shakespeare, Ballo in Quattro Parti*," being advertised for performance this evening at the San Carlo, we went to see it. Policinello had been amusing us in the afternoon; but at the Royal Theatre Policinello was distanced. No intentional fun was ever more ludicrous than the unintentional comicality of this ballet. The *libretto* was for sale at the door, and in itself was abundantly amusing. The story had been transferred into Italian from the French, but it had gathered glory in its progress. Its full title was, " Shakespeare, or the Dream of a Summer's Night," — and the translators warn their readers that it is not a translation of one of Shakespeare's plays. The piece opens at the Mermaid Tavern, where a room is filled with sailors making merry. Suddenly a person enters, also in a sailor's dress, but understood to be Shakespeare in disguise. He joins the others in their drinking and laughing, " *improvvisando alcune storielle interessanti.*" But, indulging himself in some gallantries with the pretty bar-maid, he excites the jealousy of a character named Tom. This increases the good-humor of the poet. He proposes a toast in honor of Queen Elizabeth, which is accepted with enthusiasm by all except Tom, who refuses to drink it. Shakespeare hereupon grows angry, and invites him to what the translator calls " *una partita di boxes.*" Tom is thrashed by the adventurous dramatist in the best ballet style; and immediately afterward Shakespeare is reminded, by some words of the landlord which he happens to overhear, that a great supper is to be given in that very tavern, and on that very evening, " to the luminary of England, William Shakespeare," a fact which that luminary had unaccountably forgotten. He retires in haste to prepare himself for the banquet; and, as he goes out, Falstaff, the guardian of the Royal Park at "Richemont," enters, to see that all is in order for the feast, of which he has the charge. While he is repeating his orders, two masked ladies are driven by a tremendous storm to take shelter in the tavern. These ladies are the Queen and Miss Olivia, who had been at the theatre to witness the performance of "Macbeth," and who, in coming out from it, had been separated by the violence of the storm from their attendant cavaliers. The guests begin to arrive, and the ladies, desirous to avoid encountering them, are hidden by Falstaff in a side room. After various adventures, Shakespeare appears again upon the stage, half drunk; he discovers the ladies, declares that they shall not go away, alarms Miss Olivia by drawing his sword, and receives a severe rebuke from the Queen. She, however, feels profound compassion for that genius which is being miserably lost through want of the aid of a friendly and protecting hand. She speaks to him of his future of glory, warns him of the waste of his talents, and exhorts him to make better use of them. Shakespeare, probably of opinion that he could not much improve upon "Macbeth," replies, that, betrayed by love and by glory, he has now but one comfort, namely, the bottle, which he immediately produces and empties. The effect of this draught, in addition to the wine he had previously taken, is to cause him to drop suddenly asleep. Elizabeth takes the opportunity to escape, having decided, however, to save him from the abyss into which he stands ready to plunge.

This is the outline of the action in the first part of the ballet. Dances are introduced, which add to the effect of reality. Shakespeare is a beautiful youth, with long, thin legs, and glossy black hair. The remainder of the piece is, perhaps, equally amusing. The Queen arranges a vision in the park for Shakespeare's reformation, which is happily accomplished. The poet appears at court. "Elizabeth presents to him a rich casket; he opens it, and beholds a crown of laurel. 'Oh! I am not worthy of it,' exclaims the great poet, in confusion, bending one knee to the ground. 'Yes, you are,' replies the Queen. She encircles his forehead with the rich crown, and orders that the day shall be celebrated on which the Queen of England, in the name of the country, thanks Shakespeare for his works. Elizabeth takes Shakespeare by the hand, and introduces him, to the sound of music, into the great dancing-hall."

This is fame. "Shakespeare. Un Ballo in Quattro Parti. Napoli, 1855."

NAPLES, 15th April, 1856.

I bought, to-day, at a bookstall, a volume of some four hundred pages, with the following title: "Giesù Bambino, o sieno Ragionamenti per modo di Meditazioni sopra i Dolori ed Allegrezze, ch' ebbe il Cuore di Giesù Cristo nell' Utero della Madre; come altresì sopra le Virtù da Lui esercitate mentre stava ivi racchiuso: Composti dal Padre D. Antonio De Torres, Preposito Generale della Congregazione de' Pii Operarj." The contents of this book appear to be worthy of the title, — and a character-istic specimen of the coarse materialism that prevails in Neapolitan theology.

CIVITA CASTELLANA, 2d June, 1856.

From the appearance of the children in the streets of this ancient and dirty town, it may well be doubted, whether, if a second Camillus were to besiege it, any traitorous schoolmaster could now be found to deliver the boys into his hands. The education of the lower classes in the Roman States is professedly superintended by ecclesiastics. But, in a country where public spirit is stifled, as being equally troublesome to its possessor and to the State, — where the government is in the hands of a class whose interest it is to keep all other classes in sub-jection to themselves, little is effected for the enlighten-ment and the improvement of the poor. The Roman Church claims to have done much in past times for the interests of scholarship ; but her general tendency has always been against popular instruction. She has her catechisms for religious teaching ; she has her Sunday classes ; she gathers the children of the poor together to instruct them in their duties, especially in those of faith and obedience ; she gives them stories out of Scripture history ; and she codifies for them the laws of God into the simple direction, — " Do as I bid you, and you will go to heaven ; disobey me, and you will go to hell." Such has been, and such is, the instruction given by the Church. The mass of the people, say those in authority, are not fit for other teaching than this. What is called education is dangerous. The priest and the schoolmaster are rival powers. The alphabet is the first step toward the free exercise of thought. Republicans are always readers. And when a man once begins to read, no one can tell how far he will accept what his priest gives to him as truth. The Church is logical; she possesses the knowledge of truth; she has souls to save, therefore let her prevent these souls from gaining any knowledge but such as she may teach them.

Three or four miles from Civita Castellana are the ruined walls of the city of Falerii Novi, — walls over which antiquaries have contended with as much fierceness as ever was displayed by the old besiegers and besieged who fought around them. They are all that now remain of an Etruscan city. The ride to them is by a rough path over broad upland fields, broken here and there with deep and beautiful ravines, whose sides, lined with vines, elders, and young oaks, are hollowed with tombs long since despoiled. Nightingales were singing in the trees that overhung a brook which ran through one of these ravines, and a cuckoo was calling from one of the great park-like oaks that stood in a wide field of grain. In the midst of a plain rise the dark red walls of the old city, built of squared blocks of tufo, so solid, and so well set, that, in great part, they seem as firm to-day as when first laid. The line of the northern and eastern sides is but little broken; the upper courses of stone have, however, mostly fallen or been thrown down, so that the height of the wall is irregular, sometimes rising to more than thirty feet, sometimes to scarcely more than ten or twelve. At regular intervals, hardly more than a lance-throw apart, stand low, solid, square towers, flanking the wall along its whole length, and affording a vivid illustration of the old mode of attack and defence. Here and there the whole structure has been overthrown, and the stones lie in a heap covered with clematis, poppies, and ivy. The ivy climbs, too, in masses of dark glossy green, over the red blocks of the standing wall; grass grows close up to its base; and above it rise oaks that have planted themselves on the banks within. There is no house in sight, no sign of habitation, — only this great wall standing solitary in the wooded fields, with Soracte for its magnificent and unchanging background.

Many of the old gates are now blocked up. A path through a gap in the wall leads to what was once the interior of the city, — a field waving with grain, and a meadow in which men were raking hay. The only building within the circuit is the ruin of an ancient Lombardic church, that was itself built out of the still earlier ruins. Its roof is gone, — the mullions of its round-headed windows all gone, — the marble mouldings of its portals broken and defaced. Within it a fig-tree is growing down from one of its chancel-windows, and a screen of ivy half hides the poor remains of a faded fresco. A portion of the roof of the apse still remains, and underneath this shelter girls and women were storing the hay which they brought in upon their heads from the adjoining meadows. The roofless aisles have been used for the stabling of cattle, and the fluted columns, once those of some heathen temple, serve for the barnyard posts. On a block of white marble, at one side of the great door, are the words, " *Laurentius cum Jacopo filio suo fecit hoc opus.*" As they built on the ruins of the old city, did the thought ever come to them, that their fine work, too, would fall to ruin, — that the priests and congregation would desert it, — and that the twitter of swallows, the cluck of hens, and the lowing of cows would take the place within its walls of the responses of the clerks and the chants of the choristers? A worse enemy than Goth or Vandal has driven away the people from their church, — an enemy who is now knocking at the very gates of Rome, and seems, year by year, to gain new force, — the Malaria.

Two of the smiling, good-humored girls who were bringing in hay came up to me to beg. They were not beggars by profession; but the poor people regard all foreigners as lotteries, in which it is worth while to take a ticket, on the chance of its turning up a prize, — especially as the ticket is to be had only for the asking, or rather, consists only in that. While they were begging, a man offered me some late Roman copper coins, which he said he had found in the fields. As usual, one of them was of Maxentius, who seems, by the number of his ugly coins that are turned up, to have inundated the land with his brass. One of the girls said she had an old silver coin at home, but her home was two miles off, and it was too late in the afternoon to wait for her to go and fetch it.

Just outside the southern wall runs a little torrent, by whose side is a rocky bank, in which are many tombs, Etruscan and Roman. The shepherds use them now for shelter, and the entrances of many of them are half closed with the thick growth of grass and shrubs. They possess little distinguishing interest ; — they are only the tombs of the unknown people who lived in the city close by. There are some Etruscan inscriptions between here and Civita Castellana, but no one has made out their meaning. It is a strange thing to know so much as we do of the external life of the Etruscans, and so little of their inner life, and of the events in their history. From their tombs, their bronzes, their vases, and their jewelry, we may read something of their character, learn something of their art and of their religion ; but, after all, it is very little, and the past shuts down around them like a mist over a distant mountain.

PERUGIA, 5th June, 1856.

Not long since, an evening school, similar to those in Rome, was established here by some private persons interested to do what could be best done for the poor of Perugia. It was kept for boys who were employed at work during the day. The authorities found it inconvenient, and suppressed it.

In 1849, the old fortifications that command the city, built by Pope Paul III., expressly " *ad coercendam Perusinorum audaciam,*" were dismantled by the people during the short time in which they held their own. The present government is now restoring them.

To-day being market-day, a great number of peasants were in the town. In the centre of the crowd in the square was a boy with a lottery-wheel, selling numbers from it, corresponding to the numbers in a book of fortunes. He was doing a good business.

BOLOGNA, 14th June, 1856.

The character of the criticisms passed by travellers upon works of Art is generally worthless; but the extracts given in "Murray," in regard to the pictures in the Academy here, from Mr. John Bell's book on Italy, — a work not without reputation, — are more curiously and elaborately bad, as specimens of criticism, than are common. That they should be given in the only good handbook for Italy, in English, to help travellers in forming a judgment in regard to the merits of the famous works in this collection, is a striking proof how little accuracy and good sense are in general required in such criticism, how readily people yield to pretension, and how easily they are deceived by sounding words and unmeaning phrases.

The first extract from Mr. Bell is upon a picture of the Madonna and Child by Ludovico Caracci. He says that "it is an inimitable painting, in which the artist has displayed the richest stores of genius." And he amplifies this statement as follows: " St. Francis kissing the child's hand is painted in a dark tone, not to interfere with the principal figures, and is yet finely made out, as are the angels and the other accompaniments of the picture; the coloring soft and sweetly tinted, the whole being, with wonderful art and keeping, entirely subordinate to the great object of the composition." This seems a little vague. St. Francis painted in a *dark* tone! Is it a *low* tone or *dark* colors that is meant? And *yet* his figure finely made out! Pray, why should not a figure that stands prominent in a picture be finely made out? "The coloring soft and sweetly tinted, the whole being, with wonderful art and keeping, entirely subordinate to the great object of the composition." What does this mean, — this " whole " being subordinate to the object of the composition ?

But this is not equal to what follows. In his remarks upon one of Tiarini's pictures, Mr. Bell says, — " The figures are considerably smaller than life, which might be supposed to hurt the general effect; but the composition is so perfect as to leave no feeling in the mind but that of admiration." Now it happens that the figures in this picture are *not* smaller than life; but, if they were so, what an amusing and ignorant absurdity it is to suggest that figures below life-size might hurt " the general effect "! Is it needful, to produce what Mr. Bell would call a good general effect, that all the figures in a picture should be life-size or gigantic? Raffaelle's " St. Cecilia," hanging just opposite, might have taught the hastiest observer and the most thoughtless critic better. Is the picture of the Vision of Ezekiel less sublime because it is on a foot square of canvas ?

In speaking of Domenichino's "Martyrdom of St. Agnes," Mr. Bell says, — "The serene and beautiful countenance of the Saint is irradiated by an expression of rapt holiness and heavenly resignation infinitely touching." Such, undoubtedly, it would have been well that the expression of the Saint should be; but such it is not; for its coarse materialism, disgusting exaggeration, and the utter want of elevation or truth of expression, this picture is one of the worst even of the Bolognese school. But Mr. Bell goes on to say, — "The episode of the two women forming the foreground of one corner of the picture, who are represented as hiding the face and stilling the screams of a terrified child, affords a scene of fine action, very admirably delineated." No such scene as this exists in the picture. In the right foreground is a woman with a frightened child, but she is inattentive to its screams, and doing nothing to hide its face. Behind this group, and quite separate from it, are two other women, occupied with their own terrors. Such carelessness of criticism is inexcusable; but, fortunately, errors like this may be set right by the most inattentive eyes.

Again, in regard to Domenichino's "Martyrdom of St. Peter Martyr," Mr. Bell says, — "The elevated and exalted resignation painted on the features of a noble countenance, the effect of the black drapery cast around the kneeling figure, and held in one large, majestic fold by the left hand, has a combined effect of grandeur and chaste simplicity, which is inexpressibly fine." The elevated resignation and the *effect* of the drapery *has* a *combined effect* inexpressibly fine! But, unfortunately

12

for all this fine writing, there is no kneeling figure in the picture. The Saint is prostrate on the ground; the murderer stands over him, holding the Saint's black robe, but scarcely in what is to be termed a "majestic fold."

After what is intended for a piece of very eloquent and magnificent writing, in the account of Guido's "Massacre of the Innocents," in which "the outcry of one mother," "the pale, dishevelled aspect of another," "the despair and agony of a third," and "the murdered babes lying on the blood-stained marble, huddled together," are fully described, Mr. Bell concludes with the startling assertion, that these figures "*present an historical picture, perhaps the most domestic and touching that ever was painted.*" Do mothers in anguish, and murdered babes, form a characteristically domestic scene? Such writing as this is absolutely intolerable. Had it been intended as a travesty upon the usual style of criticism, it would have been considered dull extravagance; but here it passes for serious earnest, and is quoted as worth reading.

It is not worth while to go on. These passages are fair samples of the whole; and it is unsatisfactory work to expose such presumptuous imbecility.

There is great want of a good artistic guide-book for Italy. Kugler's work on Italian Art is the only one that approaches to what is needed; but Kugler is thoroughly German in his dulness, and in many of his notions about Art. Lord Lindsay's "Christian Art," and Mrs. Jameson's "Legendary Art," both in many respects excellent, are too limited in their scope to serve as guide-books,

besides being too cumbrous and expensive for the majority of travellers. In American literature there is nothing
that deserves notice as a help to the lover of Art in Italy,
and, of all travellers, Americans need such help the most.
We come abroad utterly ignorant of Art, and, with natural and national self-confidence, at once constitute our-
selves judges and critics of paintings and statues. The
audacity of our ignorance halts at nothing; and a five-
minutes' visit to the Sistine Chapel qualifies us to de-
cide on the powers of Michel Angelo. The majority
of American travellers have yet to learn that some previous knowledge is to be acquired before one can be a
judge even of the externals of Art; that it is not the
eye alone that needs cultivation, but the heart and the
intellect as well, by those who would understand and
enjoy the works of the great masters. You may judge
correctly of the merits of a poem in a language which you
do not know, as easily as you can judge correctly of the
merits of a picture while you are ignorant of those principles that are, as it were, the alphabet of Art. If you
are unwilling to accept the authority of others, it is well
to remember that the only independence of judgment
that deserves the name is that which rests upon a basis
of humility, and of desire to learn how to judge correctly. It is somewhat damaging to our national vanity
to find that the worst pictures are purchased by Americans, or for the American market. Many an American
who comes to Rome and Florence thinks it will not do
for him to go home without taking a picture from Italy,
as a proof of his taste and a record of his travels. He

puts himself into the hands of a *commissionaire*, who takes him to shops where he is sure to be flattered and cheated. He buys a black, patched-up landscape, " a real Salvator," bright with varnish, and in a carved frame ; or he purchases one of the watery copies of some picture that suits common taste, because painted on the level of common-place, uneducated feeling. His *commissionaire* makes the bargain, and receives a good proportion of the sum apparently paid for the picture. All other *commissionaires* are most dishonest rogues ; this one alone is trustworthy. Our countryman goes back to his hotel, and thinks he has made a good bargain, since he paid only twenty dollars for a head, while the poor American artist, whose studio he went to the day before, asks two hundred and fifty dollars for the picture he has just painted. Or perhaps our friend has paid a large sum for his picture ; he has got a genuine Murillo, or a real Titian, — at least, so he has been persuaded by the dealer ; and then he congratulates himself that no such pictures are painted in our days, — not knowing that pictures a thousand times better hang, unbought, in the studio of his poor countryman.

It is no matter of surprise that our best artists find but little encouragement, and that Art is considered among us generally as a matter of little importance, when one sees, by such evidence as is afforded by American travellers in Italy, the average level of American taste and the depth of American ignorance.

The doctrines of Hell and Purgatory, and of the power of the Pope to afford absolution, may be regarded as the corner-stone of the grand edifice of the Papacy. From the time that it was established as a truth of religion, that there was a hell, and that men could be saved from the consequences of their sins, that is, could escape from hell, through the intervention of the Pope, — from that time, wealth and temporal power were assured to the Church. St. Peter's was paid for by money raised by the sale of indulgences; and while the material investment appeared in the marbles and gilding of the church, the moral investment appeared in the denunciations of Luther and the progress of the Reformation. The importance of these doctrines to the Church led to the subjection of all its other religious dogmas to them. The fall of man, the offended majesty of God, the atonement, the justice of the Almighty in contradistinction to his mercy, the power delegated to St. Peter, and, through him, to the Pope, have all been made subservient to the support of a belief in the eternity of punishment, and the opportunity afforded to escape from it. The fear of hell became greater than the love of heaven; but the desire for heaven was greater than the desire for goodness. The popular imagination was easily excited by the delineation of future torments; and Art represented accurately the popular belief. As the dread of the vengeance of God increased, the worship of Mary, the "Mother of Mercy," increased. In pictures of the Last Judgment, Mary appears as if pleading

with her indignant Son. The genius of Michel Angelo
has given to these doctrines of fear their most vivid and
awful representation. God is no longer the Father, but
the unrelenting Judge condemning his children. Over
the minds of the common people of Italy these doctrines
still hold an unshaken supremacy. The love due to God
is diverted to the Virgin ; the wayside shrines are adorned
with pictures of souls in the torment of flames, and with
pictures of the Virgin as the intercessor for fallen man.
Indulgences are as much sought as ever ; crowds kneel
before privileged altars ; and the steps of the Scala Santa
are worn by the knees of constant pilgrims.

Nor does the Church weary in her teaching. Money
and power are as important to her now as ever, and consequently hell and its fires. The Padre Passaglia is
considered the best scholastic theologian in Rome. His
lecture-room in the Collegio Romano is crowded five
times a week by an audience of students in theology from
all parts of Europe, and from America. His eloquence
and zeal are like those of the lecturers of old times ; and
his authority is quoted upon points of doctrine. He has
lately published a tract, "On the Eternity of Punishments, and on the Fire of Hell," in which he exerts
himself to prove the one and the other. It is a piece
of cold, dry, unfeeling logic. His fifth theorem is, " The
eternity of punishment is proved by those texts in which
the damned are deprived of all hope of any future redemption or liberation." *   The demonstration of his

* " In Religion,
What damned error, but some sober brow
Will bless it, and approve it with a text ? "

eighth theorem, in regard to the Fire of Hell, is as follows : " The principal efficient cause of fire in the present life is God the Author and Governor of Nature ; but of the fire of hell God the Judge and Avenger of sin and sinners is the efficient cause.

" Present fire burns and is supported by chemical operations ; but the fire of hell is excited and preserved by the breath of the Lord.

" Present fire does not act upon the soul except through the body ; but the fire of hell immediately afflicts and torments the soul.

" Present fire must finally be extinguished ; but the fire of hell will last forever.

" The former shines ; the latter produces outer darkness. The former, burning, dissolves and consumes ; the latter tortures and burns, but yet does not destroy. The former may, by human art, be diminished and extinguished ; the latter makes every effort vain, and has the power of God for its support."

Another curious and interesting tract, published last year, from which something of the present character of the teaching of the Roman Church upon these points may be gained, is called, " A Catechism concerning Protestantism and the Catholic Church." * It is to be noticed that this work appears at Milan, — a city, as all the world knows, under Austrian rule, — and that the Emperor of Austria, last year, in the *concordat* made with the Pope, signed away, as far as such things can be

---

* Per Giovanni Perrotti, *Poliantea Cattolica.* Milano, 1855.

signed away, religious and educational freedom in his dominions. The first lesson is on "The Name and Origin of Protestantism." The following is one of the statements : " The name of Protestant and of Protestantism is employed to signify the rebellion of all modern sects against the Catholic Church founded by Jesus Christ ; or, which is the same thing, the rebellion of proud men against Jesus Christ, the Founder of that Church." The third lesson is on " The Doctrines of Protestantism," and ends with the pupil's saying, " These doctrines strike me with horror ; — are they not, in some sense, worse than those of the pagans ? " To which the teacher replies : " You are right ; neither pagans nor Turks have ever reached such impiety of doctrine." The fourth lesson is on " The Authors and First Promulgators of Protestantism," of which the following extract will serve as a specimen : " Luther was an apostate. After he had married a nun, he had, as his first disciples, Carlostadius, Melancthon, Lange, and others of the same sort, — all of a piece. Carlostadius was an apostate, and he also took a wife. Melancthon was a hypocrite, a dissembler, cruel, a blasphemer, and devoted to judicial astrology. Lange was an ex-friar, like Luther ; and he, too, married. . . . . Calvin died madly blaspheming, and invoking the Devil." There is much more matter as remarkable as that here quoted, serving to illustrate the ideas prevalent among the supporters of the Catholic Church in regard to Protestantism, and the mode adopted to deter the young religious inquirer from adopting a form of belief so pernicious. A curious description is given of the signs by which the disseminators of Protestantism are to be recognized, in which it is stated that " you should know, that, in England, within a short time, the desire has been frequently expressed of renewing the executions practised for about three centuries upon the poor Catholics." But it is Lesson XV. that is most important to our present purpose. This lesson is, " On the Certain Damnation of Apostate Catholics "; and the teacher asserts in the course of it, that " it is certain with the certainty of faith, that all Catholics who become Protestants are irretrievably damned for all eternity, except in case of sincere repentance before death, accompanied with the abjuration of their errors." This portion of the Catechism closes with the statement, that " there is nothing in these pages which cannot be confirmed with irrefragable proofs and arguments."

Such is a specimen of the authorized teaching of the Church in 1856. Is it strange that superstition still prevails in Italy? Christianity is degraded into a creed of fear; and, to the lively imagination of the Italian, the horrors of hell are pictured with such force as to form the prevailing motive of his so-called religion.

" A woman went through the streets of Alexandria, in Egypt, — her feet bare, her hair dishevelled, with a torch in one hand, and a jar of water in the other. She said, — ' With this torch I will burn heaven, and with this water put out hell, that man may love God for Himself alone.' "

VENICE, 5th July, 1856.

The mosaics in the vestibule of St. Mark's are, perhaps, the most interesting of the long series of these
works with which the roof of the cathedral is covered.
They comprise some of the best mosaics of the thirteenth,
and some of the best, also, of the sixteenth century; and
the sharp contrast between them shows, at a glance, the
course of Art during this interval of three centuries, from
its first struggles to free itself from the bands of Byzantine swaddling-clothes, to the near period of its decrep-
itude and decline.   They afford, also, curious incidental
illustrations of the character and spirit of the workmen
of the one time and of the other.

In the intention of the early builders of the church,
the vestibule, or atrium, was regarded as that portion of
the sacred building which was appropriated to those who
had not been received into the full standing of members
of the Church of Christ.   It was for the unbaptized, and
for new converts, and perhaps, also, for such as might
have fallen into sin, and who, as penitents, sought for a
second admittance within the fold.   The subjects to
which the attention of such persons was to be directed
were, for the most part, chosen from the Old Testament,
and the old mosaics in the vestibule of St. Mark's represent scenes taken from the Books of Genesis and
Exodus, beginning with the Creation and the Fall of
Man, and going on through the histories of Noah, Abra-
ham, Joseph, and Moses, ending with the representation
of the miracle of the Fall of Manna.   The series of subjects is similar to that which is found in like places in

many other cathedrals; but there are few where the designs are so numerous, or where the story is so regularly carried forward.

The earliest in the order of arrangement are those on the right hand of the main entrance. In the cupola in the roof, over the door, of which the bronze valves were brought from Constantinople, is a series representing the Creation and the Fall of Man. The popular belief, derived as much from favorite apocryphal stories as from the account in the Bible, is here curiously exhibited. The second subject, for instance, is that of the Creation of Angels, by whom the Creator is accompanied in the after works. The quaint simplicity and honest straightforwardness of treatment, combined now and then with a sudden and surprising attempt to express some poetic conception or vivid imagination, in which the hand of the designer fell short of his desire, and failed him at the moment when its best skill was most needed, are often strikingly manifest. But in these very shortcomings of manual execution, as compared with the vigor of conception, lie the promise and the certainty of the rapid progress of Art. Thought had freed itself from traditional restraints, by which for centuries it had been held in check, and the hand was sure soon to become obedient to the directing will.

The cupola is divided into three bands, in the second of which occurs the picture of the Creation of Man. The Creator is seated on a throne, and is forming man from the dust of the earth. The angels stand around, looking on. Man is represented as a black, inanimate figure. This is followed by the blessing of the seventh day, in which the day appears as an angel kneeling to receive the benediction. The next is the giving of the soul to man. Man stands before the Creator, who holds up towards his mouth a little figure with butterfly-wings, — this figure being intended to represent the soul. The third range of the cupola contains the scenes in Paradise, and the expulsion from it, — all of them curious in design, but all rendered so plainly as to be intelligible to any one who had read or had heard the story from Genesis. This was the first lesson to be learned, and no one could fail to understand its meaning, written, in glowing colors, on a ground of gold, and in clear, though awkward, lines. Each of the pictures is accompanied with an inscription, taken generally from the Scripture narrative.

The place of the old mosaics over the main door has been filled by later ones; and it does not appear what were the subjects of the earlier works. They probably did not belong to the series of subjects from the Old Testament, but were detached and separate works, representing, it is not unlikely, Death and the Judgment, Heaven and Hell.

The remaining spaces of the ceiling of the atrium are occupied with subjects from the Old Dispensation, and there appears to have been an obvious and impressive meaning, as has been pointed out by Mr. Ruskin, in the conclusion of the series with the miracle of the Fall of Manna. It was to direct the thoughts of the disciple to the words of Christ, — " Your fathers did eat manna, and are dead"; and to lead him to remember that living bread which "if any man eat, he shall live forever." And this thought would be still more strongly impressed upon him, when, returning from the northern end of the vestibule, where this miracle was represented, he entered the central door of the church, and, turning, saw above it, on the wall, a grand and solemn mosaic of the Saviour "enthroned, with the Virgin on one side, and St. Mark on the other, in attitudes of adoration, — Christ being represented as holding a book open upon his knee, on which is written, 'I AM THE DOOR: BY ME IF ANY MAN ENTER IN, HE SHALL BE SAVED.' On the red marble moulding which surrounds the mosaic is written, 'I AM THE GATE OF LIFE: LET THOSE WHO ARE MINE ENTER BY ME.' Above, on the red marble fillet which forms the cornice of the west end of the church, is written, with reference to the figure of Christ below, 'WHO HE WAS, AND FROM WHOM HE CAME, AND AT WHAT PRICE HE REDEEMED THEE, AND WHY HE MADE THEE AND GAVE THEE ALL THINGS, DO THOU CONSIDER.'" *

The mosaics were thus designed, not merely for the adornment of the church, but also for the instruction of the people. Every part had a religious significance, either in plain words or in symbolic suggestion. "The visible temple was a type of the invisible Church of God."

From the eleventh to the fifteenth century, mosaic-workers seem to have been employed with few intervals upon the church roof. It does not appear at what period

* *Stones of Venice*, ii. 111, 112.

the whole was completed, but it was probably during the fifteenth century that the last mosaic of that series which had been commenced almost four hundred years before was finished, and the great design of the original builders fulfilled.   With the sixteenth century a new period begins.   Some of the oldest mosaics had been injured by time and accident.   The resources of painting had been wonderfully developed ; the old designs looked poor and meagre, beside the splendid work of the new school of Venetian painters.   The meaning of the early artists was now no longer read, or, if read, was but little regarded.   No reverence was felt for their pious work ; and the procurators of St. Mark's determined, that, instead of restoring those of the old mosaics which stood in need of repair, they should be removed, and their places supplied by entirely new work.   The best artists were employed on these new mosaics, and their names have come down to us, not only in the records of the works, but in the inscriptions which they took care to place on the pictures themselves.   The most famous of them were the brothers Francesco and Valerio Zuccato, both of them the friends of Titian, who seems to have had for the elder of them, Francesco, a more than common regard. To these brothers was intrusted the work of making fresh mosaics in the vestibule over the main door of entrance ; and here may now be seen their brighter colors and richer and more skilful designs, contrasting with the older mosaics on each side.   In the lunette over the door is a figure of St. Mark.   He is represented as standing with his arms raised, and his face turned toward heaven, from which a hand appears, in the act of blessing. He is dressed in rich vestments, and the whole ground upon which the figure is relieved is of gold. This is the first mosaic that strikes the eye of the stranger as he enters the vestibule through the outer central door. Its colors are as glowing and fresh as when it was first set in its place. There is, perhaps, no more highly finished work of the kind in the whole church than this. The design for it is said to have been given to the Zuccati by Titian; and the internal evidence afforded by the figure of the Evangelist is such as to give authority to the tradition. The hardness of line, the too great sharpness of light and shadow, the want of softness and harmony in color, which are faults often to be found in mosaics of all ages, have been so far successfully avoided in this, that the proud inscription which the artists placed under the feet of St. Mark appears not as a piece of vaingloriousness, but rather as a just claim on the applause of all who may look at their work, and a fit expression of their own assurance of its excellence. MDXLV. UBI DILIGENTER INSPEXERIS, ARTEMQUE AC LABOREM FRANCISCI ET VALERII ZUCATI, VENETOR., FRATRUM, AGNOVERIS, TUM DEMUM JUDICATO. "When you have carefully looked and recognized the art and the labor of Francis and Valerius Zuccato, brothers, of Venice, then finally judge."

But if this inscription be pleasant to read, in view of the merit of the work and the satisfaction of the workmen, it is far otherwise when one considers the place in which it is set, and the incongruity between it and the inscriptions on the more ancient mosaics. The entrance to that house which men have dedicated to the Most High is no place for the exhibition of pride in their own work, and for boastfulness of its excellence. There is no more forcible illustration of the difference in the spirit of the earlier workers and that of the workers of the sixteenth century, to be found in all Venice, (and such illustrations are by no means uncommon here,) than is to be found in these inscriptions. The one was the spirit of an age of faith, in which men considered the best that they could do as but a poor offering to God, and took delight in their calling as a means of expressing their deepest convictions, — an age, not of pride and self-satisfaction, but of comparative simplicity and self-forgetfulness. The other was the spirit of an age of formal reverence and real infidelity, in which men worked with reference not so much to the glory of God as to their own ambitions and petty fames, and by their example and their works led on that period of debasement in religion, in philosophy, and Art, from which we are now so imperfectly and tediously struggling out. The decline of Art is to be dated from the time when artists began to work for purely worldly ends. Men of genius, it is true, prepared and disciplined by the works of those who had preceded them, using the slowly accumulated experience of many generations, and freed from clogging conventionalisms, accomplished, after the period of faithlessness had begun, works more splendid in color, more accurate and rich in design, more complete in what are technically called artistic qualities, than any that had been accomplished before. But their greatness had the seeds of decay within itself; and a wise critic, contemporary with Titian, Michel Angelo, and Raffaelle, might have foretold, judging from their works alone, that they were the immediate forerunners of the decline and fall of Art.

On the other side of the vestibule, opposite their figure of St. Mark, the Zuccati executed a mosaic of the Deposition from the Cross, and under it placed the inscription,

NATURÆ SAXIBUS, ZUCATORUM FRATRUM INGENIO,

which may, perhaps, be translated, "Made with the stones of Nature by the genius of the brothers Zuccati." The inscription is curious, not merely for its bad Latin, but for the results which followed this error in declension. The success of the Zuccati was so great, and the approval of their mosaics so general, that the directors of the works on St. Mark's increased their salary, and allotted to them new and important places, where the old mosaics were to be removed, and new ones substituted. The magician had come with his new, bright lamps, which he offered in exchange for the dull and ugly old one. How often in the history of Art has the magic lamp been flung away, without getting even so much as a common new one in exchange!

But the brilliant fortune of the Zuccati excited the jealousy of the other mosaic-masters who were employed on St. Mark's, and reports were spread to their discredit, which, being brought to the ears of the procurators, determined them to institute an investigation to discover the truth. The most important of the charges brought

13

against the brothers was that of having increased the effect of their mosaics by painting; but it was also said that the stones were badly set; that they worked out of season, in unfair competition; and, more than this, Valerio was charged with not understanding his art, and with spending his time in his shop, making designs for coifs, vestures, and open-work, instead of being at work at St. Mark's. In support of these charges, one of their rivals, Bartolommeo Bozza, who had formerly been one of their pupils, pointed out some little buildings, in the hand of an angel, that were painted, and certain clouds above and below the Evangelists, in the vestibule between the two doors, which were made with the paint-brush, and not with colored glass or stones, as they should have been, according to the orders of the procurators. The other mosaics were then washed with a sponge and sand, to discover if there were painting upon them. In going over that of the Deposition from the Cross, a bit of paper that had been pasted upon a part of the inscription was washed off. This was regarded as a further proof of the deceptions practised by the Zuccati; for it appeared that the error they had committed in the word *saxibus* having been pointed out to them, they had corrected the mistake by putting a bit of painted paper, with the right word upon it, over the wrong. The mosaics, however, on the whole, stood the test well; and finally, on the 9th of May, 1563, the most distinguished painters in Venice, having examined the works, were called upon for their opinion. Such a jury of great artists has seldom een gathered together. It was composed of Titian, Tintoret, Paul Veronese, Schiavone, and one Jacopo Pistoia, whose name is hardly known except for this mention of it. There was little disagreement among them. Titian was warm in his praise of the works, and in defending the Zuccati; and all declared, that, although it could not be denied that in some places the paint-brush had been used, yet, after the color thus applied had been removed by washing, the mosaic had apparently lost nothing; and that their design, and the skill with which they were made, were in the highest degree worthy of praise. After such testimony to their merits, the accusations that had been brought against the Zuccati were reduced to their just value; and the procurators, satisfied with the general excellence of the work, condemned the brothers only to remake, at their own expense, in mosaic, such parts as had been painted, and suspended the salary of Valerio until he should give new proof of understanding his art. Valerio showed, as a proof of his knowledge, the half-figure of St. Clement, over the right-hand door leading from the atrium into the church, which he had made by himself; but it had been made many years before, and some new work was now required from him.[*] It does not appear that the Zuccati ever remade the portions of their work which had been painted; and any one going into St. Mark's may read the word *saxibus* still plain in the inscription, — a memorial of their unsuccessful trick to hide their bad Latin, and of the praise given to their mosaics by the greatest masters of Venetian

[*] George Sand has made this story of the Zuccati the basis of her tale of *Les Maîtres Mosaistes.*

Art. And any one walking up and down the atrium, over the beautiful, time-worn, uneven pavement, may see, in the earlier and the later mosaics, not only works of Art well worthy his regard, but firm-set and enduring types of the rise and of the fall of Venice.

ROME.

As I entered Rome once more, just before sunset this
evening, Shakespeare's words were running in my memory,

> " Was't not a happy star
> Led us to Rome?"

and the suggestive ruins and dark aspect of the narrow
streets, full of remembered interest and of power over
the imagination, brought to mind the greeting of Titus
Andronicus to the city,

> " Hail, Rome, victorious in thy mourning weeds!"

Then I went on to think what else Shakespeare had
said of historic or prophetic application to Rome.

The batteries of the castle of St. Angelo pointed upon
the city, and the French sentinels at its gate, told of disquiet and insecurity, of passions repressed by force, of
ill-will between rulers and people, of oppression and
of hatred.

> " Why, foolish Lucius, dost thou not perceive
> That Rome is but a wilderness of tigers?"

It does not require a long stay in the city to discover that

> " Here is a mourning Rome, a dangerous Rome ";

while the beggars, the priests, the monks, the idlers, who fill the streets, cause one to exclaim,

> " What trash is Rome,
> What rubbish, and what offal ! "

One needs but to

> " Look round about the wicked streets of Rome,"

to feel as if it were true indeed that

> " The sun of Rome is set," —

that the ancient mother of so many noble men, of so many heroes and poets,

> " Has lost the breed of noble bloods."

Years of suffering and disappointment have quenched the old spirit, and from

> " The sad-fac'd men, people and sons of Rome,"

little is to be hoped of wise counsel, of hearty resolution, of vigorous effort.

> " Romans now
> Have thews and limbs like to their ancestors;
> But, woe the while ! their fathers' minds are dead,
> And they are governed with their mothers' spirits.
> Their yoke and sufferance show them womanish."

And yet Rome may, perhaps, again be Roman. All hope is not dead. Tyranny and falsehood are not eternal. And even though in their fall they crush the city utterly, and leave its hills desolate, then, if need be, for their destruction,

> "Let Rome in Tiber melt, and the wide arch
> Of the rang'd empire fall! Kingdoms are clay."

ROME, 18th December, 1856.

The old column for the new monument in the Piazza di Spagna, in honor of the Virgin of the Immaculate Conception, and in memory of the promulgation of the dogma, was raised to-day and set upon its base. The architect who directed the work adopted much the same means of operation as Fontana employed for raising the obelisk in front of St. Peter's, about which the famous story of "Wet the Ropes" is told. For some weeks the Piazza has been blocked up at the end near the Propaganda with a clumsy and enormous inclined plane of timber, for the purpose of rolling the column up to a level with the top of the base of the monument. The immense extent of timber-work gave rise to a pasquinade in which there was some humor: "Lost, an architect, supposed to have missed his way in the forest in the Piazza di Spagna!"

There was no religious ceremony connected with the raising of the column; and the Pope, although greatly interested in the work, was not present even as a spectator. The people say he stayed away on account of his evil eye. A large proportion of the spectators, both in

the square and in the neighboring houses, were foreigners. The Romans do not like the monument; — it costs
too much money, and their taxes are heavy. The windows of the Propaganda were occupied by cardinals,
while Queen Christina, no fear being felt of her evil eye,
was looking on from one of the windows of the Spanish
palace.

A troop of soldiers was stationed around the board
fence which inclosed the monument, to keep the crowd
at a proper distance, and within the inclosure were the
city firemen, in their blue dresses and brass-topped caps,
manning the windlasses by which the column was to be
hoisted. Before the work began, the ropes, already
damp with the morning rain, were well wet, and then,
at the sound of a trumpet, the men began to turn the
windlasses, and the great mass moved slowly. As the
column rose and the creaking ropes bore the strain,
the clouds broke, and, just as it settled down upon the
base prepared for it, the sun came out brightly. A band
played a march, the people quickly dispersed, the draperies were pulled in from the windows, and the workmen
unwound the covering of ropes in which the pillar had
been bound, showing the fine green veins of the *cipollino*
marble. Next summer four statues of the prophets are
to be set at its foot, and it is to be crowned with one of
the Virgin *sine labe concepta*. It promises, when finished,
to be as ugly as most of the public monuments of Rome.
When will architects and artists learn that a column is
not a proper pedestal for a statue?

Two facts connected with this column are curious. It

once belonged to a building of the Empire, and has been lying for centuries on the Quirinal. In repolishing it for its present use, it was found not to be sound, and it has been cased, for security, nearly half way up, in bronze open-work. The statue of the Virgin on its summit will afford a curious type of the Roman Church itself, based upon unsound supports derived from heathen times.

ROME, 19th December, 1856.

As I was riding this afternoon beyond the noble old basilica of San Lorenzo, one of the Papal *gendarmeria* came up behind me on a stout, black horse, and joined me with a salutation of " Good day, Excellency! " — I responded, and praised his horse. — " Yes, Signore," answered he, " he is a good horse, but he has twenty years. I bought him last year for eighteen *scudi ;* but he brought me from Tivoli last night, and will go back to-night, and will eat well." — " Are the roads quiet, now ? " — " Ah, Excellency, the poor must live, and the winter is hard, and there is no work ! " — " But how was the harvest ? " — " Small enough, Signore ! There is no grain at Tivoli, and no wine ; and as for the olives, a thousand trees have not given the worth of a *baiocco*." — " And what does the government do for the poor ? " — " Nothing, nothing at all." — " And the priests ? " — " *Eh ! vivono benone, sempre benone ; godono questo mondo, — ma ? "* (They live well, always well ; they have a good time in this world, — but ?)

Rome, 22d December, 1856.

To-day, as I was passing the steps of Santa Maria Maggiore, a beggar called out to me, " Excellency, give me a *baiocco*, and I will go up the Scala Santa for your profit." This was a good offer, for he who devoutly ascends the Scala Santa on his knees gains nine years of indulgence for each of its twenty-eight steps, — and thus, for a *baiocco*, I might have gained vicariously two hundred and fifty-two years' indulgence. As I continued my walk, and came in sight of St. Peter's dome, I was reminded of the traffic by which the Papal treasury had been supplied with means for the completion of the great church, — and it seemed to me that this church might, in some sort, be regarded as the monument erected in Rome, in memory of the principles of the Reformation.

But those principles have made little advance in Rome itself. Take this matter of Indulgences, for example. Although the public sale of them is no longer continued, and although many of the abuses connected with them have been done away, yet, among the common people, they are regarded in the same way as of old, and the beggar's speech shows that they still afford the means of private, if not of public gain.

As in so many instances of ecclesiastical doctrine and discipline, the teaching of the Church upon this subject is not properly understood by the mass either of Romanists or of Protestants. The Church teaches one thing in formal words, and allows another in common practice and belief. This creates confusion, and affords a loop-hole of escape from the reproaches of adversaries. But even taking the most favorable view of the doctrine of the Church in the matter of Indulgences, as it is declared at the present day, it will be found to afford ample room for the starting-point of a new Reformation.

There is a book, easily obtainable at Rome, called "A Collection of those Prayers and Pious Works to which Holy Indulgences have been conceded by the Popes." * The copy which I have is of the twelfth Roman edition, published in 1849, with the express sanction of the Cardinal Prefect of the Congregation of Indulgences. Its five hundred and twenty-seven pages are occupied only with those Indulgences which have been granted *in perpetuo;* all those which are limited in time, or to a special place, with the exception of a few in Rome, being excluded.

Prefixed to this list is a short essay on Indulgences, and on the conditions required to obtain them. It may be considered as an authoritative statement of the present doctrine of the Church upon this matter. According to this doctrine, sin produces two results in the soul, — the guilt which deprives us of the grace of God, and the punishment which prevents us from enjoying him in Paradise. This punishment is either eternal or temporal. From the guilt and the eternal punishment we are wholly freed through the infinite merits of Christ in the sacrament of Penitence, provided we receive that

* *Raccolta di Orazioni e Pie Opere per le quali sono state concedute dai Sommi Pontefici le S. Indulgenze.* Decima seconda Edizione Romana. Corretta ed accresciuta di altre Concessioni del Sommo Pontefice Pio IX. Roma, 1849.

sacrament with proper dispositions.   But as to temporal punishment, as we are commonly not wholly relieved from it by means of that sacrament, a great part
remains to be made up for in this life by good works or
by repentance, or in the next life to be suffered in the
fires of Purgatory.   " But Christ conferred upon his
Church from its origin the power of making us par-
takers in its treasure of holy Indulgences, by virtue of
which we may, with the slightest inconvenience to our-
selves, pay in full to the Divine Justice all that we owe
it for our sins, — they being already pardoned, so far as
regards the guilt and the eternal punishment.   For this
is a treasure which endures in the sight of God, — the
treasure of the merits and satisfactions of Jesus Christ,
of the Blessed Virgin Mary, and of the Saints, — or, in
other words, the sum of the satisfactions offered by our
Divine Redeemer, which were superabundant and infinite, and, still further, of those of the most Holy Mary,
of the Martyrs, and the other Saints, which were not
needed by them for the expiation of their own faults."
These treasures suffer no diminution, however much they
may be drawn upon.

Indulgences, or drafts upon this treasure, are of two
classes, — the partial, and the plenary.   A partial indulgence remits the temporal punishment for a limited
time.   That is, if a tolerably small sin be charged against
us with forty-nine years of Purgatorial fire, seven partial indulgences of seven years would discharge us of
this debt.   But by a plenary indulgence all the temporal
punishment due for all our sins is remitted to us, — " sc

that, if one should chance to die after having worthily gained a plenary indulgence, the theologians affirm that he would go directly to Paradise."

Nor are indulgences confined to the living; for, although the Church does not dispense indulgences for the dead absolutely, or so that they certainly accrue to the advantage of any given individual, she does so by way of suffrage, as it is called. That is, one who desires to relieve a soul from Purgatory may gain a plenary indulgence, — for a partial one would seem hardly worth gaining, when plenary are to be had with equal ease, — and may then offer it to God, praying Him to apply it to the benefit of some special soul. But he cannot be certain that God will so apply it; he cannot "make the indulgence over to that soul, as if it were his own to bestow."

The conditions, by fulfilment of which indulgences are to be gained, are, first, that whoever desires to obtain an indulgence must be in a state of grace. This is secured by true repentance combined with confession and communion. If, however, for any reason, it is impossible to confess previously to fulfilling the special conditions attached to an indulgence, it is well to have a firm intention to confess, in order to recover the Divine grace, should it have been lost. A weekly confession is sufficient to secure the benefits of all such indulgences as are to be gained from day to day, unless one should be conscious of the guilt of a mortal sin committed since the last confession, in which case a new confession becomes necessary.

In the second place, all the special conditions attached

to any indulgence must be accurately performed. As, for instance, one must not stand when the indulgence has been granted for an act upon the knees. To ascend the Scala Santa on one's feet would be an act of impiety ; to go up its steps upon one's knees — a not difficult labor, except for the stout or the rheumatic, for whom easier modes of indulgence are provided — gains the remission of two centuries and a half of Purgatorial fire.

And, finally, in the third place, to obtain plenary indulgence, it is needful that one should hold his sins in detestation, and should lay aside every inclination towards them. And it is furthermore to be desired that the undertaking to gain indulgences should be accompanied by the worthy fruits of penitence, the good works and penances of piety and devotion, in order to give some satisfaction to the Divine Justice for the faults which have been committed.

Such is the general theory of Indulgences. The Dedication of this Collection of Prayers affords a curious illustration of practical opinion in regard to their efficacy. The Dedication is addressed (and it is to be remembered that this book has the highest ecclesiastical sanction) to the Holy Souls of Purgatory. The editor of this twelfth edition recalls to their remembrance the fact, that the original compiler of the work dedicated it to them as a token of gratitude for the many graces and favors which they had obtained for him, and also because the work itself was of special interest to them, on account of so many indulgences being applicable to them by way of suffrage. " Accept, then," he goes on, " accept, dear

Souls, this little offering, and consider the end that I propose and the affection with which I offer it. Spread over me, Elect Souls, your most efficacious protection, . . . and may this work bring to you that entrance for which you sigh into the kingdom of glory!"

Over the doors of many churches in Rome, and in other cities, is to be seen an inscription, often bearing much the character of a sign-board, with the words, " Plenary Indulgence every day," — signifying, that, by some Papal concession, plenary indulgence is to be gained by attendance on the Mass at some special altar in the church, or by the repetition of certain prayers at this altar, on any day of the year. This sign has the value of a recommendation of the church to the faithful, and affords a means of attracting worshippers, whose alms increase the revenues of the ecclesiastics attached to it.

It might be supposed that the ease with which plenary indulgence is to be obtained would diminish the zeal in seeking for partial indulgences. But such is not the case. The occasion of this may be that the imagination is less affected by the thought of a complete remission of the penalty due than by the consideration of shortening the period of punishment by a definite number of days or years. Few minds can grasp the indefinite conceptions of eternity with the vigor which may render them as satisfactory as those which are bounded by the known limits of years. So that, while the church of St. John Lateran offers plenary indulgence daily at its altars, they are less frequented by the common people, than the steps, just across the way, of the Scala Santa. The tendency

14

in this respect, is toward material rather than spiritual conceptions.

The special observances attached to the obtaining of various indulgences afford many illustrations of the prevailing opinions in regard to the worship and the doctrine of the Church. Thus, in the list contained in the Collection, there are but five forms for the gaining of indulgence connected with the worship of God, in contrast with thirty-five connected with that of the Virgin, — and of the former, but one is immediately and exclusively devoted to the Supreme Being.

One hundred days of indulgence were granted by Pius VII. to whoever devoutly and with contrite heart should recite the following ejaculation, as often as he might recite it: "Jesus, Joseph, and Mary, I give you my soul with my heart!" This indulgence is also applicable to the souls in Purgatory. A more attractive form of indulgence for the same period is offered to those who repeat the famous hymn, *Stabat Mater dolorosa*, — while those who daily recite, at morning, noon, and evening, the *Angelus Domini* and three *Ave Marias*, acquire, not only a hundred days' indulgence by each repetition, but once a month plenary indulgence in addition.

In many churches, especially in those frequented by the lower classes, a Protestant is often shocked by representations of the crucified Saviour, carved or painted of the size of life, and in a style which betrays the utmost brutality of conception and the deadness of all true reverence. The bloody horrors and abjectness of these figures are beyond description. The more physically disgusting they are, the better do they seem to be esteemed. Their object is to stimulate dull imaginations and to inflame stupid hearts. Possibly this object may in some instances be attained ; but a more common effect, more common because more natural, is to degrade the popular conceptions of the character and the sufferings of the Saviour, to substitute the coarsest fancies for the most solemn and pathetic truths, and to minister to a diseased craving for unnatural and detestable excitements. In connection with these images, and appealing to the same low principles of superstition, are a series of prayers to which great indulgences were affixed by Pius VII., addressed to "the Most Holy Wounds." They are five in number. Too shocking to bear translation, (and yet they may be found translated in English books of the devotions of the Roman Church,) it is enough to read the words with which they open, " *Vi adoro, Sacratissima Piaga del Piede sinistro del mio Gesù. Vi compatisco del dolore acerbissimo sofferto.*" It is enough to read these opening words, and to know that they are among the most commonly used acts of devotion, to gain an ineffaceable impression of the mournful perversion of the conceptions of prayer, the destruction of its holy sentiment, the loss of its spiritual influences, in those who are taught to use such forms, and are instructed by the Church which claims absolute subjection to its teachings, that these prayers are among the means of salvation.

I do not mean to say that many pious and pure-minded

persons may not use these prayers in a spirit which may render them a true act of worship. I do not mean to deny that they may derive a certain feeling of comfort from their use, nor that the soul may often, in times of weakness, be stimulated to a fervor of sentiment resembling real strength of religious feeling, by such material images and words as these. But even in such instances, the prayers and crucifixes of this sort address themselves only to the morbid side of human nature. The Roman Church is in nothing more skilful than in enlisting the weaknesses of human nature in her cause. The blood and the wounds of Christ are appeals to the imagination, to be heightened by the scenic effects of superstition. I have seen in a Roman church a painted representation of souls burning and tortured in the fires of Purgatory, while above was the Saviour on the cross, and from the wounds in his hands and feet and side the blood was pouring in streams upon the flames below. Immediately at the side of this picture was a money-box with an inscription asking alms for masses for the souls in Purgatory, for whom the Saviour had died. Is it strange that one turns away from the system of Rome to the Gospels with a sense as of turning to its very contrary?

Equally familiar to all visitors of Roman Catholic churches are the representations of the Stations of our Lord, as they are called. These are usually cheap colored engravings, fourteen in number, depicting our Saviour before Pilate, — the scenes where he paused on his way from the house of Pilate to Calvary, according to the tradition of the Church, — the Crucifixion, the Depo sition, and the Laying in the Sepulchre. With these pictures is connected the holy exercise of the *Via Crucis*, which consists in passing from one to another of these stations in their order, with meditation, hymns, and prayers, in memory and imitation of the Saviour's progress. Perhaps there is no devotional service more popular than this, joined in as it is at appointed times by processions of the people and pious confraternities, and its observance being connected with the amplest indulgences. Its origin is of ancient date, and, according to the Roman authorities, it was instituted by the Virgin herself. Adrichomius, in his famous "Theatrum Terræ Sanctæ," says, — "Pia habet traditio majorum Beatam Virginem, quæ cum suis cruenta Filii sui vestigia ad crucem usque soquuta fuit, post ejus sepulturam huc redeuntem, primam Viam Crucis ex devotione calcâsse, unde et Christianorum processiones ac crucis gestationes originem habere videntur." And in that book of marvellous, though sanctified coarseness and impiety, "The Revelations of St. Bridget," the Saint tells us that the Virgin declared to her that she constantly visited the places of the sufferings of her Son, — "Omni tempore post ascensionem Filii mei, visitavi loca in quibus Ipse passus est." * The Popes have liberally dispensed those treasures of the Church, which are not to be diminished by any profuseness of expenditure, upon those who practise this ancient form of service; and one of the most striking sights in Rome is due to the regard in which the *Via Crucis* is held.

* Lib vi. cap. 6

It was in 1750, a year of Jubilee, that Benedict XIV. instituted a confraternity of both sexes, under the name of the Lovers of Jesus and Mary, and gave to them in perpetuity the charge of the fourteen stations, and of the crucifix which he had that year erected in the Colosseum. The confraternity still exists, composed of lay members, who practise charitable works, and, on the afternoons of Fridays and Sundays and the feast-days of the year, assemble within the walls of the Colosseum, and, after an exhortation from a Franciscan friar, make the circuit of the stations with hymns and prayers. The men are dressed in long gray robes, with cowls that completely conceal their features. The scene and the service are impressive. The loud, clear voice of the friar resounds through the dark arches and mounts over the broken walls of the amphitheatre. The contrast in associations between the memories that belong to the place and its present use is strong and affecting, even in this city, where the frequency of similar, but less effective contrasts, wearies the feelings. The sermon over, the friar descends from his platform, and puts himself at the head of the irregular procession. He sings, as he advances to the first station, —

> " L' orme sanguigne
> Del mio Signore
> Tutto dolore
> Seguiterò."

" The bloody steps of my Lord in grief will I follow. And the people answer, —

"Vi prego, O Gesù buono,
Per la vostra Passione,
Darmi il Perdono!"

"O good Jesus, we pray thee, by thy Passion, give us pardon!"

The sound of the singing of the people fills the vast area of the Colosseum, — that space which has been so often filled with the shrieks of the victims of Imperial or popular cruelty. For the time, I join in the service, and I seem to hear the voices of the martyrs who suffered for Christ's sake within these walls, taking part in the hymn which the worshippers now kneeling are singing in honor of our common Master and Lord.

"*Adoramus te, Christe, et benedicimus tibi!*" sing the voices, while others take up the words and respond, "*Quia per Sanctam Crucem tuam redemisti mundum.*"

There is no nobler church in Rome than this, with the sky for its dome, with the wall-flowers and the wild trailing plants for its draperies, with the wind for its great organ, and the sun for the lights of its altar, — with its soil sanctified by the blood of those who died for the Faith, — with its ruinous walls telling of the fall of one superstition, and foretelling the fall of another; — sky, and sun, and wind, and earth, and failing human walls, all prophesying of the time, near in the sight of God, though far off to our eyes, when truth shall prevail, and the Church of Christ be but another name for the world.

But the fervor of the imagination is chilled, and its hopes are driven back worsted into the heart, as the sun goes down behind the Palace of the Cæsars, and, the service over, the masked brother clinks his money-box at the exit of the amphitheatre. The realities of Rome again prevail.

One might suppose, that, with so many and such easy opportunities for gaining indulgences during life, few persons would put off till their last hour the means necessary to be taken for securing themselves against the penal consequences of their sins. But such does not seem to be the case, and the Church has provided plenary indulgence *in articulo mortis* for all who may then receive the priestly benediction. The efficacy of a deathbed repentance is unquestioned, particularly when accompanied with devout bequests. Money left for masses for the repose of the soul of the dead paves the way to eternal bliss; and in one of the noblest Italian cathedrals I have seen a priest on a high festival day sitting at a table with an account-book before him, entering in it the sums received from the poor worshippers who crowded about him, with their money in their hands, to purchase masses for the souls of their beloved dead. The money-changers had returned to the temple.

The discussion with regard to the utility of indulgences, and the attacks upon the whole system, have been going on for centuries, and have engaged the forces of the ablest controversialists. That the practice of the Church has not been more greatly changed in this respect by such persevering assaults affords strong ground for believing that a system productive of such scandals would not be maintained, unless profit resulted from it to the ministers of the Church. The system, moreover, is maintained with comparative ease, because it harmonizes with the weakness of uninstructed human nature, affords a pleasant retreat to vice, renders immorality compatible with the practices of religion and with the hopes of Paradise, — and also because, so far as Italy is concerned, there is no freedom of discussion, and men's minds are not stirred with the suggestions of other and more rational forms of belief and modes of worship.

But to an observer stationed outside the Church, and watching without passion the course of affairs within, the practical results of this doctrine present themselves under two aspects. The lessons of past history are repeated in present experience; and the old debate is reopened in the latest words of to-day.

" Ne croyons pas," says Massillon, " que les grâces de l'Église nous aient purifié, si elles ne nous ont pas changé ; ne comptons sur son indulgence qu'autant que nous pouvons compter sur un sincère repentir." * In his noted treatise, " Sulla Morale Cattolica," written in reply to Sismondi's charges against the morality of Roman

---

* *Mandement pour la Publication de Jubile*, 15 Nov., 1724. But the doctrines of the eloquent Bishop of Clermont may be seen at large in his *Instruction sur le Jubilé*; one sentence of which will show to what conceptions of the nature of God, to what practical and revolting heathenism, even good men are led by the teachings of the Roman Church. " Ah! l'Église autrefois elle-même, plus indulgente sans doute que le Dieu terrible, puisqu'elle n'étoit occupée qu'à l'apaiser, qu'à adoucir par les rigueurs canoniques la sentence du souverain Juge, et qu'elle ne punissoit ses enfans que comme une mère; "Église elle-même, pour un seul crime, imposoit autrefois de longues années de travaux et de pénitence."

doctrine, in the " History of the Italian Republics," Manzoni says, " Dire che le Indulgenze ottengono la remissione della pena, senza la conversione del cuore, e la brama di soddisfare, è empietà, che, grazie al Cielo, non è insegnato da alcuno nella Chiesa." * " To say that Indulgences obtain the remission of punishment, unless there be conversion of the heart, and desire to make satisfaction, is an impiety which, thanks be to Heaven, is taught by no one in the Church." Such is unquestionably the case. The teaching of the authorities of the Church is now uniform upon this point. The enlightened Catholic receives indulgence as a gift which is to be gained only by sincere repentance, by leaving and utterly casting off his sins. Indulgence is to him as the manifest proof of the grace of God, ever ready to welcome back the prodigal with full forgiveness ; and all the sweet parables of the mercy of the Lord seem concentrated into a personal experience by means of this consoling testimony of pardon. The Church assures him of that forgiveness which he has been taught to seek through her. The Church stands between him and God. And here lies the chief evil of this doctrine in its application to the better sort of men. It substitutes a material and visible form for a spiritual condition. It withdraws the imagination from the things of the Spirit. It conforms to the tendency of human weakness to draw God down to itself, instead of lifting itself to God. It interferes with the close relation of the soul and its Father, and mediates between them as if they were or could be parted.

* Cap. XI. *Delle Indulgenze.*

But the second aspect under which the practical results of this doctrine exhibit themselves is even more conclusive against it. The teaching of the Church is not in the hands of careful thinkers alone, and of those who are called authorities, anxious to preserve its doctrines from abuse. The teachers it employs are not all Bossuets and Massillons, but far more generally men of imperfect education, and elevated only by the title of Priest above the common run of men. The abuses of doctrine often tend to the advantage of ecclesiastics. The poor and the ignorant receive little instruction which may enable them to attain even that moderate degree of spiritual enlightenment by which they might gain a true comprehension of the conditions attached to indulgences. It is not to be disputed that the mass of the people in Rome, who seek and suppose themselves to acquire indulgences, have a very imperfect notion of the nature of penitence. It is generally supposed to be a state of regret for past sin, — not a determination to depart from sin in future. An indulgence wipes out the temporal penalty of past sin, — and practically it is too often considered as a good starting-point for the commission of sin, which may, in its turn, be confessed, repented of, and easily expiated. With many, an indulgence is an indulgence to sin. This is deplored by enlightened Catholics themselves. And no one can be well acquainted with the condition of the lower classes in Italy, without seeing that the system of indulgences has a direct tendency to weaken the sense of moral obligation, to confuse the popular notions of Divine justice, to destroy purity of heart, and to promote a general immorality.

ROME, 5th January, 1857.

The gardens attached to the Vatican palace have but little beauty at this season. There is an utter want of taste in the manner in which they are laid out; and as gardens, they are on a level with the palace as a palace. They contain some interesting pieces of ancient sculpture; but the object of chief interest within them is the pine-cone of bronze which was originally on the summit of Hadrian's Mausoleum, which was afterwards placed as an ornament in front of the old basilica of St. Peter, and which, on the rebuilding of the church, was removed to the place it now occupies in the quiet garden of the Belvedere. It is one of the few objects in Rome which Dante has commemorated. He saw it when it belonged to the church; for he says that the face of the giant Nimrod seemed to him as long and large as the pine-cone of St. Peter's at Rome.[*]

The gardens are inhabited by a race of shuffling, pertinacious old gardeners, of the same nature as the guardians of the sculpture gallery, save that their hands are dirty with earth and snuff, instead of with snuff and dust. There is also here a tribe of cats, — black, black-and-white, brown, gray, tortoise-shell, yellow, — some half-asleep in the sun on the terrace, some snarling at each other, some prowling through the hedges, some rubbing themselves against broken marbles, some licking themselves into comfortable sleekness, and some hiding in holes in the walls. My theory concerning their existence is, that they are cardinals transmigrated, — cardinals

* *Inferno,* xxxi 59.

of the tabby order, — some with claws sheathed, some
with backs up and claws out, some lazy and well fed,
some winking and dozing here as of old on the benches
of the Sistine Chapel, some with half-shut wily eyes, —
all transformed to the similitude of what they were.
There is a sly Dominican in his black-and-white robes,
and by his side a dirty-brown Capuchin, — and there is a
demure black Jesuit lying asleep with one eye open.
Such is the transmigration of the souls of cardinals !

ROME, 6th January, 1857. The Epiphany.

Instead of going to the Ara Celi to see the procession
of the Bambino, the pleasant-looking but dirty crowd,
the bad monks, and the curious exhibition of superstition
and credulity on the part of the performers and the spectators, I went to San Luigi de' Francesi, to hear a
French preacher who has been attracting large audiences
for the past fortnight, and who, to-day, was to deliver his
last sermon, before his return to Paris.   He is the Père
Petitot, and he is said to be of most holy life.   He is the
present head, as I am told, of the Oratorians in France,
an order based on the rule of San Filippo Neri, with
certain modifications in discipline.   The audience was a
very large one, consisting mostly of French residents in
Rome, French soldiers, and other strangers.   There
were few Romans present.   The preacher had, obviously, heard that many Protestants had been attracted to
hear him ; and on entering the pulpit, he began his discourse by saying that he regarded this as the most im-

portant occasion on which he had spoken from that place, — that he was about to preach on some of the differences between Catholicism and Protestantism, and, in doing so, to address the heart rather than to exercise the reason. His voice was sweet, its tones full of pathos, and his manner direct and earnest. Before beginning, he said he desired to pray, and to have his hearers join him in prayer, for the blessing of Heaven upon his words, — upon which, the people knelt upon the pavement, and for a moment engaged in prayer. He then said that the main purpose of his sermon would be to present the consolations possessed by the Catholic in his religion, of which the Protestant was deprived; that he should do this in the spirit of love and charity, — for that without love no soul was ever won, no true convert ever made, — and that, if the heart were rendered bitter by one who desired to bring it to God, his work was not only vain, but unchristian. Then he began.

"Think, in the first place, *mes très chers frères*, of what surpassing consolation those who do not share in the Catholic faith are deprived, in not having the presence of our Lord in the Eucharist! We receive him bodily there; we know him to be there, as we know him to be in heaven; he is close to us, — in our company; he lives with us in real presence, as he lived with his apostles." He then went on to speak of the Protestant being without the consolation of a spiritual father and guide upon earth, possessed by those within the Church who rested upon his counsels and listened to his voice with the conviction of its absolute authority and truth; without the consolation of those blessed gifts of the Church, confession and absolution, so that they can never *know* that their penitence is accepted and their sins forgiven; without the consolations afforded by the Blessed Virgin, without a Mother in heaven, unto whose tender heart her children can always come to repose, who comforts them in their sorrows, and whose prayers and tears are always interceding for them; without the Saints, so that they have no communion with holy spirits, and are under the care of no holy protectors, — "not supported, as we are, by the living and acting presence of the martyrs and saints of all ages." "Take from the Sister of Charity her rosary, her Virgin, and her Saints, and see what she would become!" Without belief in a guardian angel; — "and what a belief, rich in consolation and delight, is this, — to be accompanied through life by a celestial friend! Before I came here this afternoon, I prayed to my guardian angel to direct me in what I should speak; I feel his presence with me. I prayed to the guardian angels of those who hear me that they should cause my words to reach hearts made ready to receive them." Without the consolation of praying for the dead; so that the memory of the dead is desolate. And without the consolation of the crucifix and the worship of the cross. "*Ah! mes très chers frères*, what a joy has the Christian in his crucifix! — to hold your dying Saviour in your hand, to look on your God face to face, to press him to your heart, to bathe him with your tears, to speak to him, to kiss those beloved features, and to feel his love enter into your heart with a kiss! Ah!

dear brothers who are not Catholics, let me implore you
to get for yourselves a crucifix, to gaze upon it, to bear it
with you, to place it on your pillows, and to see if my
words are not true, of the strength, the happiness, the
consolation it will give you!"

After preaching for an hour in this strain, with many
passages made eloquent by the fervor of his feeling, as
well as by skilful oratory, he said, — "I have one word
to say before I conclude, one word of logic, the only one
in my discourse. If, as I have declared, and as all
Catholics will declare with me, these consolations of
which I have spoken are the most precious that our religion affords us, — if they are what most raise and rejoice
our souls, — if they are to us the very essence of spiritual life on earth, — then I say that they are of God,
they are not man's inventions. It is not possible for
man to surpass God Himself in those things which are
the best that religion brings to us. All our happiness is
from God ; and because these are our choicest blessings,
we know them to be from Him."

It was dark before the Père Petitot had ended his sermon ; but the congregation had stayed, listening with the
utmost attention. It was thought a very beautiful and
very powerful discourse. It certainly afforded a remarkable illustration of the prevailing tendency in Catholicism
to materialize the immaterial, and to substitute the Church
for the Gospel. The step from such a sermon as this to
the worship of the Bambino, or to any lower and more
superstitious observance, if any such there be, is but a
short one. Yet it is not to be doubted that Père Petitot

laments the errors of such superstitious observances, and is a devout, and what would be called an enlightened Catholic.

——, the German sculptor, who has been long in Rome, told, the other day, a story which illustrates well the mode in which small affairs are managed here. In 1849, in the course of some excavations on the Vicolo delle Palme, in Trastevere, the bronze head of a horse, now in the Capitol Museum, was discovered, and with it the magnificent statue of the Athlete scraping himself with a Strigil, which is in the Braccio Nuovo at the Vatican. One or two fragments of other works were found at the same time, and, as the grounds of the Anician family had once occupied this portion of the city, it was reasonably believed that further excavations would bring to light other precious works of Art. The government proposed to purchase the land, but the owners, stimulated by the discoveries already made, asked a price which was considered exorbitant, and the government declined to go on with the bargain. The owners determined to continue the excavations on their own account, but the authorities at once laid an interdict on their proceeding. If the government could not have the land, they could at least prevent its being dug over! And so the matter has stood up to the present time. After a statue has been buried a thousand years or more, it matters, perhaps, but little to it that it should lie underground ten or twenty years longer; but it is of some consequence to the lovers of Art of this generation whether it be kept hidden from them or not. The chance of finding a statue after Lysippus is not to be slighted. This *Strigilatore* is supposed to be a copy in marble of the famous bronze statue by that sculptor, which was set up by Agrippa before his Baths near the Pantheon, and which was so much admired by Tiberius, that, shortly after he became emperor, he caused it to be removed to his bed-room, and another statue to be put in its place. But at this, the indignation of the Romans was aroused, and, with great clamor, they demanded that their favorite statue should be restored to them, and Tiberius was forced to yield it up, *quanquam adamatum*.*

That other relics of ancient Art, of equal worth with this, might be found in the same locality is no extravagant supposition. " The marbles of the Anician palace," says Gibbon, " were used as a proverbial expression of opulence and splendor." †   From the reign of Diocletian to the fall of the Western Empire, the Anician family was unsurpassed among the great houses of Rome, in wealth and in reputation, — and its glory expired only with the death of Boëthius, the last famous descendant of the long line of Senators and Consuls.

Modern Rome is built upon ruins. What war and fire and the ravages of barbarian conquerors left of ancient splendor, the Romans themselves, still more barbarian, — people, princes, and popes, — have conspired to destroy.

---

* Pliny, *Nat. Hist.*, Lib. XXXIV. xix. 12. The statue was then known under the name of the *Apoxyomenos*.

† *Decline and Fall of the Roman Empire*, c. 31.

Nicholas V. pulled down the magnificent tomb of one of the greatest of the Anician family, which stood in his way upon the Vatican, and only the memory of its inscriptions and its sculptures is preserved in the dry pages of the ecclesiastical annalist. Beneath the very pavement of the streets and squares of Rome lie buried treasures of Art. The words which Cicero uses, in speaking of the city, have now a double meaning: " *Quacumque enim ingredimur, in aliquam historiam vestigium ponimus.*" "Which way soever we walk, we set our foot upon some history." It was but the other day, that, as I was watching the men digging a trench for the gas-pipes near the Fountain of Trevi, I saw them turn up a handful of rust-eaten Imperial coins. In excavating for the foundation of the new column in the Piazza di Spagna, the bust of a Dacian king was found, which, after its long interment, is now placed on show in the Vatican Gallery. Of the host of ancient statues and works in marble in the museums, almost all have been discovered underground. The bosom of the earth has been, and is still, the great storehouse of sculpture. Happily, an interdict cannot be laid on all digging. The Roman gardeners, in making their trenches for cabbages or cauliflowers, will still find some long-hidden marble or turn up some broken inscription. Or, if digging be stopped, the rains will do a partial work. It was on New Year's day, as I was walking toward Rome from the Torre de' Schiavi, — near which I had been picking up bits of the ancient mosaic of the Gordian villa, laid bare by the late rains, — that I saw by the side of the road, half-washed out of the bank, a

bit of white marble. I took it up, and found that it was
part of the leg of an old statue; and a few steps farther
on, seeing a flat piece of statuary marble lying in the
cart-track by the side of the main road, I turned it over,
and found on its under side a portion of a bas-relief of
Leda, not unskilfully worked. Such discoveries as these
— worth much to one who comes from a land whose soil
is barren in carved stones — will be made by every one
who frequents the Campagna. My table is already
loaded with bits of marble, pieces of inscriptions, fragments of brick ornament, and parcels of mosaic, that I
have picked up in the fields, on my walks during this
last month.

There is many a wall in Rome made of old materials strangely joined together, — bits of ancient bricks
stamped with a Consular date, pieces of the shaft of some
marble column, fragments of serpentine, or even of *giallo
antico*, that once made part of the polished pavement of
a palace, — now all combined in one strange harmony by
Nature, who seems to love these walls, and to reclaim
them to herself by tinting their various blocks with every
hue of weather-stain, and hanging over them her loveliest
draperies of wall-flower and mosses. In one of the pre-
cepts of his "Trattato della Pittura," Leonardo da Vinci
says, " Se riguarderai in alcuni muri imbrattati, o pietre
di varii mischi, potrai quivi vedere l' inventione e similitu-
dine di diversi paesi, diverse battaglie, atti pronti di figure, strane arie di volti ed habiti, ed infinite altre cose."
" If thou wilt look at old stained walls, or at stones vari-
ously mixed together, thou shalt see on them the sugges-

tion and similitude of landscapes, of battles, of lively
actions of figures, of strange aspects of face and dress,
and numberless other things." Nor thus are the suggestions of the Roman walls exhausted. The landscapes
which the fancy discovers on them are of the Campagna
before it was desolate; the battles which one sees are
those in which the statues were hurled down, whose
broken fragments are built into the wall; and the lively
actions and strange aspects which the wandering lines of
rain and the cracking heats of the sun have traced for
the imagination upon the stones seem those of the foreign
conquerors and the frightened people in whose struggles
Rome was ruined. The whole history of the decline and
fall of the city is to be read in these unconsciously monumental walls. Out of the chance materials that offered
to his hand, the ignorant bricklayer has built up many
a memorial, on which is recorded, not in words, the fortunes of the Roman State. There is no end to the
stories on these walls. All the strange things they have
heard, the whispers, the sighs, the screams, the crackling
of fire, the shouts of soldiers, the sobs, the prayers, — all,
" and numberless other things," are to be found in their
stones, and, as Leonardo goes on to say, " by these confused things the fancy is roused to new inventions."

ROME, 20th February, 1857.

The cheap literature of Rome all passes, previously to
its publication, under priestly supervision. Indeed, no
book, no pamphlet, no placard is printed at Rome with-

out the ecclesiastical *imprimatur.* Books cannot be
entirely done away with; but the evil consequences resulting from unlicensed printing may be diminished; and
to this beneficent end the Church bends her powers, and
suppresses, alters, blots out whatever may lead her subjects astray. It is a common story, that the man who
lights the cross on St. Peter's dome, on occasion of the
illumination, receives absolution before setting about his
dangerous task. It may be hoped, that, with some equal
provision of mercy, the Church protects those of her cen-
sors whom she employs to detect what is bad in books,
and who thus generously peril their own salvation for the
sake of the common safety. The "Athenæum" came to
us the other day with the article on Milman's "History
of Latin Christianity" carefully blotted out; from the
"Revue des Deux Mondes" of the fifteenth of January,
the article on "Italie: Son Avenir," etc., is gone; and
from the "Revue" of the first of February three leaves
are cut out of the middle of Montegut's article on Miche-
let. This care in regard to what is read and what is not
read by the Romans gives special interest to certain
classes of books which are permitted, inasmuch as they
may be regarded as containing such views, opinions, and
statements as are deemed to be of importance to the people, or at least to have no vital error and no evil tendency.
One of these classes of books, and perhaps the one which
has the greatest popularity, is the literature relating to
the saints and to miracles. It takes much the same
place as the literature of quack medicines with us, —
its aim being similar, and its appeals being addressed

to that large body in every community who have more credulity than sense. The art of puffing a saint or a miraculous image for the celerity and variety of the cures effected by them has been carried to a high degree of excellence by the authors of these works.

I have here a little yellow-covered pamphlet, called " Historic Notices of the Most Holy Mary of the Child, venerated in S. Augustine at Rome." It was published in 1853, and is a fair specimen of its class. The statue which is the object of veneration stands near the main entrance to the church. It derives its name of Santissima Maria del Parto from the fact that it represents the Virgin seated with the Child standing upon her lap. Its origin is uncertain, but it is commonly attributed to the chisel of the Florentine sculptor, Giacomo Tatti, who assumed the name of Sansovino in honor of his master, and who died in 1570. The opinion of those who regard this work as being a likeness of Agrippina with the young Nero in her arms is considered to be ill founded. It appears that for many years this statue had received only that general regard which all images of the Virgin receive in greater or less degree from Roman worshippers, until, in 1820, a devout youth proposed to set up a lamp to burn before it day and night, and paid the sacristan of the church a *baiocco* and a half a day to keep it well supplied with oil. Others of the faithful soon imitated the example of this good youth, and the piety of the common people who attended the services of the church was speedily awakened toward the statue by the number of lamps and candles burning around it. The feeling thus aroused was soon quickened into enthusiastic devotion by the report of miracles wrought through the intercession of the Virgin here worshipped. Crowds gathered round the marvel-working statue. Many persons dipped their fingers into the oil of the open lamps, regarding it as of sacred virtue; and the drapery of the figure became so dirtied by the dripping of the oil, that the guardians of the church were obliged to interfere, to regulate the number of lamps that should be burned, and to suspend them beyond the reach of the worshippers. But in order that such piety should not be frustrated, bits of cotton soaked in the oil and wrapped in paper were provided for sale to the devout. Votive tablets commemorative of cures and deliverance were hung around, and offerings of money, either in gratitude for favors received or to purchase such favors as prayers would not obtain, were laid before the Virgin, until at length it was thought fit to place a money-box near the statue for the reception of these offerings. This gave rise to suspicions, which are declared to have been unjust, of the desire of the Augustinians to make money for themselves out of their good-fortune in having so powerful a statue, — but, in spite of the calumny, the money-box was not removed. So great were the crowds, and so noisy in their cries to the Virgin, that scandal followed, and the church was the scene of many irreverent displays, until the modes of worship were at length properly regulated.

Meanwhile frequent acts of grace exerted by the Virgin strengthened the reverence in which the statue was held. The first case narrated at length is that of Ger

trude Palombi, a girl of nineteen years old, who, after
long suffering from an aneurism and inflammation of the
lungs, having been brought to death's door and given
over by the physicians, was suddenly restored by being
anointed with oil from the lamps. The medical details
of her case are given at great length, and are followed,
in the usual place of the medical certificate, by a Latin
decree of the Vicariate, declaring the miraculous nature
of the cure.

The next is a still more remarkable case, owing to the
peculiar complication of disorders from which the patient
suffered, — namely, extreme pains in the stomach, an
enormous tumor on the shoulder, sciatica, convulsions,
swelling of the limbs, hemicrania, fever, paralysis, and
lockjaw! So near had she approached to death, that the
parish priest was sent for to administer the last offices
of the Church. But the girl had committed herself to
Maria del Parto, a picture of whose image was hanging
by her bedside, and at this last moment she was anointed
by her faithful attendants with oil from the lamps. She
at once fell quietly asleep, and when she awoke she declared that the Madonna, such as she was seen in the
church of St. Augustine, had appeared to her, and with
her own hand had anointed her with oil. At the same
moment all her diseases left her; she rose cured from
her bed, and the next day proceeded to the church, accompanied by her relations and friends, to render thanks
for so signal a grace. A process was instituted to investigate the case, and in 1827 a decree was issued by the
Cardinal Vicar, of which the following is a portion

" Itaque, audita relatione, viso processu, lectis testium examinibus, juribus et documentis, iis sedulo matureque consideratis, consultationibus quoque requisitis theologorum, medici physici deputati, aliorumque virorum, juxta formam Sac. Conc. Trident. sess. 25, de invocat. venerat., et reliquiis sanctorum, et sacris imaginibus, diximus, pronuntiavimus, et definitive declaravimus, *plene constare de vero insignique miraculo* a Deo opt. maximo, intercedente Beata Maria Virgine, patrato, videlicet, instantaneæ perfectæque sanationis Constantiæ Tondini a multiplici gravissimorum ac diuturnorum morborum congerie, qui eam ad obitum trahebant, cum integra·virium restitutione, nulloque crisis interventu." The authority appointed for the purpose, and speaking with all the weight of infallibility, thus declared that a true and wonderful miracle had been wrought, and an order was given that the relation of this miracle should receive the widest publicity.

So formal a confirmation of the virtue of this image naturally increased the reverence in which it was held, and numerous wonders followed rapidly from the trust reposed in the Virgin represented by it. Many of them are reported at length. One more is, perhaps, worth repeating here, because of a different kind from those which precede. Vincenzo di Gennaro had fallen asleep one summer's night, when a spark from the lamp burning by his bedside fell upon his clothes, which were lying in a heap on a chair. Flames were quickly kindled. " In a moment," says the account, " they would have seized the bed and devoured it, together with him who lay on it, sleeping in ignorance of his danger of being stifled and burned before he was aware; when all of a sudden a shake from an invisible hand awoke him. He leaped from the bed, beheld the flames, and succeeded in extinguishing them. His clothes were in ashes, — all burned, save the pocket of his waistcoat, in which was a paper containing a rag that had been dipped in the oil of the Madonna del Parto, — a substance most prone to combustion. He recognized the double favor of the Madonna, in arousing him, and in preserving him unhurt by the fire, by means of the marvellous oil!"

After the narrative of wonders has extended over many pages, the reader is called upon to admire the innumerable gifts which have been made to the image, and to regard them as proofs of the efficacy of the intercession of the Virgin worshipped under it. The gifts show that avarice yields to gratitude. Rich and poor have equally brought their offerings. Queen Maria Christina of Spain has bestowed a great chain of gold, and the wealthy Torlonias have presented many magnificent ornaments. Necklaces, bracelets, diamonds, and other precious stones attest the devotion or the hopes of their givers. The familiar definition of gratitude may be supposed to hold good in many of these cases. "Behold hung around, in silver and in gold, hearts, arms, legs, hands, feet, eyes, ears, and the rest, — and on all thou wilt read P. G. R., — *Per Grazia Ricevuta:* For Favor Received."

To such fame did the statue rise, that, in 1851, by a solemn decree of the Chapter of St. Peter, it was ordained that it should receive the honor of a coronation, the final and highest testimony of the Church to its miraculous virtues. The services connected with this ceremonial were performed by illustrious cardinals, with great pomp, with the bestowal of plenary indulgence, and with general rejoicing and concourse of the faithful. A golden crown was placed on the head of the Virgin, and another on that of her Son, on the festival of the Visitation. Since that time these wonders have not ceased.

Such is a specimen of the art of puffing, as practised at Rome. The difference between the quacks of the Papal city and those of Protestant countries is that of their professions. The ecclesiastical is more dangerous than the medical impostor.

I would not be understood as implying that many of the cases reported in this class of publications are not reported truly. The influence of imagination is undoubtedly one of the great curative powers, and faith in remedies is one of the frequent precursors of recovery. Imposture and credulity, it was long ago remarked, go hand in hand. It was one of Lord Bacon's shrewd observations, that, "although they appear to be of a diverse nature, the one seeming to proceed of cunning and the other of simplicity, yet certainly they do for the most part concur." Nor would I be understood as asserting that the processes of examination adopted in regard to the evidence of these marvels, before the dogmatic sanction of them as miracles, were careless, hasty, or unfair. I have no doubt that the testimony to the facts was ample, consistent, and honest. But there are conditions of belief, resulting from education and prepossession, which may affect the value of men's testimony upon large classes of subjects, — which may, indeed, render their testimony utterly worthless, without affecting its sincerity.

But that such a state of things should exist at the present time in Rome is a proof of the continuance there of what we are apt to suppose ceased with the Middle Ages, — that condition of general belief, and those mental habits, which gave to those ages their common appellation of Dark. The Roman people belong to the Dark Ages. Even Bacon, writing more than two centuries ago, in a passage in the "Advancement of Learning" which follows close on the sentence just quoted, could speak of the " too easily received and registered reports and narrations of miracles " wrought by saints, relics, or images, as already passed. They had " had passage for a time, by the ignorance of the people, the superstitious simplicity of some, and the politic toleration of others, holding them but as divine poesies; yet, after a period of time, when the mist began to clear up, they grew to be esteemed but as old wives' fables, impostures of the clergy, illusions of spirits, and badges of Antichrist, to the great scandal and detriment of religion."

The earnestness with which miraculous intervention is sought, the confidence in its frequent occurrence, and the ease with which stories of miracles are received, are proofs not merely of the prevalence of superstition and false notions of the nature of God, but also of a state of general opinion in which the usual laws of probability as applied to evidence no longer hold good. In a state of society in which miracles are expected to be of not infrequent occurrence, and where the antecedent improbability of such an event has no weight in determining the final judgment in regard to an interruption of the common courses of Nature, no amount of common human testimony would be sufficient to establish the fact of a miracle.   Where miracles are expected, events which bear enough of their external characteristics to be mistaken for them by the mass of the people will be easily met with.   That a man believes a miracle to have taken place in himself is no proof that one has actually taken place.   Few men are able to trace the causes of effects in their physical system, — still fewer in their mental processes and their spiritual experiences.*   The whole history of Revivals — a history which painfully exhibits the lowness of the religious spirit and character of many Protestant communities — is full of instances of

---

* In that most confidential of books, *The Diary of Mr. Samuel Pepys*, its excellent author makes the following entry, under date of 20th January, 1664-5: "Homeward, in my way buying a hare, and taking it home; which arose upon my discourse to-day with Mr. Batten, in Westminster Hall, who showed me my mistake, that my hare's foot hath not the joint to it, and assures me he never had his cholique since he carried it about him; and it is a strange thing how fancy works, for I no sooner handle his foot, but I become very well, and so continue."

The next day he writes, — "Now mighty well; and truly I can but impute it to my hare's foot."

And on the 26th of March following, he enters upon his journal, — "I never was better in my life. . . . . Now I am at a loss to know whether it be my hare's foot which is my preservation; for I never ad a fit of the collique since I wore it; or whether it be my taking of a pill of turpentine every morning."

imperceptible causes working the most extraordinary results. But because the natural causes cannot be discovered, it is not therefore to be argued that they are supernatural. Such, however, is the popular mode of reasoning, among the ignorant ; it is the mode among the Romans. From their infancy, the Romans are taught to believe that the Virgin and the Saints are not only their spiritual consolers and guides, but protectors from earthly perils, healers of bodily maladies, and guardians of worldly goods. Two plain results follow from this, — superstitious devotion, and blasphemous irreverence. The Virgin and the Saints who fail to answer the prayers that are made to them are cursed with a heartiness proportioned to the fervor of the previous petition.

It is not difficult to see to what advantage such a spirit may be turned by the priests. There are many good priests in Rome, — but not all are good. Where superstition prevails, the offerings to the Church will be large. Fear and hope open all purses.

It is not strange that the censorship is strict, nor that it allows such publications as the account of the Madonna del Parto to circulate freely.

ROME, 7th February, 1857.

This afternoon, Dr. Manning, formerly so well known in the English Church as Archdeacon Manning, delivered the first of a course of three sermons, at San Carlo al Corso. He is a man of tall and striking presence, with an intellectual head, dark eyes, and the look of an ascetic. His personal influence is great, and his reputation at Rome very high. The church was filled with a large audience. Before the service, I copied the following inscription from an altar in the right aisle : " Ogni volta che in questo altare, dedicato alla B^{ma} Vergine, sarà offerto il santo sacrifizio della Messa per l'anima di qualsivoglia fedele, Innocenzo XI. P. M. ha conceduto che venga essa liberata dalle pene del Purgatorio." " Every time that on this altar, dedicated to the Most Blessed Virgin, the holy sacrifice of the Mass shall be offered for the soul of any faithful [Catholic], by concession of Pope Innocent XI., that soul shall be freed from the pains of Purgatory."

This inscription was a favorable introduction to the sermon, which was on the honor and worship due to the Virgin as the Mother of God. Dr. Manning's simple and finished manner, his careful and occasionally poetic diction, his quiet fervor, and his fine voice, give him uncommon power as a pulpit orator. His style of thought is subtle, he is an acute pleader, and he makes much use of the forms of logical reasoning. " In strictest truth," is a phrase which he frequently uses. There was, however, no attempt in his discourse to avoid those doctrines of the Church which are most repugnant to reason and most contrary to Christianity. He spoke of the Eucharist as " the real, actual, living, breathing, palpable presence of the Lord." He spoke of the *deification* of the Saints. " Do not startle," said he, " at the word ; it belongs to them by participation in the nature of Jesus Christ." He argued, that, as the Virgin was the mother of Christ, and Christ had called us his brethren, she was

our actual mother. He urged that she deserved reparation for the past neglect with which she had been treated.
and for the scoffs of those who did not honor her. He
declared that the Church had not pronounced the doctrine of the Immaculate Conception to be *true ;* but that
it announced this dogma as revealed from Heaven,
through the Divine Spirit which dwells always infallible
in it. " I know," said he, " that it is often objected that
there is very little about all this in the Gospels. Very
little of this in the Gospels? In a spark that darts from
a burning mass there is the whole essence of fire. If
there were but one word in the Gospels concerning the
Blessed Virgin, in that word would be concentrated the
whole force and spirit of the New Testament. If I
found only the words, ' And the mother of Jesus was
there,' I should find enough to learn devotion, reverence, and worship for her. I do not forget that Origen
has said, ' No man can understand the spirit of the gospel who has not, like the Apostle John, lain on the bosom
of his Lord, and had the mother of his Lord given to
him for a mother.' " The use of this passage was skilful
and eloquent. Throughout the sermon there were many
sentences of great beauty. One expression struck me
as remarkably fine : — " The affections have a *federal* nature ; you cannot love the Lord and not love what he
loves."

Rome, 10th February, 1857.

It is one of Montaigne's claims to affection, that he
loved Rome so well. He was a member of a greater

16

church than the one which calls itself Catholic, — for he belonged to that inclusive church of the Independents in which have been numbered many Romanists, in spite of councils, synods, and decrees. How delightful is what he says of Rome! "Rome, as it stands now, deserveth to be loved, — being the only common and universal city. . . . Both French and Spaniards, and all men else, are there at home. To be a prince of that state, a man needs but be of Christendom, wherever it be seated. There's no place here on earth which the heavens have embraced with such influence of favors and grace, and with such constancy. Even her ruin is glorious with renown and swollen with glory." And as one walks up and down the Roman streets, it is pleasant and cheering to remember his adoption by the city, and how he says, that, "amongst the vain favors of Fortune, I have none doth so much please my fond, self-pleasing conceit, as an authentic bull, charter, or patent of denizenship or burgesship of Rome, which, at my last being there, was granted me by the whole Senate of that city, — garish, and trimly adorned with goodly seals, and written in fair golden letters, bestowed upon me with all gracious and free liberality."

It was in 1581 that he was thus made citizen of Rome; and the fact was recalled to me to-day by seeing in the "Index of Prohibited Books" the following entry, which still prevents his writings from having that freedom of the city which was bestowed upon their author: —

"De Montaigne Michel. Les Essais. Decr. 12 Junii, 1676."

Another instance of prohibition, curious from circumstances connected with the book itself, is that of Bacon's treatise, " De Augmentis Scientiarum." This work is in great part only a translation into Latin of "The Advancement of Learning," which was published some years previously. But as in this latter treatise there were many passages which might cause some offence to the Roman Church, Lord Bacon, desirous to give to his more important thoughts free circulation, carefully altered or omitted in the translation all expressions which he supposed could excite the active hostility of Rome. In a letter sent to King James with the " De Augmentis," he says : " I have been also mine own *Index Expurgatorius*, that it may be read in all places. For, since my end of putting it into Latin was to have it read everywhere, it had been an absurd contradiction to free it in the language and pen it up in the matter." Notwithstanding his precautions, however, the book was deemed by the ruling powers at Rome unfit for their subjects to read; and, by decree of the 3d of April, 1669, a decree still unrepealed, it was put among the prohibited books.

I have been obliged to send to Florence, this winter, for a copy of Martini's translation of the New Testament, which is in some sort an authorized Italian version. There is a general prohibition in the Index "of all versions of the Bible in any vulgar tongue, unless authorized by the Apostolic See, or published with Annotations taken from the Fathers of the Holy Church, or from learned and Catholic men." Among the one hundred and one propositions condemned as heretical in

1713, by Clement XI., in the famous bull, Unigenitus, were the two following: "That the reading of the Sacred Scripture is for all"; and "That to interdict to Christians the reading of the Sacred Scripture, especially of the Gospel, is to interdict the use of light to the sons of light, and to make them suffer a kind of excommunication." These were heretical propositions. The Church declared, and still declares, that the reading of Scripture is not for all. But Martini was Archbishop of Florence, and too good a churchman to do anything contrary to the decrees or the interests of the Church. He accordingly accompanied his version of the New Testament with an elaborate commentary, to counteract the ill effect that might be produced by the perusal of the simple text. His work met the approbation of the Pope, Pius VI., who, in 1778, granted him a brief expressive of his satisfaction in the work. This brief, prefixed to the subsequent editions of the translation, gives to them the highest sanction of the Church.

But on the 17th of January, 1820, a decree was issued by the Sacred Congregation of the Index, which contains the following words: "Sacra Congregatio . . . habita in Palatio Apostolico Quirinali damnavit et damnat, proscripsit proscribitque, vel alias damnata atque proscripta in Indicem Librorum Prohibitorum referri mandavit et mandat opera quæ sequuntur: Nuovo Testamento secondo la Volgata tradotto in Lingua Italiana da Monsig. Antonio Martini. Livorno, 1818. Idem, Italia, 1817."

I did not at first know how to account for this condemnation of a book which the Pope had sanctioned; but having by chance found here in Rome a copy of the prohibited edition which bears the imprint of Italia, 1817, I find that it is a reprint of the text alone, — the Archbishop's copious notes being omitted. The necessary inference from this is, that the meaning which Rome draws from the Gospels must be taught by commentaries, and is undiscoverable by the unassisted reader of the text. Nor is it surprising that the pure and simple words of the New Testament should be obnoxious to the Sacred Congregation, "qui damnavit et damnat, proscripsit proscribitque Novum Testamentum in lingua Italiana." One of the notes of the Florentine dignitary will show what was lost by the omission of his comments. On the words in the nineteenth verse of the sixteenth chapter of Matthew, " And I will give unto thee the keys," he says, "The keys signify supreme authority and power to govern. All that power is, therefore, here given to Peter which is necessary for ruling the kingdom of Christ, that is, the Church. One act of this supreme power is explained in the words which follow, — *whatsoever thou shalt loose,* — in which words full power is promised to Peter of loosing in general from sins, from spiritual penalties, from vows, and from all those things from which Christ himself, dwelling upon earth, could have loosed men. With the power of loosing that of binding is united, that is, of fastening sins, [*di ritenere i peccati,*] of punishing men even with spiritual punishments. This fulness of power is transferred to the successors of Peter, the Roman Popes, according to the doctrine of all times and of all Catholics."

It is an old teaching in the Church, that the Commentators are better than the Text. Luther says somewhere in his "Table Talk," that one of the Austin friars in the monastery at Erfurt, seeing that he was constantly reading the Bible, said to him one day, — "Brother Martin, what is the Bible? Let us," said he, "read the ancient teachers and fathers, for they have sucked the juice and truth out of the Bible. The Bible is the cause of all dissension and rebellion."

ROME, March, 1857.

On the slope of the Quirinal Hill, in the quiet inclosure of the convent of St. Catharine of Siena, stands a square, brick tower, seven stories high. It is a conspicuous object in any general view of Rome; for there are few other towers so tall, and there is not a single spire or steeple in the city. It is the Torre delle Milizie. It was begun by Pope Gregory IX., and finished near the end of the thirteenth century by his vigorous and warlike successor, Boniface VIII. Many such towers were built for the purposes of private warfare, in those times when the streets of Rome were the fighting-places of its noble families; but this is, perhaps, the only one that now remains undiminished in height and unaltered in appearance. It was a new building when Dante visited Rome; and it is one of the very few edifices that still preserve the aspect they then presented. The older ruins have been greatly changed in appearance, and most of the structures of the Middle Ages have disappeared, in the vicissitudes of the last few centuries. The Forum was then filled with a confused mass of ruins and miserable dwellings. with no street running through their intricacies. The Capitol was surrounded with uneven battlemented walls, and bore the character and look of an irregular citadel. St. Peter's was a low basilica; the Colosseum had suffered little from the attacks of Popes or princes, neither the Venetian nor the Farnese palace having as yet been built with stones from its walls; and centuries were still to pass before Michel Angelo, Bernini, and Borromini were to stamp its present character upon the face of the modern city. The siege and burning of Rome by Robert Guiscard, in 1084, may be taken as the dividing-line between the city of the Emperors and the city of the Popes, between ancient and modern Rome. But a wide space on either side of this line is obscure. The thousand years from the fall of the Empire to the revival of letters have left little trace of their passage either in records or in monuments. A few isolated characters and events are still held in remembrance; but even the brilliant years of Rienzi's comet-like course show only a narrow track of light, which leaves the darkness on each side but more apparent.

The whole period was one of destruction rather than of creation. The buildings of the past were perishing, and few new ones were rising to take the place of the old. The architecture of the time was almost confined to towers and to churches; but the towers have been mostly thrown down, and the churches have been rebuilt, modernized, or otherwise defaced, within the last three or four hundred years, so that their original construction is in scarcely a single instance to be seen complete. Rome was in a state of too deep depression, its people were too turbulent and unsettled, to have either the spirit or the opportunity for great works. There was no established and recognized authority, no regular course of justice. There was not even any strong force, rarely any overwhelming violence, which for a time at least could subdue opposition, and organize a steady, and consequently a beneficent tyranny. The city was continually distracted by petty personal quarrels, and by bitter family feuds. Its obscure annals are full of bloody civil victories and defeats, — victories which brought no gain to those who won them, defeats which taught no lesson to those who lost them. The breath of liberty never inspired with life the dead clay of Rome; and though for a time it might seem to kindle some vital heat, the glow soon grew cold, and speedily disappeared. The records of Florence, Siena, Bologna, and Perugia are as full of fighting and bloodshed as those of Rome; but their fights were not mere brawls, nor were their triumphs always barren. Even the twelfth and thirteenth centuries, which were like the coming of the spring after a long winter, making the earth to blossom, and gladdening the hearts of men, — the centuries which elsewhere in Italy, and over the rest of Europe, gave birth to the noblest mediæval Art, when every great city was adorning itself with the beautiful works of the new architecture, sculpture, and painting, — even these centuries left scarcely any token of their passage over Rome. The sun, breaking through the clouds that had long hidden it, shone everywhere but here. While Florence was building her Cathedral and her Campanile, and Orvieto her matchless Duomo, — while Pisa was showing her piety and her wealth in her Cathedral, her Camposanto, her Baptistery, and her Tower, — while Siena was beginning a church greater and more magnificent in design than her shifting fortune would permit her to complete, — Rome was building neither cathedral nor campanile, but was selling the marbles of her ancient temples and tombs to the builders of other cities, or quarrying them for her own mean uses.*

At the beginning of the fourteenth century, when the Popes quitted Rome for Avignon, it might have seemed as if her fortunes had reached a point of depression from which there could be no hope of recovery. But one striking feature marked this time, as it did the whole period of darkness and evil fortune, — the steady and persistent belief of the Romans in the predestined greatness of their city. If she had fallen, she would rise again. The contrast of her low estate with her remembered supremacy only quickened the anticipation of a future greatness which would far exceed the past. The

* " De ipsius vetustatis ac propriæ impietatis fragminibus vilem questum, turpi mercimonio, captare non puduit," says Petrarch, in his *Epistola Hortatoria* to Rienzi, a letter intended to be read in the full assembly of the people. " Indolent Naples is adorned with the marble columns from your temples." We have seen that much of the marble used in the construction of the Duomo at Orvieto was drawn from Rome. This explains its richness in Greek marble. See Papensor *, *Rienzi, et Rome à son Époque*, p 46

Romans looked upon Rome as the Jews regard Jerusalem, and this feeling was shared by the rest of Christendom. The tradition of authority remained long after the reality had departed, and the mere name of Rome exercised control over the imaginations of men. She was still esteemed the source of temporal as well as of spiritual power upon earth. And as she sat desolate on her hills, mumbling over her old spells, the nations still bowed down their heads before her.

Dante and Petrarch, in their various works, afford the most ample illustration of the prevalence and depth of the conviction that Rome was appointed by divine ordainment to be the centre of power upon earth. It is the basis of their political creed, and the ruling motive of their public lives. The belief, indeed, affected for centuries the politics of Europe; while at Rome itself it was clung to, amid all reverses, with superstitious bigotry, and cherished with religious zeal. But the Romans were characterized by an insolence and indolence quite as enduring as their reliance on this article of faith, and, leaving Heaven to accomplish in its own way the predestined glory of the city, they quarrelled among themselves, and carelessly watched or helped the decay of Rome.

Dante's feelings toward Rome were deep and ardent, but they were of a double nature. On the one hand was the feeling of reverence for its divinely ordered history, for its past grandeur, and for the new glory which he foresaw in its future; on the other, was disgust at its actual condition, and detestation of the vices of its rulers

and its people.* He closes a chapter of his " Convito,"
in which he has been asserting the miraculous claims of
Rome to be considered a holy city, with the words, —
" And truly I am of firm opinion that the stones which
stand in its walls are worthy of reverence, and the very
ground on which it sits is worthy beyond that for which
men praise and commend it." † But in his treatise
" De Vulgari Eloquio," speaking of the various dialects
of Italy, he declares, with vigorous emphasis, that "the
common tongue of the Romans, or, more properly, their
wretched speech, is the basest of all the common tongues
of Italy; nor is this strange, since in depravity of manners and customs they are foulest of all." ‡

* O buon principio,
A che vil fine convien che tu caschi!
Ma l' alta providenza che con Scipio
Difese a Roma la gloria del mondo
Socorrà tosto sì com' io concipio.
                    Paradiso, xxvii. 59–68.

† *Convito.* Trattato iv. cap. 6. In a letter of Petrarch's to Pope
Urban V., urging him to restore the Papal seat from Avignon to
Rome, there is a passage of similar character. Consider, he says,
whether thou preferrest to pass what time is left to thee " at Rome,
which is the very flesh and blood of the martyrs, (*quæ tota caro et
sanguis est martyrum*,) or on this rock and in this country of the
winds where thou now dwellest, — and whether thou dost not desire
to be buried in the Vatican, which of all places upon our earth is
without comparison the holiest." *Ep. Rer. Sen.* vii. 1. — There are
many other expressions of like feeling to be found in his letters. " He
who wonders that Rome is esteemed sacred," he says, " is utterly profane, and ignorant of sacred things." *Apologia,* etc.

‡ *De Vulgari Eloquio,* c. xi.

So also in various passages of the " Divina Commedia "
he displays a similar contrast of feeling : —

> " Soleva Roma che il buon mondo feo
> Duo soli aver, che l' una e l' altra strada
> Facèn vedere, e del mondo e di Dio."
>
> *Purgatorio,* xvi. 106–8.

> " Rome, that turned the world to good,
> Was wont to boast two suns, whose several beams
> Cast light on either way, — the world's and God's."
>
> CARY.

And it was this strong sense of the glory of its former
greatness that deepened the poet's grief at its present
desolation.   In the magnificent invocation to the Emperor Albert, full of earnest and impetuous feeling, he
bursts forth, —

> " Vieni a veder la tua Roma che piagne,
> Vedova, sola, e dì e notte chiama,
> Cesare mio, perchè non m' accompagne? "
>
> *Purgatorio,* vi. 112–14.

> " Come and behold thy Rome, who calls on thee,
> Desolate, widowed, day and night, with moans,
> My Cæsar, why dost thou desert my side? "
>
> CARY.

Thus in his prose and in his poetry may be traced the
opposition in Dante's mind between the ideal and the
real Rome, between the Rome of history and prophecy
and the Rome of his own time.*   She was to him the
most revered city of the imagination, and he regarded
her with a mingling of love and sad scorn, similar to that

* See, especially, *Paradiso,* c. vi.

which, deepened in intensity by personal feeling, he bestowed on his native Florence. In early life, in the natural and tender exaggeration of grief at the death of
Beatrice, he had applied the opening verse of the Lamen-
tations of Jeremiah to the desolate condition of Florence ;
in later years, he applied it, with literal directness and
the sincerity of earnest exhortation, to Rome : " How
doth the city sit solitary that was full of people ! how is
she become as a widow ! "

The number and the periods of Dante's visits to Rome
are involved in some doubt. That he went there as one
of the Florentine envoys, not long before his exile, is
certain ; and it seems likely that the news of the revolution, which rendered his return to Florence impossible,
reached him while he was still in the Papal city. In the
" Divina Commedia " there are few passages which have
to do with the outside form and look of Rome. Two
striking similes, however, are drawn from Roman objects.
The first is in the description of the Giant Nimrod, of
whom the poet says, (*Inferno*, xxxi. 58, 59,)

> " La faccia sua mi parea lunga e grossa
> Come la pina di San Pietro in Roma."

> " His countenance meseemed long and huge
> As the pine-cone of Peter's Church at Rome."

This pine-cone, of bronze, was set originally upon the
summit of the Mausoleum of Hadrian. After this imperial sepulchre had undergone many evil fates, and as
its ornaments were stripped one by one from it, the cone
was in the sixth century taken down, and carried off to

adorn a fountain, which had been constructed for the use
of dusty and thirsty pilgrims, in a pillared inclosure,
called the *Paradiso*, in front of the old basilica of St.
Peter. Here it remained for centuries; and when the
old church gave way to the new, it was put where it
now stands, useless and out of place, in the trim and
formal gardens of the Papal palace.*

But in the eighteenth canto of the "Inferno," where
Dante describes how the troops of the seducers and be-
trayers of women were scourged in opposite directions by
demons, he draws another image, of finer and more vivid
character, from a scene at Rome, of which he himself
had probably been a spectator. It was one of the most
striking sights that could have been witnessed at Rome
in that generation.

> "Nel fondo erano ignudi i peccatori:
> Dal mezzo in quà ci venian verso il volto;
> Di là con noi, ma con passi maggiori.
> Come i Roman, per l' esercito molto,
> L' anno del Giubileo, su per lo ponte
> Hanno a passar la gente modo tolto:
> Che dall' un lato tutti hanno la fronte
> Verso il castello, e vanno a Santo Pietro,
> Dall' altra sponda vanno verso il monte."

"In the abyss the sinners were naked. On this side
of the middle they came facing us; on the other side
[they went along] with us, but with greater steps: as

---

* At the present day it serves the bronze-workers of Rome as a
model for an inkstand, such as is seen in the shop-windows every
winter, and is sold to travellers, few of whom know the history and
the poetry belonging to its original.

he Romans, because of the great throng, in the year of Jubilee, have taken means to pass the people over the bridge, so that on the one side all have their faces towards the Castle, and go to St. Peter, on the other side they go towards the Mount."

The year of Jubilee, 1300, was the year to the Easter of which Dante assigns the date of his journey through the spiritual realms. The Roman Church had lost one of its chief sources of wealth, and of power to excite enthusiasm, by the loss of Palestine. The Crusades were ended, and plenary indulgences could no longer be offered to those who engaged in them. But the memory of them still dwelt in the minds of men. The seething energies of the time longed for some new outlet, and its wild and irregular impulses were cramped in the narrow spaces of European life. Men were impatient for some easy means of acquiring the assurance of salvation, and mourned that they could no longer fight their way into Paradise. Everywhere the passionate elements of society prevailed. Boniface VIII. was too able a man to allow such emotions to exist without turning them to the profit of the Church of which he was the head. The beginning of the new century brought many pilgrims to the Papal city, and the Pope, seeing to what account the treasury of indulgences possessed by the Church might now be turned, hit upon the plan of promising plenary indulgence to all who, during the year, should visit with fit dispositions the holy places of Rome. He accordingly, in the most solemn manner, proclaimed a year of Jubilee, to date from the Christmas of 1299, and appointed a similar celebration for each hundredth year thereafter. The report of the marvellous promise spread rapidly through Europe; and as the year advanced, pilgrims poured into Italy from remote as well as from neighboring lands. The roads leading to Rome were dusty with bands of travellers pressing forward to gain the unwonted indulgence. The Crusades had made travel familiar to men, and a journey to Rome seemed easy to those who had dreamed of the Farther East, of Constantinople, and Jerusalem. Giovanni Villani, who was among the pilgrims from Florence, declares that there were never less than two hundred thousand strangers at Rome during the year; * and Guglielmo Ventura, the chronicler of Asti, reports the total number of pilgrims at not less than two millions. The picture which he draws of Rome during the Jubilee is a curious one. " Mirandum est quod passim ibant viri et mulieres, qui anno illo Romæ fuerunt quo ego ibi fui et per dies xv. steti. De pane, vino, carnibus, piscibus, et avena, bonum mercatum ibi erat; fœnum carissimum ibi fuit; hospitia carissima; taliter quod lectus meus et equi mei super fœno et avena constabat mihi tornesium unum grossum. Exiens de Roma in Vigilia Nativitatis Christi, vidi turbam magnam, quam dinumerare nemo poterat; et fama erat inter Romanos, quod ibi fuerant plusquam vigenti centum millia virorum et mulierum. Pluries ego vidi ibi tam viros quam mulieres conculcatos sub pedibus aliorum; et etiam egomet in eodem periculo plures vices evasi. Papa innumerabilem pecuniam ab eisdem recepit, quia die ac nocte duc

* *Istorie Fiorentine*, viii. 86.

clerici stabant ad altare Sancti Pauli tenentes in eorum manibus rastellos, rastellantes pecuniam infinitam." * To accommodate the throng of pilgrims, and to protect them as far as possible from the danger which Ventura feelingly describes, a barrier was erected along the middle of the bridge under the castle of Sant' Angelo, so that those going to St. Peter's and those coming from the church, passing on opposite sides, might not interfere with each other. It seems not unlikely that Dante himself was one of the crowd who thus crossed the old bridge, over whose arches, during this year, a flood of men was flowing almost as constantly as the river's flood ran through below.

There is one other reference to this year of Jubilee in the " Divina Commedia." It is in the exquisitely beautiful passage, full of the tenderest feeling, descriptive of the meeting of the poet with his friend, the singer Casella, on the shore of Purgatory. † " For three months," says Casella, " for three months has the angel who brings the souls in his boat across the sea brought readily whoever wished to embark." These three months were those which at Easter had elapsed since the Jubilee began. The angel, who at other times might keep some souls waiting for their passage to Purgatory from the mouth of the Tiber, where, according to Dante's symbolical geography, all the spirits destined for Purgatory assembled, had, during this time, suffered all to enter his boat without delay, — so far did the authority of the Church

* Tosti, *Storia di Bonifazio VIII.* ii. 284.
† *Purgatorio,* ii. 98, 99.

17

extend, and such was the harmony between its earthly and its spiritual ministers in this season of rejoicing.

The castle of Sant' Angelo, beneath whose walls the crowded bridge crossed the river, had undergone strange varieties of fortune since the time when Hadrian built it for his tomb and that of his successors. Alaric, in search of hidden treasure, had burst through its bronze doors into the dark chambers in which the ashes of Antoninus Pius and Marcus Aurelius, whose names alone should have preserved it from profanation, were reposing. Theodoric the Goth had changed the despoiled tomb into a fortress. The soldiers of Belisarius had torn down the marble statues that still adorned its terraced walls, to hurl them on the heads of their besiegers. Successive Popes stripped it of its finest marbles, and carried away pilasters and columns with which to construct and ornament their new churches, — and for years it was now a fort and now a quarry, according to the needs of its possessors. The name which the castle now bears had its origin in an event, half historic and half legendary, which occurred in the year 590. Rome had been distressed by a terrible inundation of the Tiber, and this disaster had been followed by a dreadful pestilence, to which the Pope himself had fallen a victim. St. Gregory was summoned by clergy and by people to fill the vacant pontifical chair. Before accepting the charge, he called an assembly of the Romans, and, rebuking them for their sins, upon which the pestilence was a divine judgment, urged them to acts of penitence and humiliation. A day was set for a solemn procession through the city to the church of St. Peter, in the hope of propitiating Heaven. Seven processions of penitents, uttering prayers and supplications, met from various points on the way to the church. The regular clergy came from the church of St. John the Baptist, the monks from that of the martyrs John and Paul, the virgins from that of the Saints Cosmos and Damianus, the poor and the children from that of St. Cæcilia, the widows from St. Vitalis, the men from St. Marcellus, the married women from St. Stephen's. Many persons fell dead as they marched through the streets. Gregory himself walked at the head of the united bands, bearing in his hands a miracle-working picture of a black Madonna and Child, said to have been painted by St. Luke.* As the procession was crossing the bridge, the Pope raised his eyes and beheld on the summit of the Mausoleum an angel sheathing his sword. It was the angel of the pestilence, and, according to the legend, from that hour the sickness ceased through the city. The picture which the Pope was carrying still exists, and is venerated in the rich and tasteless chapel of the Borghese family, in the basilica of Santa Maria Maggiore. And still on the 25th of April in each year a procession takes place to St. Peter's, in commemoration of this miracle.†

---

* The industry of the Saint in producing copies of this portrait of the Virgin seems to have been more remarkable than his artistic skill. "Seven such pictures," says the good Benedictine Montfaucon, " exist, if I am not mistaken, in different churches of the city, — all brought from Greece." And there is scarcely a large town in Italy that does not possess one, at least, of these black Byzantine Madonnas.

† Gregory of Tours, x. 1; Nibby, *Roma Antica*, ii. 499; *Roma Moderna*, i. 401.

Not long after the marvellous vision, a little church was built on the high top of the castle where the Pope had beheld the angel. Being dedicated to the Archangel Michael, it was called by the fanciful name of *Sant' Angelo inter Nubes*, the Church of the Holy Angel in the Clouds, and by degrees its name was in part transferred to the great foundation upon which it stood.

But the church did not interfere with the use of the building as a fortress and a prison. Here, in the ninth century, the notorious and beautiful Marozia, whose lover, whose son, and whose grandson were Popes, held her seat, and tempted successive husbands with the lure of her charms, and of the hope of supremacy over Rome. Here Pope John X. was stifled to death, and John XIV. was starved, — "*famis crudelitate necatus est.*" Here Crescentius, whose character it is difficult to read through the darkness of the times, was besieged and betrayed, — and dying, left his name to his stronghold, known as the Tower of Crescentius. Here, in the twelfth century, the brave reformer, Arnaldo da Brescia, was imprisoned, and from his dungeon was led out early in the morning, before the city which had so often answered to his earnest and eloquent appeals was astir, to be burnt on the Piazza del Popolo. During successive troubled centuries, the castle was held sometimes by the enemies and sometimes by the friends of the people and the Popes, sometimes by the Popes themselves. Not long after the great Jubilee, it fell into the hands of the Orsini, who occupied it for many years, during the contentions between them and the other quarrelsome and noble houses of Rome. In those days of brutal violence, the thick-walled tombs of the old Romans were often turned into dens by their savage successors.

But let us return to the illustrations which Dante's poem affords of the condition of Rome. The ninth canto of the "Paradiso" closes with a denunciation of the greed and avarice of the Pope and the Cardinals. Their thoughts are fixed upon their privileges and their gains, "and no longer go to Nazareth, where Gabriel unfolded his wings. But the Vatican, and the other chosen parts of Rome which were the burial-places of the soldiery that followed Peter, shall soon be free from this adultery."

> " Ma Vaticano, e l' altre parti elette
> Di Roma che son state cimitero
> Alla milizia che Pietro seguette,
> Tosto libere fien dell' adultero."

On the Vatican, where the followers of Peter had been murdered in the circus of Nero, — "ferarum tergis contecti laniatu canum interirent, aut crucibus adfixi, aut flammandi, atque ubi defecisset dies, in usum nocturni luminis urerentur," — stood the church erected in honor, and believed to possess the relics, of the chief of the Apostles, but now profaned and violated by him who professed to be the successor of Peter. All around, within the city, and in the fields without its walls, were the chosen places where lay the soldiery that followed Peter, — the places where St. John and St. Paul had suffered martyrdom, and where they were buried, — the catacombs and churches full of the relics and the traditions of the faithful and persecuted disciples at Rome, now turned by licentious or infidel churchmen to the uses of worldly profit, or given over to desolation and decay. St. Peter in Paradise is filled with holy wrath at him who, claiming to be his successor, had thus forgotten the example and dishonored the memory of the founders of the church. " He who on earth usurps my place, my place, my place, which is empty before the Son of God, he has made of my tomb a sewer of blood and of filth."

> " Quegli ch' usurpa in terra il luogo mio,
> Il luogo mio, il luogo mio, che vaca
> Nella presenza del Figliuol di Dio,
> Fatto ha del cimiterio mio cloaca
> Del sangue e della puzza."
>
> *Paradiso*, xxviii. 22-26.

If the " Divina Commedia " could be expurgated, this passage would not appear in the Roman editions of the poem. But Dante is the unsilenced justiciary of Popes, princes, and people.

Nor is it only in Paradise that the evil deeds of Boniface are denounced. They are remembered against him in Hell. In the circle of the Simonists a place is reserved for him. In the very depths of Hell, where lying counsellers are punished, Guido da Montefeltro curses him from within the fire, and tells Dante the story of the evil counsel which Boniface had solicited, profited by, and undertaken to absolve. A line in his story recalls us to Rome, — where " the Prince of the new Pharisees, having a war near the Lateran, and not with Saracens or Jews, for every enemy of his was

Christian," followed the advice of deceit, and gained a triumph by " promising much and fulfilling little."

> " Lo Principe de' nuovi Farisei,
>   Avendo guerra presso a Laterano,
>   E non con Saracin nè con Guidei,
>   Chè ciascun suo nemico era Cristiano."
>   .   .   .   .   .   .
> " Lunga promessa con l' attender corto
>   Ti farà trionfar nell' alto seggio."

This " war near the Lateran " was a war with the great family of Colonna. Two of the house were Cardinals. They had been deceived in the election,[*] and were rebellious under the rule of Boniface. The Cardinals of the great Ghibelline house took no pains to conceal their ill-will toward the Guelf Pope. Boniface, indeed, accused them of plotting with his enemies for his overthrow. The Colonnas, finding Rome unsafe, had withdrawn to their strong town of Palestrina, whence they could issue forth at will for plunder, and where they could give shelter to those who shared in their hostility toward the Pope. On the other hand, Boniface, not trusting himself in Rome, withdrew to the secure height of Orvieto, and thence, on the 14th of December, 1297, issued a terrible bull for a crusade against them, granting plenary indulgence to all, (such was the Christian temper of the times, and so literally were the violent

---

[*] Dante refers to the deceit practised by Boniface: —

> " Se' tu sì tosto di quell' aver sazio
>   Per lo qual non temesti torre a inganno
>   La bella Donna, e di poi farne strazio ? "
>   *Inferno*, xix 55

seizing upon the kingdom of Heaven,) granting plenary indulgence to all who would take up arms against these rebellious sons of the Church and march against their chief stronghold, their " *alto seggio* " of Palestrina. They and their adherents had already been excommunicated and put under the ban of the Church; they had been stripped of all dignities and privileges; their property had been confiscated; and they were now by this bull placed in the position of enemies, not of the Pope alone, but of the Church Universal. Troops gathered against them from all quarters of Papal Italy.* Their lands were ravaged, and they themselves shut up within their stronghold; but for a long time they held out in their ancient high-walled mountain-town. It was to gain Palestrina that Boniface "had war near the Lateran." The great church and palace of the Lateran, standing on the summit of the Cœlian Hill, close to the city wall, overlooks the Campagna, which, in broken levels of brown and green and purple fields, reaches to the base of the encircling mountains. Twenty miles away, crowning the top and clinging to the side of one of the last heights of the Sabine range, are the gray walls and roofs of Pales-

---

* The Cardinal Matteo d' Acquasparta went, as Legate of the Pope, through Italy, scattering the Papal indulgences, and stimulating the people to take up the cross and fight against the Colonnas His laxity as General of the Franciscan Order is referred to by Dante *Paradiso*, xii. 124–6: —

"Ma non fia da Casal, nè d' Acquasparta "

His tomb is to be seen in the church of S. Maria di Aracœli, at Rome.

trina. It was a far more conspicuous place at the close
of the thirteenth century than it is now; for the great
columns of the famous temple of Fortune still rose above
the town, and the ancient citadel kept watch over it from
its high rock. At length, in September, 1298, the Colonnas, reduced to the hardest extremities, became ready for
peace. Boniface promised largely. The two Cardinals
presented themselves before him at Rieti, in coarse brown
dresses, and with ropes around their necks, in token of
their repentance and submission. The Pope gave them
not only pardon and absolution, but hope of being restored to their titles and possessions. This was the
" *lunga promessa con l' attender corto* "; for, while the
Colonnas were retained near him, and these deceptive
hopes held out to them, Boniface sent the Bishop of Orvieto to take possession of Palestrina, and to destroy it
utterly, leaving only the church to stand as a monument
above its ruins. The work was done thoroughly; — a
plough was drawn across the site of the unhappy town
and salt scattered in the furrow, that the land might
thenceforth be desolate. The inhabitants were removed
from the mountain to the plain, and there forced to build
new homes for themselves, which, in their turn, two years
afterwards, were thrown down and burned by order of
the implacable Pope. This last piece of malignity was
accomplished in 1300, the year of the Jubilee, the year
in which Dante was in Rome, and in which he saw
Guy of Montefeltro, the counsellor of Boniface in deceit,
burning in Hell.

The Pope himself died in 1303, and the Colonnas,

freed from his vindictive hostility,* pressed a claim for reparation for the losses they had suffered, before the conclave of Cardinals. Their petition has been preserved, and is an interesting document, as proving the completeness of the destruction of Palestrina, and exhibiting some of the curious fancies of the age. After suing for the restoration to them of their titles as Cardinals, they claim compensation for the ruin of their city, "*quæ totaliter supposita fuit exterminio et ruinæ,*" with its very noble and ancient palaces, "and with its great and solemn temple, which was dedicated to the honor of the Blessed Virgin, and built by Julius Cæsar the Emperor, with wide and ample steps of noblest marble, by which one might go up to the palace and temple even on horseback, and which steps were more than a hundred in number." † All these, they declare, including the palace built by Cæsar in the form of a C, on account of its being the first letter of his name, were destroyed by . the tyranny of Boniface, with incalculable loss, — for great sums of money would not rebuild them, and no reckon-

---

* The Colonnas, after the destruction of Palestrina, had fled in various directions. Those who might receive or afford them aid had been deprived, by a special bull, of all the privileges of the Jubilee. The words afford a striking instance of Christian temper: "Et qui receptabunt Columnenses eosdem, ... et qui dabunt scientes supradictis, eorum alicui vel aliquibus, auxilium, consilium, vel favorem, ... indulgentiarum hujusmodi cum non sint capaces nolumus esse participes, ipsosque penitus excludimus ab eisdem." (Tosti. ii. 288.) This was the Papal translation of "If thine enemy thirst, give him drink." What are the present pretensions of the . Church in regard to her Popes?

† Petrini, *Memorie Prenestine.* p. 429.

ing of money could restore their nobleness and antiquity.

These words in regard to the preciousness of the old buildings, from the associations which belonged to them, may be accepted as not a mere piece of rhetoric on the part of the Colonnas, to enhance their loss, but as an expression of genuine feeling. During a long period, fatal to many ancient buildings and to many monuments of past times, the Colonnas were honorably distinguished by their care and reverence for what was left of the works of the elder Romans, — and in the next generation Petrarch speaks of it as one of the glories of his friends, the Colonnas of that time, that they held their country's ruins dear.

From such a Rome as this, a Rome of wrong, violence, and bitterness, it is no wonder that Dante turned in disgust. From the real Rome he turned to the Rome of his imagination. The vision of that Rome which should bring the world into peaceful subjection, fulfilling the decrees of Heaven, and uniting divine with human authority, was a vision which consoled his exile and his solitary age, and was illuminated by his poetry and his patriotism. But there was for him also a heavenly Rome, — and to this heavenly Rome his life was but a long pilgrimage. The first gracious words that Beatrice addresses to him, at their meeting near the entrance of Paradise, are, " Thou shalt be with me forever a citizen of that Rome of which Christ is a Roman," —

" Di quello Roma onde Cristo è Romano."

ROME, March, 1857.

"From my infancy I burned with desire of seeing Rome," says Petrarch; but he was already past thirty years old, before this desire was fulfilled. In 1335, he set out from Avignon to go to Rome, not merely for the sake of seeing the city, but also to see again some of the members of the great Colonna family, whom he had known at the French Papal Court, and especially the now old, but still vigorous Stephen Colonna, the father of the chief friends of the poet. Just before his departure, he writes to James Colonna, Bishop of Lombez, then at Rome, telling him of his proposed journey, and saying, — "It passes belief how much I desire to see that city, though she be deserted, and the mere image of ancient Rome; and that I have never seen it I blame my sloth, — if it be sloth, and not necessity. Seneca, writing to Lucilius from the villa of Scipio Africanus, seems to me to exult; nor does he esteem it a little thing to have seen the place where that great man passed his exile, and where he left the bones that he refused to his country. If a Spaniard was thus moved, what do you think that I, a man of Italy, feel, not in regard to the villa of Liternum or the burial-place of Scipio, but in regard to the city of Rome, where Scipio was born and brought up, and where, victor or accused, he triumphed with equal glory; where not only he, but innumerable men of whom Fame will never be silent, have lived; — about that city, I say, one like to which there never was and never will be, and which even by its enemy was called the City of Kings? Or suppose that I were

in no wise touched by these things, how sweet is it to
a Christian soul to behold the city like to heaven on
earth, full of the sacred bodies and bones of the Martyrs,
and sprinkled with the precious blood of the witnesses
to the truth! to see the image of the Saviour venerated by the people, and his footprints in the hardest
rock, to be adored forever by the nations! to walk
round the tombs of the Saints; to wander through the
halls of the Apostles; with better cares now for companions, — the restless solicitudes of the present life
being left behind on the shore of Marseilles!"*

This passage is characteristic of Petrarch. It exhibits his somewhat stiff and rhetorical style, his love for
the past, and his reverence for the great men of ancient Rome. He had studied with enthusiasm all that
could be found written concerning them; and by his
almost unaided efforts he excited a wide interest among
his contemporaries in the learning of earlier times. He
had taken Scipio Africanus as the hero of his Latin epic
of "Africa," the poem which won the admiration of his
own age, and upon which he fancied his fame would rest.
With a scholarship really profound and liberal for the
period, he united a belief in Christianity as sincere, if
not as fervent, as his regard for heathenism, and Rome
was dear to him from its Christian associations no less
than from its pagan glories.

In a letter to the Cardinal John Colonna at the Court
of Avignon, Petrarch describes his approach to Rome.
The letter is written from Capranica, between twenty

* *De Reb. Fam. Epist.* ii. 9.

and thirty miles from Rome, the seat of Orso, Count of Anguillara, the brother-in-law of the Cardinal. Here he had been detained for sixteen days, owing to the dangers of the road to Rome. The enemies of the Colonnas were besieging all the approaches to their house, and Petrarch's letter gives a lively picture of the perilous condition of the Campagna. After speaking of the fertility and salubrity of the country,* he says, " Peace alone is wanting to it, — peace, exiled by I know not what crime of the people, what decree of Heaven, what fate, or what force of the stars. The shepherd armed keeps watch in the woods, not fearing wolves so much as plunderers; the ploughman wears a cuirass, and uses a lance as a goad for his oxen; the fowler covers his nets with a shield; the fisherman hangs his bait from a sword; and you may laugh, but even one going to draw water from a well ties a rusty helmet to the dirty rope. Nothing is safe, peaceable, or humane, among the inhabitants of these regions; but here are war and hatred, and everything like the works of devils." † The Count of Anguillara was, however, a man with whom Petrarch, if we may trust the description that he gives of him, might have been well contented to pass a fortnight; — " a lover of peace, but without fear of war, second to no one in hospitality, rigidly kind to his own people, well acquainted with the Muses, and "

---

* " *Aër hic, quantum breve tempus ostendit, saluberrimus.*" This district is now wasted by malaria. The retribution has followed the wrong-doing.

† *De Reb. Fam. Epist.* ii. 12.

(this last point may have touched the young poet) "a most elegant admirer and praiser of excellent geniuses." His wife, Agnes, the daughter of Stephen Colonna, was a woman worthy, it seems, of such a husband. "It is better to be silent about her than to say too little," says their guest; "for she is of those who are best praised by wonder and silence."

Less than two years before the date of this visit, one of the Colonnas had laid an ambush for his enemies, the then Count of Anguillara and Bertoldo of the Orsini, as they were coming into Rome to treat for peace, after long contention, with Stephen Colonna and others of his family. Their attendants were few; both the Count and Bertoldo were slain; and this was the beginning of much evil;—for before that time, in all their wars, the Orsini and the Colonnas had never slain nor wounded each other.* The memory of this treachery was still fresh in the minds not only of those who had suffered from it, but of those who feared revenge for it. Petrarch, finding how dangerous the attempt to reach the Colonnas in Rome would be, sent a letter announcing his arrival at Capranica to his friend James Colonna, asking him how he should get into the city. The Bishop speedily returned him an answer, congratulating him on his coming to Italy, and bidding him wait still a short time longer. After a day or two, — it was now the end of January, — the Bishop appeared at Capranica, accompanied by his brother Stephen. Each of them was attended by about a hundred armed horsemen, a very

---

* Giovanni Villani, *Istorie Fiorentine*, x. 220.

small number, it was thought, — for their enemies were known to have more than five hundred horse under their banners; but with this escort, and in company with these friends, Petrarch safely entered the city he had so long desired to behold.*

His next letter to the Cardinal is a very natural one. "You thought that I should write something great when I had come to Rome," he says; "and perhaps by-and-by I may; but I can write nothing now. One thing only I will say, — for it has fallen out contrary to what you supposed. You used to advise me not to come, chiefly on this pretext, — lest the aspect of the ruinous city not answering to its fame, or to my preconceived opinion got from books, my ardor would grow slack. And I, too, though burning with desire, not unwillingly put off coming, fearing lest my eyes, and the actual presence, which is hostile to great names, should reduce the idea I had formed for myself. But this presence, strange to say, diminishes nothing, but increases everything; and Rome, in truth, was greater, and her remains are greater, than I had thought." †

This is all that Petrarch tells of his first impressions of the city, and he has left no further letters concerning his first stay there. Nearly seven years passed before he visited it a second time. He was now at the height of his reputation. On the 23d of August, 1840, by a curious coincidence, two invitations reached him at Vaucluse, one from the University of Paris, the

---

* De Reb. Fam. Epist. ii. 12, 13.
† Id. ii. 14.

other from the Senate of Rome, to proceed to the respective cities to receive the laurel crown as poet. He had for a long time been desirous of this honor, and both he and his friends had used many efforts to obtain it. His fondness for the customs of antiquity, and the affectation and false taste which marked his character, had led him to set a factitious value on the ceremony, and to dwell with pleasure on the thought of reviving splendidly in himself this long extinct usage. With a blindness not uncommon to Italians in his and in our days, he did not see, that, though the old form of the ceremony might be revived, the old spirit which had given worth to it could not be called back, and that the leaves of the laurel wreath would now be but dry leaves at the best.*

* The fancies of other poets beside Petrarch had turned back with desire to the old poetic coronation. Now and then, during the century, one of the smaller cities of Italy had bestowed the laurel upon some now long-forgotten rhymer. In the first of the curious Latin eclogues addressed to Dante by Giovanni del Virgilio of Bologna, with the object of persuading him to write his poems in Latin and not in the vulgar tongue, he suggests to him that by so doing he would deserve the laurel crown, which Giovanni promises to obtain for him at Bologna. Dante, in the eclogue written in reply to that of the presumptuous Virgilio, answers, that the glory and almost the name of poet have vanished; and that, if he be crowned, it must be in his own city on the Arno, where he may cover with the leafy wreath the gray hairs once golden.

> " Nonne triumphales melius pexare capillos,
>   Et patrio redeam si quando, abscondere canos
>   Fronde sub inserta solitum flavescere Sarno ? "

And again, as all the readers of his *Paradiso* remember, near the close of the poem, to which both heaven and earth had set their hands, he says, " If ever this sacred poem may conquer that cruelty

18

Consulting his own inclination, and following the advice of his friends, Petrarch determined to accept the
Roman invitation, — and in February, 1341, set out anew
toward Rome, going first, however, to Naples, where he
desired to submit himself to an examination before King
Robert the Good, who was distinguished by his love
and patronage of letters, and whose testimony to his
fitness to receive the laurel the poet wished to obtain.
After an examination that lasted for three days, — "*triduo excussa ignorantia mea,*" — Petrarch was adjudged
worthy of the laurel, which the King urged him to accept
from his hands at Naples; but love of Rome prevailed,
and, without exciting the royal displeasure, Petrarch refused the proffered honor.   King Robert dismissed him
with letters and messages to the Roman Senate filled
with the warmest commendation.   "The royal judgment,"
wrote Petrarch, many years afterwards, "was then especially in accordance with my own; but now I do not
approve it; — love was stronger in it than zeal for the
truth."

Since the period of Petrarch's former visit, the quarrels between the Colonnas and the Orsini had been stifled
for the time by the intervention and exertions of a Papal
legate.   The poor Romans had made desperate and pathetic efforts to secure peace.   "In the year 1338," says
Giovanni Villani,* "the Romans, as if by divine inspira-

---

which bars me out from the beautiful sheepfold, I will come back to
it a poet, and will take the garland upon the font of my baptism.
Paradiso, xxv. 1-10.   See also i. 25-38.

    * *Istorie Fiorentine,* xi. 95.

tion, turned themselves to a general peace, both the nobles and the people laying aside for the love of God every offence one against the other, which was a marvellous thing." He then goes on to relate how the Romans sent ambassadors to Florence to ask for the ordinances of justice, which were made against the great and the powerful, in defence of the poor and less powerful, and for "the other good ordinances that we have, all of which were sent to Rome. And it is to be noted how conditions change; for in ancient times the Romans established the city of Florence and gave it laws, and now in our times they send for laws to the Florentines." The Romans were indeed reduced to sad straits, that they should be forced to send for laws to the city which had not lost her old character of making

> " tanto sottili
> Provvedimenti che a mezzo novembre
> Non giunge quel che tu d' ottobre fili."

During this period of comparative quiet in Rome, the two Senators were Orso, the Count of Anguillara, the former host of Petrarch, and Giordano Orsini. The latter, however, was absent from the city at the time of Petrarch's arrival, and the duty of crowning the poet devolved upon the Count. Easter Day, the 8th of April, was appointed for the ceremony. It was a holiday for all Rome, — but it was a special festival for the Colonnas; for it was the coronation not only of their friend, but of the poet who had celebrated the glories of their family. Petrarch has left a poetical description of the day. "The Capitol," he says, " was filled with a joyful murmur, and you would have thought that the very walls and the old roof joined in the rejoicing." Twelve youths, chosen from the best families of Rome, dressed in scarlet robes, opened the procession, reciting passages from the poems of Petrarch that had reference to Rome. They were followed by the poet himself, attended by six nobles in green dresses and with garlands of flowers on their heads. Then came the Senator. When they reached the Capitol, and the trumpets of the heralds were silent, and the people were still, the poet, looking down upon the throng and over the ruins of old Rome, recited a sonnet in praise of the city, and then, crying aloud, "Long live the people, long live the Senators of Rome! May God preserve their liberty!" — he knelt before the Count of Anguillara, who, with the words, "I crown virtue before all," placed a laurel wreath upon his head, amidst the acclamations of the people. Then Stephen Colonna, "than whom in our time Rome has not borne a greater man," pronounced a speech in honor of the poet, and the Senator presented Petrarch with a formal diploma, drawn out in a pedantic and elaborate style, setting forth the motives that had led to the bestowal of this honor, lamenting the decline of poetic glory, which had gone so far "that even what is meant by the name of poet is almost unknown to men, many believing the office of the poet nothing else than to make false inventions and tell lies," — and finally giving authority to him in the arts of poetry and history, "in this most holy city, which is the chief of all cities and lands, or elsewhere, to read, discuss, and interpret the writings of the ancients, and to compose new books of his own, to last, with the aid of God, through all ages." The ceremony being thus concluded, the procession was formed anew, and went through the city to St. Peter's, where Petrarch hung up his laurel wreath as a votive offering. Then returning to the residence of the Colonnas, a banquet was served, at which the Bishop of Lombez recited a sonnet, in honor of the laureate.*

The next day Petrarch left Rome, on his return. "Scarcely had I got outside the walls of the city," he writes, "with those who had accompanied me, ere we fell into the hands of armed robbers, from whom how we were freed, and obliged to return to Rome, and what a commotion there was among the people on account of it, and how under the protection of an armed guard we departed the next day, would be too long a story to tell." This little sketch of what befell him is curious enough, however, and indicates clearly the condition of the Campagna in the neighborhood of Rome.†

Rome was now dearer than ever to Petrarch. In the autumn of the next year he was again there, on his way to Naples, and we find him writing as usual to his friend the Cardinal. "Although late at night when I arrived, yet, before resting, I went to see your magnanimous father. Good God! what majesty in the man! what a

---

* This sonnet affords an early instance of the excessive hyperbole of modern Italian eulogy. It is not strange that the people of Italy gained the idea that "the office of the poet was to lie." Giacomo Colonna's sonnet begins, " Se le parti del corpo mio distrutte."

† See *Epist. de sumenda Laurea; Privilegium Laureæ; Epist. Poet.* ii. 1. *Epist ad Post.*

forehead! what a countenance! what a voice! what a manner! what vigor of mind at his age! what strength of body! He was altogether the same in appearance as when, seven years ago, I left him at Rome, or twelve years ago, when I saw him for the first time at Avignon. It is wonderful, and almost incredible, that this one man, while Rome grows old, does not grow old. I found him already half-undressed, and just going to his bed-chamber; so that, after he had made a few affectionate inquiries about you, we put off the rest till the next day. That day I passed with him, and not a single hour was spent in silence."

Stephen Colonna, the elder, was the most remarkable Roman of his time. His long life had been full of variety of fortune, and the few years that remained to him were to be more changeful than any that had preceded. Born not long after the middle of the thirteenth century, he had early entered into public life. In 1289 he was made governor of Bologna by Nicholas IV., and in 1292 was Senator of Rome. At the accession of Boniface VIII., in 1294, he was involved, with the other members of his house, in the persecution with which the Pope relentlessly pursued them. After Boniface had treacherously gained possession of Palestrina, Stephen, no longer secure within his reach, secretly fled away from Tivoli, where a dwelling had been assigned to him. He is heard of now in Sicily, now in England, now in France at the Court of Philippe le Bel, the redoubtable adversary of Boniface, — but followed always by the implacable hatred and the hostile wiles of the Pope. Sometimes orced to conceal himself, sometimes reduced to extremities of want, he never lost heart, or let his intrepid spirit sink. One day, at Arles, he fell by chance into the hands of his pursuers. "Who are you?" they asked him, not recognizing the man. He, scorning falsehood, replied, "Stephen Colonna, citizen of Rome"; and his enemies, overcome by his magnanimity and courage, did not offer to detain him. On another day, in a hard battle, when the fight was doubtful, and a great crowd of enemies was pressing round him, a stranger, who, attracted by his fame, had come to fight at his side, said to him, "Stephen, where now is your fortress?" "Here," answered he, smiling, and laying his hand on his heart. Many times, in foreign lands, he took part in the battles of his friends, unknown to either side till the battle was over. Victory seemed always to attend him, — for Nature had given him a strength of body that corresponded to his strength of soul. Often his death was reported at Rome, and then all hope for the fortunes of the Colonnas fell, for they rested on him alone.[*] At length, after many years of exile and wandering, Boniface being dead, he returned to his native city. From that time forward, for almost half a century, he held the place of the first citizen of Rome. He supported the cause of the Emperor Henry VII., the "*alto Arrigo*," and was his chief protector at the time of his coronation in 1312, when Rome was divided into two

[*] " Gloriosa Colonna, in cui s' appoggia
Nostra speranza e 'l gran nome Latino."
says Petrarch, in his tenth Sonnet.

camps, of the Emperor's enemies and friends.   Some
years later, during a time of famine and distress, when
the people rose against the existing Senator, he was
made Senator by acclamation, with Poncello Orsini as
his colleague.   And then he and Orsini, bringing out the
grain from their own storehouses into the public square,
and compelling the other nobles to do the same, distributed it to the exacting and violent people.

A family of seven sons and six daughters added to
the strength of Colonna.   All the sons were men of
more than common fortune.   The eldest, named after his
father, Stephen, was distinguished as a man of arms; *
John, the second son, was a Cardinal; and the four next
brothers were also dignitaries in the Church; while
Henry, the youngest, was a soldier.

In his old age Stefano Colonna retained the vigor of
his youth.   On one occasion, when he was nearly eighty
years old, he, with other spectators, among whom was
Petrarch, was looking on at the games and trials of
strength on horseback of his sons and other young men,
— and there was a certain "infamous" lance that no
one of them could bend, much less break.   The old man
laughingly rebuked their want of vigor, when his son
Stephen said to him, "It is very easy, father, sitting still

---

* Petrarch addressed a sonnet to the younger Stephen, on occasion
of one of his victories over the Orsini. (Sonnet 82) The poet associ-
ates his friendship for the Colonnas with his love for Laura. " A
green laurel, a noble column, have I borne in my breast, — the one for
fifteen, the other for eighteen years, — and never have I parted from
them." He calls his love for his mistress and his friends his double
treasure. (Sonnets 227 and 229)

at a window, to judge those who are working, and to run down the present with praise of the past." The ardent old soldier got up, went down to the play-ground, calling out, " Do you believe that I am not a man ? " mounted the first horse he found, put spurs to him, and, having seized the lance, broke it to splinters.* Petrarch dwells often on his kindness, declaring that the old man treated him as though he had been his own son. Once, in Rome, when there had been a quarrel between him and one of his sons, the poet relates, that, as he was walking in the afternoon with the old Colonna, he succeeded in reconciling him to his son, but that, as they were talking over the fortunes of the family, and had stopped, " leaning against that beautiful ancient marble tomb which is on the corner of the street," the old man, weeping, said, " I had hoped to leave some inheritance to my sons, but I shall be the heir of them all." † The prophetic intimation was fulfilled : one after another, all his sons died ; the glory of the house was crushed in Rienzi's short, unfruitful despotism ; and when the news of the death of his eldest son and of his grandson, fighting against Rienzi, was brought to the old man, he fixed his eyes a little while upon the ground, and then said, without a tear, " The will of God be done ! It is truly better to die than to bear the yoke of a rustic." ‡ The lonely survivor of his children and his children's children died, at length, not long before the middle of the fourteenth century.

* *Epist. Rerum Senil.* xii. 1. † *De Reb. Fam. Epist.* viii. 1.
‡ *Rerum Senil.* x. 4.

His grand figure looms up in noble and stately propor-
tions in the dusk of that dim age. In the "Triumph of
Fame" Petrarch introduces two characters of his own
time; — one was "the good Sicilian King," Robert of
Naples; the other was Stefano Colonna, —

> " Il mio gran Colonnese,
> Magnanimo, gentil, costante, e largo. "

The friendship for the poet extended to all the members of the great family. "Whoever springs from that
stock will be my master, and will also be my son," said
Petrarch. He recalls with constant pleasure his inter-
course with them. He lingers on the memory of it, and
repeats his expressions of affection. Even the cold
rhetoric of his Latin style does not conceal the warmth
of his grateful feeling. "As often as I go to Rome, I
am received more like an angel than a man." One day,
a strife having arisen in the household of John Colonna, and his people having come to blows, he became
very angry, and called before him all who were in the
house, that he might examine into the origin of the
quarrel. Each man was sworn in turn to tell what he
knew of it; the oath was administered even to his brother, the Bishop of Luni; but when Petrarch came to take
the oath, and had already put out his hand, the Cardinal
drew back the volume of the Gospels, saying, "Your
simple word is enough." * In a letter to the Cardinal,
the poet brings to mind the long walks and conversations
he had had with him in Rome, and his recollections have

* De Reb. Fam. Epist. v. 2.

a pleasing kindliness of tone. "We often used," he says, " when we were tired with walking through the immense city, to stop at the Baths of Diocletian, and sometimes to mount up to the roof of that once most magnificent building. The healthful air, the open prospect, the silence, and the votive solitude, drove away all thought of affairs and care. There was no talk of family concerns, none of the republic, which to have wept for once is enough, the fragments of whose ruins were before our eyes as we sat there. Much of our talk was of history, in which it seemed that I was more skilled in the ancient and you in the modern times; much, also, of that part of philosophy which instructs in morals; and sometimes of the arts, their inventors, and their principles." The view which these friends saw, as they sat together on the grass that covers the ruinous vaults of Diocletian's Baths, was not greatly different then from what it is to-day. The yellow wall-flower lit up with its gold the brown fissures of the old walls, and the cypresses threw down their slow and melancholy shadows over the sunlit ruin. Far off, the snow touched the gray summits of the Sabine mountains; Tivoli sparkled on its olive-covered hill; while on the other side, the great temple of the Alban Jove, yet undestroyed, looked down from its topmost crest of rock. Towers, which are now ruins, the sheltering-places of sheep and shepherds, were then seen scattered over the Campagna, little destructive strongholds, the seats of robbers who watched travellers going in and out of the city, regarding them as the flocks that they were to fleece. But in our days, with one part of

Diocletian's Baths turned into a church as bare as it is inappropriate, with another portion given up to convent buildings and cloisters, and with the remainder occupied as a magazine of forage for the French troops, there is little remaining venerableness about the mighty ruin. Michel Angelo's genius was ill employed in turning the halls of a luxurious bath-house into the aisles and transepts of a Carthusian church ; and the French, who, in the course of this century, have done so much to preserve the ancient buildings of Rome, might well have found some fitter place for storing their straw and grain.

In Petrarch's time, however, the Romans were even more indifferent to their city than they now are, and more wantonly destructive of its old remains, much as is done in the way of destruction (by restorations, so called) at the present day. " Who," asks Petrarch, " are more ignorant of Roman things than the Roman citizens? I say it unwillingly, but nowhere is Rome less known than in Rome itself, — in which I mourn not only for the ignorance, but for what is worse than ignorance, the flight and exile of many of the virtues. For who can doubt that Rome would instantly rise again, if she but began to know herself?" *

Petrarch's interest seems to have been divided in very equal measure between the remains of the heathen city and those of the early Church and the first Christians. In naming over the places in the city he had seen, he begins with a list of those which had interested him from their associations with classical times, and ends with a list

* *De Reb. Fam. Epist.* vi. 2.   See also *Poet. Epist.* ii. 5, 13.

of those which were sacred to him as the scenes of famous events in the history of the Church. Here was the Cave of Cacus; here the way infamous as that along which the wretched Tullia drove; here was the bridge from which the brave Horatius leaped into the river; here was the Tarpeian Rock; here the Curtian Gulf; here Cæsar triumphed, and here he died; here were the Portico of Pompey, the Column of Trajan, the Temple of Peace, the Tomb of Hadrian; and here were the horses of Phidias and Praxiteles, the marble bearing witness for so many centuries to the genius of the artists. But here, too, was the place where Christ met his flying vicar; here Peter was slain on the cross, and here Paul was beheaded; here Lawrence spoke, and made a place at his side in the tomb for Stephen; here John despised the boiling oil; and here Agnes, living after death, forbade her friends to weep. — These were the localities which he had sought out and visited in Rome. They are mostly familiar to the modern traveller, but at that time there was rarely a pilgrim to the holy city who cared for any but its Christian associations. Petrarch was one of the first to arouse the modern interest in classic characters and events, — and the study of the antiquities of Rome as a science may date from the time of his visit. Since the period of Julius II. and Leo X., of Michel Angelo and of Raffaelle, the classical antiquities have been investigated, indeed, with far more zeal than the Christian, and almost to the exclusion of the latter. Men have been more interested in the stories of the founders of Rome than in the stories of the founders of our faith. But the

fables taught as doctrines or received as facts by the Roman Church held a large place in Petrarch's imagination.   His critical skill had never been directed to the
examination of their evidences.   He recalls, for instance, the old and fanciful fiction, that the body of St.
Lawrence in his tomb moved and made room for the
bones of St. Stephen, when they were brought from
Palestine, to be laid at his side.   In a poetical epistle
addressed to Pope Clement VI., urging him to restore
the Papal seat to Rome, he presses upon the Pope the
sacred claims of the city, from its holy relics and its
holy places ; — relics, among which were the footprints
of Christ left in the hard rock ; the face of the Saviour
impressed on a woman's kerchief; the cradle in which
the Author of all things lay asleep, Mary gently hushing
him ; —

> " Lac quoque vel puero optatum, vel virginis almæ
> Læve puerperium; puraque ex carne recisam
> Particulam infanti; preciosaque fragmina vestis,
> Et custoditos in secula nostra capillos." *

---

* *Epist. Poet.* ii. 6.   The superstitions of the fourteenth century are
the superstitions of the nineteenth.   Any one who has spent Passion
Week at Rome will remember that one of the chief ceremonies of the
time is the exhibition of the relics at St. Peter's.   It is repeated three
times during the week.   One of those relics is the kerchief of St.
Veronica, on which the likeness of the Saviour is supposed to have
been miraculously impressed.   The reverential kneeling of the crowd,
their silence, and the stillness through the usually noisy church, render this exhibition one of the most striking scenes of this week of
stage effects.   In a little book entitled *I Sette Viaggi di nostro Signore*, of which the twelfth edition appeared in Florence in 1851, the
popular story of this marvellous likeness is told.   St. Veronica was
a noble woman of Jerusalem, whom our Lord healed of a flowing of

It was not only through her relics that Petrarch sought to awaken the feeling of the Pope toward Rome; he ap-

blood. She became the friend of the Virgin. On his way to Calvary, the Saviour sunk under the weight of the cross before her house. She, compassionating him, took a veil of linen from her head and gave it to him to wipe the sweat and dust from his face. His likeness was in this act miraculously impressed upon it. "It is the established opinion that St. Veronica handed this kerchief to the Saviour folded in three folds, and that his likeness was impressed on each, — for there are three originals venerated in our time in three places: the first in St. Peter's at Rome, called the *Santo Sudario;* the second in Andalusia, the third in Jerusalem." It appears that St. Veronica took the *Santo Sudario* to Rome by order of Tiberius, to cure him of the leprosy, — and that she died at Rome, and was buried in St. Peter's. I have a copy of the *Santo Sudario* stamped upon silk, and, accompanying it, a formal attest, under the seal of the authorities of the Church, that it has been compared with and applied to the original. In regard to another of the relics referred to by Petrarch, the *particula recisa,* there was a treatise published in Rome, with the approbation of the Holy Office, in 1802, of which I have a copy, entitled *Narrazione Critico-Storica della Reliquia Preziosissima del Santissimo Prepuzio di N. S. Gesù Cristo, che si venera nella Chiesa Parrocchiale di Calcata, Diocesi di Civita Castellana.* The whole story, and the philosophical discussions connected with it in regard to the resurrection of the body in its completeness, are of a very remarkable character, and one of the most curious examples which even the literature of the Roman Church affords of the abuse of sacred thoughts and names, and the debasing of a spiritual religion to a materialism as gross as that of pagan times. In Petrarch's day, this relic was venerated at St. John Lateran. It was stolen in the Bourbon's sack of Rome, lost for a term of years, and then miraculously rediscovered near Calcata, a little town twenty-seven miles from Rome, where it has ever since been the object of special veneration and the agent of numerous miracles. The canons of the Lateran long ago tried to recover it; but its will, as shown by miracle, was to remain at Calcata. Five Popes have issued briefs relating to it, and a list is given of thirty authors who have treated of it, from St. Thomas Aquinas downwards.

pealed to his sympathies for her neglected and ruinous churches, churches that had once been the glories of the sacred city. "As many as my churches were, so many are now my wounds." "Look at the temples of God, built with great labor, how they tremble, falling to ruin; the high altars, heaped with no treasure, and seldom smoking with incense, are silent; see how rarely a guest enters the inner places, and in what mean raiment the priest tends the shrine." *

The great church of St. John Lateran, "the mother and head of all the churches of the city and the world," — "*mater urbis et orbis*," — had been almost destroyed by fire, with its adjoining palace, and the houses of the canons, on the Eve of St. John, in 1308. The palace and the canons' houses were rebuilt not long after; but at the time of Petrarch's latest visit to Rome, and for years afterward, the church was without a roof, and its walls were ruinous. The poet addressed three at least of the Popes at Avignon with urgent appeals that this disgrace should no longer be permitted, — but the Popes gave no heed to his words; for the ruin of Roman churches, or of Rome itself, was a matter of little concern to these transalpine prelates.†

For years, indeed, the burden of Petrarch's public correspondence is mourning for the deserted city, longing for its restoration, for the return of the Head of the Universal Church to the proper seat of universal dominion,

---

* *Epist. Poet* ii. 5, and i. 2.

† See, beside the poetical letters already cited, to Clement VI. and Benedict XII., the prose letter to Urban V. *Epist. Rer. Sen.* vii. 1.

and aspiration for an independent Italy, of which Rome should be the central glory and power.

He lived long enough to see the Popes return to Rome, to behold the tide of pilgrims once more turn toward the no longer solitary city, the stream of tribute once more flow into Italian channels. But he lived long enough to see also that the return of the Popes had brought back little vitality to the shrunken veins and disordered faculties of Rome. The vile impieties and impurities, the violence, the cheatings, the perjuries, which he had so often rebuked and denounced at the Court of Avignon, continued undiminished at the Court of Rome. Something more than the Papal presence was needed to purify and restore the city, and more than Papal power was required to make Italy independent. Petrarch died in 1374, and Rome, five centuries after he last saw her, scarcely fulfils the prophetic visions of his imagination.

ROME, 6th March, 1857.

When Augustus was at the height of his power, he constructed a mausoleum for the burial-place of himself and of his family. Upon a broad base of marble, inclosing vaulted tombs, was raised a mound of earth covered to its summit with evergreens. On the top was a statue of the Emperor. Five years after it was built, its doors were for the first time opened to receive the ashes of the young Marcellus.

" Quantos ille virûm magnam Mavortis ad urbem
Campus aget gemitus' vel quæ, Tiberine, videbis
19

Funera, quum tumulum praeterlabere recentem!

.   .   .   .

.   .   .   .   Manibus date lilia plenis."

Here, too, was Agrippa buried ; and hither, at length, the body of Augustus was borne on the shoulders of Senators, and, having been burned, its ashes were placed within the tomb.   There was a man of praetorian rank, says Suetonius, who swore that he beheld the figure of Augustus rising from the flames and ascending to heaven.

For a considerable time the Mausoleum continued to be the burial-place of the imperial family.   After long exile, the ashes of the great Agrippina, granddaughter and mother of an Emperor, were placed here by her wretched son.   Some time in the fourteenth century, the *cippus* of marble which had held her cinerary urn was discovered, and it is now to be seen standing in the court-yard of the palace of the Conservatori on the Capitol. It bears an inscription striking from its condensed sim-plicity : —

OSSA

AGRIPPINÆ · M · AGRIPPÆ · F

DIVI · AUG · NEPTIS · UXORIS

GERMANICI · CÆSARIS

MATRIS · C · CÆSARIS · AUG

GERMANICI · PRINCIPIS

After Hadrian built his more splendid mausoleum, the earlier one was no longer used.   When the Goths, under Alaric, sacked the city, they did not spare the habitations of the dead, but scattered their ashes and rifled them of whatever precious objects they might contain.   " He that .ay in a golden urn," says Sir Thomas Browne, " was not like to find the quiet of his bones." During the gloomy centuries of the fall of Rome, the Mausoleum became ruinous, and at length was seized upon by the Colonnas, and held by them as a fortress during long years of intestine violence and civil broils. At one time the enraged Romans got possession of it and attempted to destroy it utterly; but the solid masonry of the base resisted their attempts, and, being retaken by the Colonnas, afforded them for a period longer a secure stronghold, from which they might issue forth at will on their freebooting excursions.

The old walls still stand, but so surrounded by close-packed houses, that but little of the ancient structure is to be seen. The central area, in which were the tombs of the Cæsars, is now hollowed out into an open amphitheatre, round which are ranges of seats to accommodate the common people of Rome, drawn thither in summer-time by the attractions of circus-riders or of Policinello. The dirty stairway which leads to the upper benches is lined with various marble slabs, bearing modern inscriptions. They are alike in character, — and one of them runs as follows : —

CESSA
LA LOQUACE TROMBA DELLA FAMA
OVE NON GIUNGE IL NOME
DI
GIOVANNI GUILLAUME
SUPERBO FRENATORE DI DESTRIERI
CUI STRAORDINARIAMENTE
PLAUDIVA LA CITTÀ DEL TEBRO
NELL AUTUNNI MDCCCLI
E MDCCCLII.

Such is the contrast between ancient and modern Rome! "Here's fine revolution, if we had the trick to see't." "Why may not Imagination trace the noble dust of Alexander, till he find it stopping a bung-hole?"

ROME, 18th March, 1857.

During the few months in 1848-9 in which Rome called herself a Republic, an illustrated paper was issued daily, except on feast-days, entitled "Il Don Pirlone, Giornale di Caricature Politiche." It was of the most liberal stamp, and turned its ridicule against the Pope and the *papalini* of every class. It came to an end when the French occupied Rome, and since that time it has become exceedingly scarce, as no citizen of Rome could with safety to himself keep open possession of caricatures so pointed and satire so merciless as its pages exhibit. It has, however, not merely a political, but also an artistic interest; and its illustrations, beside throwing light upon the popular feeling and spirit, show as well the instant effect of freedom in giving life and vigor to the expressions of Art.

The utter sterility and impotence of mind which have long been and are still conspicuous at Rome, the deadness of the Roman imagination, the absence of all intellectual energy in literature and in Art, are the necessary result of the political and moral servitude under which the Romans exist. Where the exercise of the privileges of thought is dangerous, the power of expression soon ceases. For a time, — as during the seventeenth century in Italy, — the external semblance of originality may remain, and mechanical facility of execution may conceal the absence of real life ; but by degrees the very semblance disappears, and facility of execution degenerates into a mere trick of the hand. The Roman artists of the present time have not, in general, the capacity even of good copyists. They can mix colors and can polish marble, but they are neither painters nor sculptors.

Living surrounded by the noblest works of classic Art, constantly frequenting a school in which Raffaelle and Michel Angelo are the teachers, they have not the power even to imitate correctly the great works of the past, much less to create anything of their own. This wretched impotence cannot be the result of national or natural deficiency. The Italians are of the same race as their predecessors ; the climate and soil of Italy are the same now as formerly. But in the days when Italy contained great men, capable of great works, the political life of the people had not ceased, and the authority of the Church had not penned up their minds within its narrow walls of creed. Florence, which, during a period of three centuries of political turbulence and activity, produced a succession of the most distinguished poets, historians, and artists, has not, during the last two hundred years of political servitude, given birth to one genius of the first order. A modicum of liberty is essential for the development of literature and Art. When political and spiritual despotism combine, a vacuum is produced in which thought and imagination die out, and all the qualities of manly character dwindle and decay.

But a little breath of liberty is sufficient to revive them; and these numbers of " Il Don Pirlone " which are lying before me are of especial interest as showing how quickly imagination exhibited itself, and expression became vigorous, even here, in this stagnant Rome, when for a moment men felt the exhilaration of freedom. There is more power in the hasty illustrations of its daily issue, more truth, more genuine feeling, than in the contents of all the modern galleries and studios of Roman artists put together.

Take, for instance, the illustration in the number for the 21st of May, 1849, entitled " Un Matrimonio Segreto." Within the walls of a church, above whose altar may be read the legend, " *Ad minorem Dei gloriam,*" are seen a bride and bridegroom kneeling at a desk, before which stands the Pope, pronouncing the blessing on the marriage. The bridegroom is a figure in military uniform, but his head is that of the Gallic cock, and on his crest hangs the imperial crown; the bride, with a woman's fair form in flowing robes, but with the double head of the Austrian eagle with rapacious beak and cruel eye, is reaching out her beautiful hand to receive the wedding-ring. On the desk, in place of the sacred emblems, are carved a skull and cross-bones, an axe and a whip. There is no classic formalism in this picture. Its meaning and its lesson are plain.

Or look at the issue of the next day. On a wide plain is spread a broad sheet, at the head of which stand

the words, " *Trattato del '15*," " Treaty of 1815," — over
which a comic figure of the Emperor of Austria, with a
headsman's axe at his side in place of a sword, and with
folded arms, is striding with great paces. At each edge
of the broadside are seen the words, " *Confini Austriaci*,"
" Austrian boundaries," and underneath the picture is
read, "*Facciano pure Ungheresi, Italiani, ma qui saremmo
sempre Noi l' Imperatore*," " Let the Hungarians and the
Italians do what they can, on this we will forever be
Emperor." There is no lack of fresh invention in a
picture like this.

On the 29th of May appeared a caricature still more
humorous. It is called " Effetti d' Impressione." One of
King Bomba's timorous soldiers, in the mask and slippers
of Pantaloon, is seen seated at table about to take a solitary meal. But his attitude and face express the utmost
consternation ; for all around him, before his bewildered
eyes, appears the terrible name Garibaldi. It is on the
wall, on every beam of the ceiling, on the tiles of the
floor, on the leg of the table, on the back of the chair,
on an old portrait ; — it is stamped on the loaf, it is in
the wine, on the blade of the knife, and the wasps buzz-
ing round the unprotected head bear it on their wings.
Nothing but Garibaldi, — the name alone of the patriotic
popular leader striking terror into the cowardly assailants
of Rome.

But on the 1st of June appeared a picture of intense
dramatic energy and truth. That it is a picture which
presents an unfair view of character and history, and contains the essence of Mazzinian spite, detracts in no degree

from its force. It is called "The Wandering Jew." Flying to the verge of Europe, where the Atlantic washes the shores of Portugal, is seen the tall figure of the unhappy Carlo Alberto, driven by skeleton ghosts, over whose heads shine stars with the dates 1821, 1831, 1848. In the midst of the sky, before the fugitive, are the flaming words, "*A Carignano* * *Maledizione Eterna!*" "Cursed be Carignano forever!" — to which a hand, issuing from the clouds, points with extended forefinger. The grim and threatening skeletons, the ghosts of those whom Carignano had betrayed, the tormented look of the flying King, the malediction in the heavens, the solitude of the earth and the sea, display a concentrated power of imagination rare in Art. It is a picture that avenges many wrongs, — and, when read by the light of Carlo Alberto's death, and with the remembrance of the misinterpretations and confusions which have wrought such woe for Italy since 1849, the indignation and the hate which its aim is to excite turn to the deepest pathos and compassion.

But the engraving which appeared on the 13th of June was the one of the whole series which excited the deepest feeling at the time of its publication, and is, perhaps, unsurpassed in the display of imagination and in fulness of suggestion. The sale of the number containing it was so large, that the first issue was speedily exhausted, and a second impression scarcely satisfied the popular demand. The Pope is beheld celebrating Mass. In place of the attendant priest is seen Oudinot, the gen-

* Carlo Alberto bore the title of *Principe di Carignano* before he became king.

eral of the French forces, kneeling on the step of the altar, holding up the pontifical robe. Around are standing military officers, and behind them is a file of bayonets. The bell of the Mass is in the shape of an imperial crown. The Pope is just raising the consecrated wafer, — but the Christ of the crucifix upon the altar has detached his arms from the cross and covers his face with his hands, as if to shut out the sight of the impious sacrifice. Lightnings dart from the cross, and a serpent raises his hissing head from the cup that should hold the blood of the Lord. The candles on the altar take the form of bayonets. Beneath the picture are the words, " *Ha incominciato il servizio colla messa ed ha finito colle bombe,*" "The service began with the Mass and has ended with Bombs." The minor details of the design fill out its meaning, and add a cumulative force to its satire.* The drawing is hasty and inaccurate, but vigorous ; the draftsman has made his thought clear to whoever has eyes.

The French took possession of Rome on the 2d of July, 1849, and on that day " Il Don Pirlone " appeared for the last time. His spirit had not abated with the

---

* Thus, the soles of the boots of General Oudinot, seen as he kneels, bear, one the words, "*Articolo V. della Costituzione,*" — the other, "*Accomodamento-Lesseps*"; thereby representing him as trampling upon the Constitution of the French Republic, the *Constitution-Marrast*, whose fifth article contained the following words: " *La République française n'emploie jamais ses forces contre la liberté d'aucun peuple,*" — while at the same time he tramples upon the arrangement entered into with the Roman Triumvirs on the 31st of May, by M. de Lesseps, the French Minister, in the spirit of the article just cited.

fall of Rome. A naked female figure, with the cap of liberty upon her head, is seen lying, apparently dead, upon the ground. Near by stands a dunghill cock crowing vociferously, while a man in a general's uniform is engaged in throwing earth upon the corpse. The words with which the design is accompanied have a sting, the point of which the French may well have felt on that day, and which has not lost its sharpness even yet: — " *Ma, caro Signor Becchino, siete poi ben sicuro che sia morta ? ?* " " But, dear Mr. Gravedigger, are you quite sure that she is dead ? "

One closes the pages of " Don Pirlone " sadly, — for they end with the end of liberty in Rome. They illustrate not merely the course of events and the popular feeling of the time, but, on a small scale, they show the working of eternal principles, and explain the degeneracy of modern Italy. French soldiers and Italian priests have ruled Rome since the summer of 1849. The grave of the Republic was the grave of much more than a form of government. From such graves there is in time a resurrection.

ROME, April, 1857.

The fourteenth century was at once the evening of the Middle Ages and the dawn of the Renaissance in Italy. Dante stands at its beginning, Boccaccio at its close, marking the separation between the old ideas and the new. Never was a book more in earnest than the " Divina Commedia," — rarely one less so than the " Decameron." The new era is inaugurated with a laugh, — but it is a

laugh at once conscious and ironical. The invisible and
the spiritual were losing their hold over the imaginations
of men, while the visible and the material were continually gaining a larger share in the desires and the belief
of the age. Faith in God and in Christ, in heaven and in
hell, in virtue and in retribution, faith even in the Church
and in the future regeneration of Italy, exists in full
strength at the beginning of the century; but as the
century advances, faith disappears, and infidelity looks
out even from under the cowl of the monk.

The gloom of the Dark Ages was breaking away.
Those ages had been marked by the excesses of rude
passions, by intensity of feeling, by sincerity of expression, and by capacity of hearty and permanent enthusiasm. But as they closed, passions were becoming
subjected to the control of manners, expression was
losing its force under the relaxation of refinement, enthusiasm was yielding to indifference. The rough sin-
cerities, the hard fights, the hearty loves and hates, the
coarse life, the brilliant shows, the long romances of
feudalism and chivalry, were drawing to an end. Force
of arm and force of soul were exhausted by long effort.
Weakness was gaining a victory over strength. The individual was becoming less absolute, less distinct, absorbed
more and more into the general life, — while the community was increasing its resources, and developing those
arts and appliances of modern civilization which depend
on the combination of many different elements in one
compact mass.

As the fifteenth century advanced, Italy was neither

quiet nor at ease; but her disturbances were not the result of the conflict of moral principles, or the clash of personal passions. There was a general aimless restlessness. A hundred years before, it had seemed as if there were still a possibility of the existence of an Italian nation, still a chance for community of national sentiment and effort, still a hope of union for the preservation of Italian freedom. But the scattered fires of liberty went out one by one, or were put out by those who dreaded their flames. The old hopes died away. Even the old hereditary party-hatreds became extinct, for no men were left capable of nourishing them. Civil wars, carried on by independent bands of mercenaries in the interest of the prince or tyrant who could pay them best, took the place of the struggles of rival states, and of the battles of citizens fighting for what they themselves held dear. Indifference to the higher things of life had gained possession of Italy. Even trouble and misfortune failed to rouse her to energy. She had lost the capacity of moral suffering,[*] and she sought relief from harass in self-forgetfulness among the delights of sensual enjoyment.

The Church no longer exercised its ancient authority over the imaginations of men. Its thunders had become empty voices. The Papacy itself was in dispute. At

---

[*] " Cette incapacité de souffrir moralement, qui deviendra de plus en plus le trait de l'Italie, et la cause permanente de son esclavage." E. Quinet, *Les Révolutions d'Italie*, ch. ix.

This eloquent and imaginative book contains many striking and profound reflections upon Italian history and character.

the opening of the fifteenth century, Boniface IX. was Pope in Rome, Benedict XIII. at Avignon. A few years later, there were three rival Popes, each claiming to be the true successor of Peter and the supreme ruler of the faithful, each denouncing his opponents with threatenings of divine vengeance in the bitter language of human wrath. The popular reverence for the sacred office, rudely shaken by such contests, was weakened still further by the characters of the rival prelates. The lives of the highest dignitaries of the Church were infamous with crime. Balthasar Cossa, known as Pope John XXIII., was better known as pirate, tyrant, adulterer, and liar.* The vices and crimes of the higher clergy were paralleled on a lower scale by those of the inferior. " If any one is lazy, if he abhors labor, he flies to the priesthood." " The priests live more after the doctrine of Epicurus than of Christ." Such was the contemporary testimony. But the vices of the clergy excited less indignation than ridicule, and there is no completer proof of the deadness of moral feeling in Italy than that she made jests of the immoralities of her

---

* When, on the 25th of May, 1416, he was formally deposed by the Council of Constance, one of the articles of the act of deposition charged him with being " pauperum oppressor, justitiæ persecutor, iniquitatum columna, Simoniacorum statua, carnis cultor, vitiorum fex, a virtutibus peregrinus, infamiæ speculum, et omnium malitiarum profundus admonitor; adeo et in tantum scandalizans ecclesiam Christi, quod inter Christi fideles vitam et mores cognoscentes vulgariter dicitur Diabolus incarnatus." Yet in a few months Balthasar was restored to the dignity of the Cardina'ate. The pretensions of the Church could hardly stand firm against such blows levelled at them by its own high Council.

priests, and turned away indifferent at the profanation
of her altars.

As confidence in the ministers of the Church was lost,
so also departed regard for what they taught. When
Braccio Montone, the leader of a free company of
troops, had reduced Martin V. to his power, he was
charged with having boasted that he would make the
Pope say six masses for a bit of silver. " Six masses,"
replied he, " for a bit of silver ! I would not give him
a bit of copper for a thousand." The illusions which
had gathered round the Church were dispelled, — and
the ties which now bound the Italian people to the
Papacy were those of worldliness rather than of religion.
That ecclesiastical sway should extend from Italy over
the world was a matter of national ambition and pride.
The Italians remained attached to the Church because
the Pope had his seat in Rome. But the services of
the Church were neglected, and the examples which it
held up for imitation disregarded. The time was not
propitious for saints. So far did the indifference to matters of religion extend, that even heresy died away; for
there was no rebellion against doctrines which were not
believed, but held with mere formal acquiescence. On
feast-days, when there were great shows, or during periods of calamity, the churches were frequented ; but even
the lingering superstitious reverence for Mass and office
did not succeed in filling them at common and regular
seasons. As the century advanced, the prevalent un-
belief deepened into irreverence. In 1443, that clever
and dissolute intriguer, Æneas Sylvius, who himself was

Pope but fifteen years afterwards, gives the character of
the times in a sentence in one of his letters. " We all,"
be wrote, " have the same faith with our temporal rulers.
If they worshipped idols, we also should worship them.
If the secular power should urge it, we should deny not
only the Pope, but Christ himself. Charity is cold;
faith is dead." Faith is dead, and the future Pope sings
the requiem over her body.

The force of national character declined in corresponding measure with the decay of faith. It is only
when men in this world are in conscious spiritual relation with another, that their characters acquire dignity
and strength, and their works possess enduring vitality.
The period of original creative power seemed to be at
an end in Italy ; for the capacity of spiritual energy and
of enthusiasm was almost extinct. In an age of indifference and pleasure-seeking, great achievements may be
admired, but will not be imitated. The cathedrals of
Venice, of Siena, of Orvieto, the church of Assisi, the
chapel of the Arena at Padua, were built and adorned by
men whose souls were warmed into fervor by the coals
upon the altar of sacrifice. Cathedrals, churches, and
chapels such as these were henceforth to be impossible.
Such genius as was left — and genius lingered on in Italy
for nearly two centuries longer — was to occupy itself in
works which had their source, not in the fresh fountains
of the imagination, but in currents derived through newly
opened channels from the past. The fifteenth century
was the first of the centuries of imitation. The Renaissance, the re-birth of the old life of the world, began.

In poetry, in scholarship, in painting, sculpture, and architecture, men set themselves to copy the style of ancient times. The masters of the ancient world were made the despots of the modern.

This spirit of dependence on the past, which had its origin in deep-lying moral deficiencies, was increased and fostered by certain external and seemingly fortuitous circumstances. Since the middle of the twelfth century, knowledge of the excellence of classic Art had been slowly increasing in Italy. The sculptors of the pulpit at Pisa, of the Doge's palace at Venice, of the bas-reliefs of the Duomo at Orvieto, had seen and studied to good purpose some remains at least of ancient work in marble. The Venetian and Pisan galleys brought home, now and then, rare pieces of sculpture, which quickened the perceptions and widened the scope of native artists. Petrarch, with the weight of his personal influence and the charm of his style, had imparted his own zeal to others in the study of the remains of classic literature. As the fifteenth century came in, the search for the lost books of the ancients was beginning to show fair results. "It was a circumstance productive of the happiest consequences," says the philosophic Mr. Roscoe, "that the pursuits of the opulent were at this time directed rather towards the recovery of the works of the ancients than to the encouragement of contemporary merit, — a fact that may serve to account in some degree for the dearth of original literary productions during this period." Whether this was "a happy consequence" may well be questioned. Many precious works, of which nothing had been known for centuries, were, indeed, recovered. There were no bounds to the extravagance of the esteem in which the ancient authors were held. Little judgment was exercised in regard to their essential merits. Their claim to reverence was regarded as unquestionable. The labors of commentators and translators were prized above all other literary work. Those authors of the time were most admired who best succeeded in imitating the ancient writers; but the critical skill and taste of scholars were imperfect and debased, so that the faults no less than the excellences of the classics were praised and reproduced in modern writings. Original thought was discouraged, and the knowledge of the classics served to stifle fresh and independent works of mind. From about the middle of the fifteenth century may be dated the rise of that spirit of pseudo-classicism which has blighted Italian literature from that day to this. Then began the Academies, whose members hid their own names under highsounding Latin appellations, — asses dressing themselves in lions' skins, and exhibiting their own feebleness by their very disguises. Then was established that code of false taste, whose laws, gaining gradually more and more authority, brought by slow degrees every department of literature and Art under their despotic and degrading control, and have not yet ceased to exercise a most injurious influence upon the national mind.

The Councils of Ferrara and Florence, at which many of the learned prelates of the Greek Church were present, and still more the fall of Constantinople in 1453, by which the scholars of the East were driven to Italy,

20

promoted, in extraordinary measure, the prevalent admiration for antiquity, not only by giving to Italian scholars a knowledge of many works of the Greek authors, of which they had been ignorant, but also by supplying them with masters who could make that knowledge available. Men of letters learned to have faith only in what was dead.

Nor was this the worst result of the rehabilitation of antiquity. With pagan literature came an influx of pagan sentiment. The practical disbelief of Christianity, as taught by Rome, led the way to the easy reception of heathen philosophy and principles of life. It was no mere scholarly impulse that led to the foundation of Platonic academies, to the setting of Plato side by side with Christ as a teacher of the truth, to the professed admiration of the doctrines of Epicurus. The Church had nothing to offer to counterbalance the attractions of the new-found doctrines. The systems of her schoolmen and divines appeared narrow, dry, and hard, when brought face to face with those of the great masters from which they professed to be remotely derived. The philosophy which she taught was of no better quality than the religion. She had succeeded in making both the one and the other despised. Nor was this all. The immorality of the period found not only a stimulus, but an excuse, in the old literature now extolled as divine. The authority of antiquity was invoked in favor of a looser code of morals, and of a more accommodating philosophy, than those which had Heaven and Hell for their final terms.

It is true that many of the fathers of the Church —

Basil and Chrysostom among them — were now brought, for the first time, to common knowledge in the West. But they could avail little against the powerful fascinations of the heathens, their old enemies, whom they had long ago left for beaten and routed.

While heathen antiquity was thus promoting the corruption of taste and of morals, and making the literature of the day stamp itself as counterfeit, its influence extended by force of natural relations over the domain of Art. The beauty and the artistic perfection of the works of ancient Art were brought into open comparison with the imperfect execution of modern productions. The spell of unidealized beauty was thrown over the imaginations of painters and sculptors. In estimating the influence of antiquity upon this period of Italian history, the charm of classic beauty must be considered as one of its chief elements. It satisfied a deep-felt want; it afforded a relief from the obscurity of symbolism, and from the intense moral consciousness of the works of the Middle Ages. It gratified the love of external life, did something to redeem sensuality from grossness, and corresponded with the general tendency to find the things of this world all-sufficient for content. Venus revealed herself to Italy as she had once done to Paris, and Italy made the choice of the shepherd on Mount Ida, while Minerva stood by and approved.

In the first half of the fifteenth century, the earth, the great treasury of sculpture, began to yield up the ancient statues and carved sarcophagi which it had long protected. Poggio Bracciolini, the Florentine, who died in

1459, seems, indeed, to have known not more than five statues in Rome; but there were many scattered works of ancient sculpture throughout Italy; and shortly after the middle of the century the collection of such works was set about in earnest. Blondo Flavio published, previously to 1447, the first regular treatise on the topography and antiquities of Rome. Even early in the century, it was the habit of the sculptors and architects of the northern cities of Italy to study the Roman remains. Vasari says of Ghiberti, that " he was the first who began to imitate the things of the ancient Romans." The good use to which his own fine genius and his patient labor enabled him to turn his study of classic Art appears in the unsurpassed beauties of his Gates of Paradise. But genius is not given to many men in one age in such measure as to enable them to overcome the unmanning effects of a professed system of imitation; and to one who looks behind the marvellous excellence of the external and purely artistic qualities of Ghiberti's work, there appears some lack of the depth of meaning, of the simple and serene piety, the pure and concentrated expression of the works of the earlier masters. He had gained by his study of ancient models, or by the study of living examples to which he was led through them, variety and animation of composition, mastery of form, attitude, and motion, — he had gained command over the body, but he had lost something of sympathy with the soul of his work.

A still nobler genius than Ghiberti, his contemporary, Brunelleschi, exhibits in a still more positive manner, in his grandest work, the effect of a return to ancient models. It was about the year 1403, that he, still a very young man, sold a little estate which he owned near Florence, in order to obtain money for a visit to Rome, where he desired to study the remains of the ancient buildings. "And there," says Vasari, "he gave himself up to his studies, taking no care about either food or sleep, devoted entirely to architecture, which at that time was extinct, — that is, I mean, the good ancient orders, for the German and barbarous style was still much used." Vasari, however, is wrong in this last assertion ; for at this time "the German and barbarous style," as he calls it, was as dead as " the good ancient orders." Gothic architecture never took strong root in Italy. It was a style that did not correspond to the genius of the Latin race. It was always an exotic, and betrayed continually its foreign origin. Though it produced, in the course of the twelfth and thirteenth centuries, some of the noblest buildings that ever rose upon Italian soil, it underwent modifications in their construction to fit it to Italian taste, and displayed in them a luxury of polished marble and a wealth of colored adornment such as it never elsewhere exhibited. Even these buildings were due to that period when Italy, in great part settled by conquerors and emigrants from the North, experienced that strong thrill of energy which ran through her veins as she awoke from her prolonged slumber in the Dark Ages.

It is a coincidence worth noting, that the corner-stone of Santa Maria de' Fiori at Florence, in its original design the grandest of all the Gothic cathedrals of Italy, was laid in the boyhood of Dante, the only Italian who has

shown a capacity to sympathize to the full with the
Gothic genius, — and that, after advancing rapidly for a
few years, the work upon it ceased at about the time of
his death.   For a century, this beginning, worthy of the
magnificent spirit of Florence in her best days, lay incomplete, a reproach to the city.   At last it was determined to finish the building.   But who now could execute
what Arnolfo had designed?   Architects were summoned
from all parts of Europe.   In 1420, the master-builders
met in Florence.   Many plans were suggested for the
vaulting of the Cathedral.   The wildest schemes were
brought forward and discussed; for the enormous span of
the arch to be thrown over the point of junction of the
nave and the transept presented a difficulty which few of
the builders of the time knew how to overcome with the
legitimate resources of their art.   Brunelleschi, however,
profiting by his study of Roman buildings, and confident
in his own power, undertook to construct what was
needed.   His proposal was at first universally derided,
as that of a madman ; but, after long discussion, the
work was committed to his charge.   The result was
the almost unsurpassed dome which crowns Florence,
and which even Michel Angelo could hardly do more
than rival.   Splendid as a work of genius, wonderful
as at once the first and almost the finest of modern
domes, as the perfect renewal of a style lost for a thousand years, — nevertheless, this dome of Brunelleschi's
went far to destroy the beauty, and did ruin the sym-
metry of the cathedral which it surmounts.   It is inappropriate as a completion of the original structure.   It

is a Roman head set upon Gothic shoulders. Arnolfo's problem was not solved by the answer which Brunelleschi gave to it. The work of the later architect bore the stamp of the later time. In the building, as Arnolfo had left it, there was an unexampled opportunity for a true Gothic dome, — grand arches leading up to a grander dome within, concentric story above story without, rising with forests of pinnacles clustered around the tall central spire, to outmatch the snowy peaks of Milan, to surpass the aspiring beauty of Strasburg or Cologne. The sense of the preëminent value of a completion that should be harmonious with the beginning of the Cathedral seems never to have been felt by Brunelleschi. No conception of the sentiment peculiar to Gothic architecture held back his hand from his bold and great undertaking. Henceforth the Gothic was banished from Italy, as a " German and barbarous style." The last stone of the lantern of Brunelleschi's dome was laid in 1461, fifteen years after his death, and from this may be dated the rise of that imitative architecture which reached its highest glory in St. Peter's, and which then rapidly ran down into the deformities of the Jesuit churches of the following centuries.

The same influences which affected the character of sculpture and of architecture with continually growing force impressed themselves upon the painting of the time. It would be a false supposition, indeed, to imagine that all the artists of the fifteenth century exhibited in their works the prevailing characteristics of the period. In the infinite diversity of the natural qualities and of

the circumstances of men, there will always be found ex
ceptions to prevailing rules. In every age, there are
many individuals who stand in opposition to its most
marked direction. Moreover, a course of national decline or progress is not established or confirmed at once
and at a definite epoch. It often exhibits itself at first
only in slight under-currents. The decay of the vital
forces of a people may be altogether concealed for a time
from the eyes of outside observers by shows of splendor,
by lustre of genius, brilliant, though perverted, and, indeed, by actual advance in material development, corresponding in some measure to the loss of spiritual
energy. Such was the case in Italy during a great
part of this time. The luxury of habits had vastly increased. Living was both easier and more civilized than
before. But living is not life.

No works of Art were ever created with a purer
spirit, with a sweeter piety, than those of Fra Angelico,
who died in 1455. The air of heaven is fanned by
the bright wings of his angels; the peace of heaven is
in their countenances. No spot of earth dims the shining colors of their robes. Such pictures as those of
the monk of Fiesole prove that in some retired corners of the earth Faith still had her abiding-place.
But Fra Angelico had preserved his piety only by
withdrawal from the world. " Although he might well
have remained in the world," says his biographer,
"yet, for his own satisfaction and quiet, being of a
tranquil and good disposition, and especially in order
to save his soul, he chose rather to make himself a

monk of the order of the Preaching Friars." The convent-gate shut out from him the knowledge of mankind. His life was solitary and exceptional, his character more refined than strong.

While Fra Angelico was showing in the features and the gestures of his saints and angels the religious affections of his soul, and exhibiting the human countenance in the exalted expressions of purity and devotion, Masaccio was carrying forward painting in another direction, by a mastery of light and shade, and a power of representing the free action of the human figure, such as had never been attained by earlier artists. The pictures which he painted in the Braneacci chapel at Florence are, perhaps, the first in modern Art that show entire freedom in execution united with variety and power in design.* They were the first truly natural pictures, free from the restraints of imperfect methods and incomplete knowledge of drawing. They showed the result of careful study of antique Art, modifying and directing study from life. In them men assume their real attitudes and gestures, devoid of constraint, and

* The fame of Masaccio has been raised too high, by attributing to his hand the finest of the works in this chapel. The late investigations of Gaye, of the editors of the Le Monnier edition of Vasari, and others, leave little doubt that the *St. Peter in Prison visited by St. Paul*, and the *St. Peter and St. Paul before the Proconsul*, which are not surpassed in excellence by any other pictures in the chapel, and which have been popularly ascribed to Masaccio, were in fact painted some forty years after his death by Filippino Lippi. There can be no question, however, that Masaccio's influence is visible in these later works, and that he deserves all credit for opening new ways of excellence in Art.

equally devoid of exaggeration. The Brancacci chapel was one of the chief schools of Michel Angelo and of Raffaelle. Many of the figures which he found there Raffaelle transferred, without improving them, to his own pictures.

But although Masaccio thus led the way to a rapid development of the powers of Art, although its materials were increased almost at the same time by the discovery and use of oil-colors, and although in many ways the science of painting was vastly improved, yet neither Masaccio nor any of his immediate followers showed a corresponding development in the more intimate and spiritual parts of their art. On the contrary, while the manner and method of painting were improving, the thought and feeling expressed by it were losing in meaning, in depth, and in truth. Compositions were gaining in fulness, variety, and grace, but were declining in simplicity and in dignity.* It seemed as if, while the

---

* A striking instance of this fact is to be observed in comparing the recently uncovered fresco by Giotto in the church of Santa Croce, in Florence, representing the Incredulity of Jerome, with the same subject as painted by Ghirlandaio in the church of Santa Trinità. Giotto's picture was painted early in the fourteenth century, Ghirlandaio's toward the end of the fifteenth. The first has lately been engraved from a drawing by Mignati. The second may be found in outline in Kugler's *Handbook of Painting in Italy*, where it is called "The Death of St. Francis," and is very highly praised as possessing "simple arrangement," "artless, unaffected dignity," "noble and manly expression." But the fact is, that the main features of the composition are taken bodily from Giotto's work, with the introduction of some needless figures and injurious accessories. The terms which Kugler uses in regard to Ghirlandaio's are appropriate to

secret of the beauty and glory of this world had been found, the more precious knowledge of the divine beauty, of which earth affords but the outward image, had been lost. Art was no longer the handmaid of piety, no longer the expression of purity. It was sinking to mere decorative purposes. Chapels were now, as formerly, adorned with painting; but the new pictures had often little that was sacred, except their subjects, and served to awaken no feelings of devotion, of religious tenderness, or awe. In the Campo Santo at Pisa, where, a hundred years before, Orcagna had painted his solemn pictures of the Four Last Things, Benozzo Gozzoli now painted on the opposite walls lovely compositions taken from the stories of the Old Testament, and full of the pleasantness, the gladness, even the mirth of life. Across the narrow green strip of graveyard, the two painted walls looked at each other, revealing the gulf that lay between the past century and the present.

As Painting decorated herself with new and unwonted charms, and as she came down from the contemplation of heavenly things to delight herself in the graces and accomplishments of sensual life, dilettantism, which had already begun to exhibit itself in literature, and which takes the place of passion in an age of indifference and skepticism, added another to the many existing influences

Giotto's picture. In the later work, the simplicity, the dignity, the tenderness of the earlier are greatly diminished. The one is instinct with deep feeling and true piety, — the other with conventional expression and Romanized faith. The history of the decline of Italian spiritual life lies between the two.

which were joined to reduce the level and aim of Art
Painting, sculpture, and architecture were, indeed, stimulated to remarkable productiveness by the growth of
private patronage, and by the demand which was made
upon them to minister with their delights to the luxurious spirit of the times. They answered readily to the
call, and lavished themselves in decorative displays, in
the construction and adornment of the halls and chambers of private palaces or the chapels of private devotion. They took their part in the open and gay world,
and learned easily to accommodate themselves to its
desires. The pencil that had designed virgins and saints
turned now to the depicting of Venuses and Cupids.
The licentious figures of heathenism were reproduced
in modern statues, — and painting and sculpture lent
themselves to be the panders of voluptuousness.

The discovery of printing, followed by the great mari-
time discoveries in which Italian navigators led the way,
roused the already active intellectual spirit of the last
half of the century to still more untiring and restless
exertions. But the art of printing, in making books
more generally accessible, and diffusing a knowledge of
letters, seems rather to have depressed than to have
stimulated the development of original thought. There
was a strange contrast, during this period, between the
greatness of physical achievements, the vast increase of
knowledge from sources external to the mind of man,
the extraordinary intellectual activity, and the deficiency
of intellectual force. Intrinsic feebleness corresponded
to a hitherto unexampled rapidity of material prog-

ress. In the midst of discoveries of startling grandeur, the Italian imagination grew cold, and rarely showed itself, save in the range of science and physical investigation. Literature lost dignity, and seemed to lose even the consciousness of morality. The poetic fancy appears in the rhymed satire of Pulci, in the mock pastorals of Lorenzo, in the Latin verse of Politian. The so-called golden age of Italian letters, the age of Lorenzo de' Medici, upon which the flattery of historians and essayists has been lavished, till its praise has become one of the rhetorical commonplaces of literature, was in truth a gilded, rather than a golden age. Lorenzo is called the patron of letters and of Art; but when letters and Art need a patron, it is because they have lost their own natural vigor.

Only one great genius, one whose power all the world recognizes and honors, belongs to the Art or literature of Italy of the last half of the fifteenth century. Leonardo da Vinci stands apart from his time, unapproached, alone. The illegitimate son of a country notary, he waited for no patron to stamp him with the mark of vulgar approbation. While other men were growing up in the conformities of faithless pietism, he learned to know the presence of God among the blue mountains that encircle Florence, and in the crowded market-place of the infidel city. The eternal and silent teachers of truth taught him a religion which had no place in the hearts of the men around him. " Such were his caprices," says Vasari, who believed in Christianity after the manner of the Popes, " such were his caprices, that, philosophizing about the things of Nature, he came to understand the properties of plants, and was continually observing the motions of the heavens, the course of the moon, and the goings of the sun; by which there arose in his mind a conceit so heretical, that he united himself to no special religion, thinking, perhaps, that it was better to be a philosopher than a Christian." * Little did the worthy biographer know of the heart of that man, who painted a head of the Saviour so tender and so sorrowful, with such depths of manly sympathy and strength, that in itself it gives testimony that the love of the Lord had entered into and taken possession of the heart of the painter. There is no other work of the last half of the century to be put by the side of Leonardo's picture of the Last Supper.

While this picture stands in express opposition to the temper of the times, the result to which the discipline of the age had brought the ablest intellects is displayed, perhaps, nowhere more clearly than in the works of Machiavelli. Their freedom from passion and from personal feeling gives to them peculiar value as illustrations of . prevailing principles. They are the cool deductions of an able man of the world from wide and various experience. They do not so much exhibit the existence of vice among men as the absence of virtue. They are not immoral, but simply unmoral. They are the works of a modern heathen philosopher, calm in tone, clear in statement, recognizing neither right nor wrong as abstract qualities, exhibiting the modes and system of tyranny,

* This passage occurs in the first edition of Vasari's Life of Leonardo; — it was omitted from the second.

without justifying, but equally without condemning them.
The end justifies the means, the world is to be dealt with
in worldly ways, and policy does not necessarily coincide
with justice and with truth.

" Faith is dead " at the middle of the century; — the
moral sense of man had died before its end. " Iniquity
and sin had multiplied in Italy," writes the Florentine
Benivieni, of the last decade of these hundred years,
" because the land had lost the faith of Christ. . . . .
All Italy, and especially the city of Florence, was given
over to skepticism. Men and women returned to heathen
customs, and took delight in the study of the poets, in astrology, and in all superstitions." In the year 1490, in
the midst of this society, in Florence itself, the enthusiast
Savonarola began for the second time to preach Reform.
The words in which Benivieni describes the rottenness of
Italy are not so strong as those in which the ardent Dominican depicts the crimes and vices of his hearers. If
one would learn what Italy had become, he may learn
it from the passionate sermons in which the undaunted
monk, filled with the spirit of prophecy, denounced woe
upon the people, unless they turned from their evil ways.
There was doubtless much exaggeration, much false zeal,
in the heated sentences of his irresistible invective ; but
beneath all the extravagances of his visionary and exalted eloquence lay a broad and deep foundation of truth.
For a time, the fervid spirit of Savonarola lighted up the
flames of repentance in the hearts of the fickle Florentines. In the Carnival season of 1492, they built a pile
.n the public square, heaping upon it their ornaments

masks, gaming-tables, licentious books, voluptuous pictures and carvings, and consumed them all. The next year the temporary passion for sacrifice had died away, — another fire was lighted, and the man who had ventured to preach repentance and reformation to people, to priests, and to Pope, was burned as the reward of his audacity. The smoke rising from his funeral-pile spreads in a dark cloud over Italy. Alexander VI., Borgia, Pope without a rival in infamy, was at the head of the Church. Paganism was enthroned at Rome, and crowned with the triple crown.

The sixteenth century was to develop the chief results of the principles in Art, in literature, and in religion, which had had their birth in the fifteenth. Over the gateway through which it is entered are the words, LET US EAT, DRINK, AND BE MERRY, FOR TO-MORROW WE DIE. For two hundred years Italy has lain dead.

CPSIA information can be obtained
at www.ICGtesting.com
Printed in the USA
LVHW081041300323
743029LV00002B/147

9 781017 532630